1984

Newspaper
Layout and Design

Newspaper
Layout and Design

BY DARYL R. MOEN

THE IOWA STATE UNIVERSITY PRESS/AMES

DARYL R. MOEN is managing editor of the *Columbia Missourian* and professor in the School of Journalism, University of Missouri, Columbia.

Composed and printed by the Iowa State University Press, Ames, Iowa   50010

First edition, 1984

Library of Congress Cataloging in Publication Data

Moen, Daryl R.
    Newspaper layout and design.

    Bibliography: p.
    Includes index.
    1. Newspaper layout and typography. 2. Printing, Practical—Layout. I. Title.
Z253.5.M63   1984   686.2'252   83–6237
ISBN 0–8138–1226–7

Contents

III

NEWSPAPER DESIGN

Preface

DURING THE SUMMER SPENT WRITING this book, I worked in the office of Earl English, dean emeritus of the Missouri School of Journalism. On his wall hung an inscribed picture from his friend, Frederic Goudy, the most prolific type designer this country has ever produced. That Dr. English had known Goudy so well was a reminder to me of how young much of our industry is. Although we are now in our fifth century of using type in the Western world, it was not until the last century that we were presented with a wide variety of typefaces and the research to guide our use of them.

We now have the technological ability to do almost anything on our newspaper pages. This presents us with the opportunity for great improvement as well as great disasters. That is why we need journalists who know how to make words and visuals work together.

We also have the incentive to ensure the survival of the print medium. Newspaper publishers are marshalling all the tools available to reach the reader. Design is one of many tools, along with thorough reporting, good writing, intelligent marketing, and efficient distribution. These are all equally important. The seeming emphasis on design—60 percent of U.S. newspapers made some change in appearance in 1978–1979 alone—reflects an industry catching up after nearly 200 years of graphic stagnation.

The goals of the newspaper industry and of this book are the same: to produce newspapers that are legible, use visual elements to communicate, and are organized for the reader's benefit.

To achieve those goals, I have integrated legibility and reader-preference research study results throughout the text to give students and professionals a basis for their decision making. The method is distinctly how-to; this is a book for people who want to learn layout and design principles as well as how to apply them better or differently.

We do need to do it better.

Just as the 12-year-old carrier who fails to deliver the paper on time can nullify the efforts of the greatest editors, so too can ignorance of basic legibility findings prevent us from getting messages to our readers. One only has to pick up a newspaper to find numerous examples of type that is too small or set too wide or set in imaginative but unreadable shapes to know there is work to be done in spreading the gospel of legibility. Or one can pick up a week's worth of any newspaper and see how many times the weather, Ann Landers, and the sports section appear in the same place every day and realize how badly many of our papers are organized. We can look at any newspaper and see how many opportunities editors have missed to tell a story more effectively by using photos, illustrations, maps, charts, and graphs or combinations of all these. When we have journalists on our newspapers trained to ask, "What is the best possible way to tell this story?" and the ability to respond by using combinations of text with other visuals, we will begin achieving the potential of the newspaper as a visual medium.

To help train people to reach that potential, I have organized this book from the simple to the complex. The first seven chapters set the foundation by showing how to lay out a page. Once the basic philosophy is understood and mechanical steps have been mastered, we move to aspects of design — the process and the thinking that are necessary to reach the print medium's potential as a communications tool.

In this progression, I have used examples of failures and successes from numerous newspapers. My work as a consultant and workshop conductor brings me into contact with hundreds of newspapers and journalists. I am indebted to many of them for permitting me to share with you their anec- dotes and their pages.

This book is intended to be immediately useful to students and professionals. However, even if students are unable to complete the text in one semester, it should remain useful to them as they encounter more complicated work such as designing logos and flags, let alone entire newspapers, and using color. Every other text discusses color in black and white. We are particularly proud that we have been able to use color to teach color, an increasingly important part of the newspaper.

My work with students and professionals has convinced me that there is a sincere interest in learning how to communicate more effectively in the print medium. To the extent that we are successful, we will be perpetuating the life of print.

That would please Goudy. He expanded the messages we can send with type; now it is up to us to combine type with all the other visual elements to ensure that our subscribers read with understanding.

*   *   *

The avid newspaper readers in my own family — my wife Nancy and my children, Chad, Mia, and Marisa — waited patiently for my time while I worked on this book. Many of my colleagues at the University of Missouri and throughout the industry contributed in formal and informal ways. To them, and to Jack and Berneice Kelly, with whom I started in this business, thanks.

I
Introduction

Evolution of design

NO MATTER how great the author's wisdom or how vital the message or how remarkable the printer's skill, unread print is merely a lot of paper and little ink. The true economics of printing must be measured by how much is read and understood and not by how much is produced.

Herbert Spencer
PHILOSOPHER

IN 1875, the *American Journalist* commented on the size of the Toledo *Blade:* "The weather is too cold to read it in the apple orchard, and the paper is too large to unfold in any ordinary house in Ohio." Now, more than 100 years later, the size of the newspaper page is again decreasing. The reason for the change, then as now, is not reader convenience but economics.

Publishing costs have shaped the size and texture of newspapers ever since *Publick Occurrences,* a 6- by 9½-inch paper, was published on September 25, 1690. One of its four pages was blank, perhaps because the editor ran out of news or decided to leave room for a mailing address. Many years would pass before white space would be used so extravagantly again.

The evolution of American newspaper design in the nearly 300 years since *Publick Occurrences* was published includes stories of economic courage, improved technology, and responses to competitive pressures. Gutenberg borrowed money to print the Mazarin Bible, was unable to repay it, and lost his press and type. He may have been the first publisher to go bankrupt, but he was not the last. In 1964, two years after becoming the first competitive metropolitan daily to try offset printing, the Phoenix *Arizona Journal* folded.

Nearly 400 years passed before there was a significant improvement in

Gutenberg's press. In the next 150 years, several generations of presses and composition machinery were invented and discarded as obsolete. In the next ten years, we will see still another revolution in the printing process – the introduction of pagination and virtual elimination of the composing room. Whether electronic delivery of the news will ever completely replace the newspaper is doubtful, but its impact will be enormous. Public preference will determine the format and design of news presentation, whether it is delivered on newsprint, television screen, or both. Technical developments will have a continuing influence on our ability to meld words and visuals; they expand our opportunities when we control them but hinder us when they limit our ability to perform the necessary journalistic functions.

To trace the evolution of design, it is necessary to study four areas of the production system: paper, presses, type and typesetting, and photographs.

Paper

The supply and cost of paper have a direct effect on newspaper size and quality. For example, colonial journalists increased page size in response to a tax levied on the number of pages. The revolutionary war eliminated the tax but reduced the supply of newsprint, which was made from rags. Some papers shrank to approximately 8½ by 11 inches. Newsprint was rough in texture and often blotched or gray (Mott 1945). By 1800, with the war over, the supply of newsprint had returned to normal and newspaper pages began increasing in size. Although most newspapers enlarged their pages to 15 to 16 inches in width, in 1853 the New York *Journal of Commerce* was 3 by 5 feet, which was unusually large and undoubtedly impossible to handle. Newspaper pages usually contained 6 or 7 columns of type set 15 to 17 picas wide.

The Civil War again interrupted the supply of newsprint, and the price soared to $440 a ton (Emery and Emery 1978). Soon after the war ended, wood pulp replaced rags as the raw material in newsprint and changed the economics of printing. With new mills and cheap forestland, the price of paper declined to $42 a ton in 1899. It was only $8 a ton higher 40 years later. Cheap newsprint, much of it supplied from Canada, continued to aid the development and growth of the newspaper industry until the late 1960s and early 1970s when increasing demand and labor strikes in the newsprint manufacturing industry collided. Newsprint, hard to obtain for about two years, shot up in price. Newspapers lowered the percentage of the paper devoted to news, reduced type size and pictures, dropped syndicated services, and reduced or eliminated some comics. Coming soon after editors had realized the value of white space, the newsprint shortage was a setback to design because material had to be shoehorned into the paper. The newsprint industry gradually caught up to demand, but the new pricing structure made many publishers wary. As they incorporated the new costs into the newspaper's pricing system, publishers eased up slightly. However, they continued to maintain tight papers, and design had to respond to this need.

Already reeling from increasing newsprint prices, publishers in the 1960s and 1970s faced the additional threat of declining circulation. The industry responded with special-interest sections, most of which had open covers. Design flourished in these sections, and the experimentation done there had an effect on the news sections of many newspapers.

The pressures of price continue to exist. Studies show that a significant portion of potential subscribers cannot read a newspaper because of the small type size, but editors are reluctant to use larger text type because an increase from 9- to 10-pt. type means an 11 percent loss of newshole. Readers with bad eyesight had a champion in John S. Knight, former editor of Knight-Newspapers, Inc., who said, "To mix a few metaphors, get on the soapbox, sound the trumpets, ride a white horse, and lead the way to emancipation of the readers from eyestrain and possible circulation malnutrition" (Editors Exchange 1980).

The company Knight helped found is presently concerned, along with several other publishers, about the proposed drop in paper weight. In an effort to slow the speed at which newsprint prices are increasing, the manufacturers are lobbying publishers to permit them to decrease paper weight. A lower weight, however, means a flimsier newsprint and lower printing quality. Consequently, there is more show-through from one side of the page to the other as well as more paper breaks during printing.

Researchers are trying to determine if the use of kenaf, a fibrous plant, can lower newsprint prices as dramatically as wood pulp did more than 100 years ago. In an Arizona test, kenaf grew to a height of 14 feet in four months. Unlike trees, which require years of growth, kenaf is harvested annually. Although newsprint made from kenaf has been tested successfully in several newspaper plants, it is not yet known whether farmers can make enough profit to justify substituting it for their other crops or if newsprint mills can buy it cheaply enough to justify changeover costs. If the economics prove favorable for both farmers and newsprint producers, kenaf may soon start replacing wood pulp.

Regardless of whether newsprint is made from wood pulp or kenaf, the size of the newspaper page will shrink. In the late 1970s, with newsprint at $500 a metric ton, most newspapers were 30 to 32 inches wide. An industry effort to standardize page sizes to accommodate national advertisers and cut paper costs resulted in a recommendation for a 28-inch width. Although this size is easier for readers to handle, legibility is decreased slightly because of narrower column widths.

Presses

Journalism historian Frank Luther Mott described how newspapers were produced in the 1700s: "The type was inked by a sheepskin ball filled with wool and attached to a hickory stick; a boy wielded two such balls, transferring the ink from the slab on which it was spread to the form and often bedaubing himself" (Mott 1945, p. 46). Printing was slow, and the quality poor. In 1980, that boy with the hickory stick would be awed by the giant contraptions spewing out newspapers at speeds up to 70,000 impressions an hour. But this progress has its price. It takes a letterpress press that weighs more than 400 tons and consumes about 750 horsepower to put one-fifth of an ounce of ink on 64 pages of newsprint (Puncekar 1980). Enormous amounts of space are required to house these presses. Today, researchers are working on smaller, lighter presses with better reproduction quality. If history is any guide, smaller presses will be developed to meet the needs of increased speed and quality. That's the way it has been ever since 1825 when the *New York Daily Advertiser* installed America's first steam-driven cylinder press and forced the boy with the hickory stick out of a job.

Steam-powered presses printed 2,000 papers an hour and increased production to 4,000 an hour less than ten years later. The next breakthrough came in 1847 when the revolving printing surface was invented. Curved type forms were locked on the cylinder and fastened with wedged or V-shaped column rules. Speed reached 20,000 copies an hour, but editors could not use headlines more than 1 column wide because the type had to be locked in. Stereotype plates solved that problem in 1861. Instead of locking the actual type into a form, a metal impression — stereotype, or metal plate — was made of the type, curved to fit the rollers, and put on the press. Vertical makeup continued out of habit, and probably preference, for many years, but the mechanical justification for it was gone.

Further press developments came rapidly. In 1863, the first web-perfecting press was installed in an American newspaper. It was called web because the paper was fed onto the press from a roll rather than in sheets and perfecting because the paper was printed on both sides as it passed through the press. By 1890, a Hoe press could print 48,000 twelve-page papers an hour. By 1920, improved presses increased production to 60,000.

Until 1940, all papers were printed on letterpress presses. This is a direct printing method in which paper and ink are brought together under pressure to make an impression. Unfortunately, the reproduction quality, especially of photographs, is not good on such presses. The problem was solved in 1939 by offset printing, a method in which the inked image is transferred from the plate to a rubber blanket and then to the paper. With a finer halftone screen, a little higher grade of paper and ink, and less plate pressure, offset produces better tones. This method of printing became popular with small newspapers and was usually accompanied by cold type composition, a photographic process that does not require metal type. As manufacturers increased press speed, papers with larger circulation went offset. In 1965, the Dubuque (Iowa) *Telegraph Herald* installed an offset press (Goss Metro) that printed 50,000 papers an hour. To show off the printing quality, offset papers increased the size and number of photographs, and photographers flocked to them. Photojournalism — reporting with a camera — had existed ever since the Spanish-American War, but it was refined on the small- to medium-sized dailies during the 1960s and 1970s, and the photographer began to be integrated into the newsroom.

While editors and photographers were changing the face of smaller papers, publishers of metropolitan papers were looking for ways to improve the quality of their letterpress printing without investing several million dollars for new presses and changeover costs. Research spearheaded by the American Newspaper Publishers Association Research Institute produced a photo-imaged relief plate that permitted letterpress papers to use cold type or photocomposition techniques and eliminate stereotype plates. This breakthrough improved reproduction at the big dailies.

In 1968, the Research Institute produced the DiLitho system that uses aluminum offset plates on a specially altered letterpress unit. Eighty dailies had adopted DiLitho by 1980 and achieved near-offset-quality reproduction. By 1980, 99 percent of American dailies were printed by offset, DiLitho, or a refinement of DiLitho.

In 1979, 1,283 of the nation's 1,768 (72 percent) dailies were offset. Since then a number of larger newspapers, including *Newsday,* the *Chicago Tribune, Houston Post,* and *Free Press* and *News* in Detroit, have switched to offset. Speed is up to 70,000 impressions per hour, and some of the larger newspapers have bought two complete units to double their output.

The presses no longer inhibit design, but the future will bring further refinements and perhaps even a new system. Ink-jet printing, in which ink is sprayed directly onto the paper through computer-driven presses, will eliminate plates, save time, and allow editors to change the content without stopping the press. The ink-jet system is already being used in some commercial printing applications but is only at the testing stage for newspapers.

Type and typesetting

The necessity to cut type from wood by hand inhibited the development and use of type for the first 150 years of American newspapering. Wood type was followed by metal type that was cast by hand at first but produced by machine in 1822.

Even though display type was more readily available, editors did not use headlines consistently until the Mexican War in 1846 when they often appeared with several decks. Until stereotype plates were introduced in 1861, headlines were restricted to 1 column to keep the type from flying from the form during printing. Makeup remained vertical for a long time, even after the advent of stereotype plates. During the Civil War, headlines were still 1 column with 6 to 12 decks descending from them. Often, six different kinds of type were used. The yellow journalism practiced in the 1890s brought with it big, black Gothic headlines. It was the first time that headlines were consistently used wider than 1 column. Historian Mott commented, "There was, however, so much lawless variety in front-page makeup that it amounted to monstrous confusion" (Mott 1945, p. 544). The type was crudely hand drawn because none was available in the several-inch-high sizes that were used.

About that time, the Linotype was introduced. Until then, all the text type was set by hand. Several people, including Mark Twain, who went broke in the effort in the 1890s, had been trying to produce such a machine. Ottmar Merganthaler finally succeeded where the others had failed. Type quality improved, and the setting speed increased dramatically. That in turn improved newspaper typography. As Mott commented, "Better taste of both type founders and makers of Linotype faces made for greatly improved typography in the newspapers" (Mott 1945, p. 602).

In 1892, 22 typefounders consolidated to become the American Type Founders, a company that improved type and type use. Cheltenham was designed in 1902 and immediately joined the ranks of other popular typefaces such as Bodoni and Goudy. Ionic, Excelsior, and Ideal were introduced for text use in the 1920s and 1930s. All were highly legible and held up under the punishment of rotary presses. With Corona, they remain among the most popular newspaper text faces today. Futura and Times New Roman were cut after World War I and have also lasted in newspapers. In the 1940s, Univers, Helvetica, Optima, and Palatino were introduced. Few new typefaces were designed in the 1960s and 1970s because photocomposition was being introduced and companies were too busy converting their type stocks to film to meet the requirements of the new production process.

Another deterrent to new typeface design was the lack of copyright protection. In 1970, the International Typeface Corporation (ITC), was formed. When ITC buys the rights to a typeface, it licenses that face to any company that wants to produce it under its own name. In its first ten years, ITC produced 34 new typefaces, including Avant Garde Gothic, Franklin Gothic, Zapf Book, and Tiffany, all of which appear regularly in newspapers but not necessarily as the basic display face.

Photocomposition has improved the use of type even though it slightly damaged the design of individual letters. When type was produced in metal, each size had its own proportions; when it is produced for photocomposition, one size, approximately 5 points, is stored on film. When 10-pt. type is desired, the image is magnified by a factor of two; for 30-pt. type, the magnification factor is six. Consequently, subtle changes cut into metal type as it increased in size were lost in photocomposition. That shortcoming was rectified with introduction of digitized cathode ray tube typesetting, in which each character in a font is stored as computer information and broken down into overlapping strokes. The more the type is broken down, the better it looks when reproduced. Autologic, which breaks type down up to 2,880 lines per inch, produces a high-quality letter (see left "i" in Fig. 1.1).

Fig. 1.1.

Photocomposition equipment also permits designers to control the amount of space between letters, between lines, and between headlines and copy. Control of the spacing between letters was not possible with metal type, and the designer had to accept the spacing built into the typeface. Kerning (setting type so letters touch each other) can be done more easily by adjusting computer programs. This is especially useful for correcting the optically incorrect amount of space that occurs, for instance, when a capital *T* precedes a lowercase letter. Because of the cross stroke (top of the *T*), the next letter looks like it is too far removed from the stem (Ti). Using the computer, such letters can now be moved closer to the stem to be more pleasing optically (Ti).

Photocomposition machines that produce both display type and text copy at the same time can be programmed to provide the correct amount of space between headline and copy. Because that space should change as the size of the headline changes, phototypesetting equipment offers time-saving flexibility as well as improved quality of reproduction. (Specifics of handling type are treated in detail in Chapters 10, 11, and 12.) In addition, it can produce type at speeds up to 1,250 11-pica lines per minute. However, phototypesetting equipment is not used everywhere; in 1980, type was still being hand set at the Marlinton (W.Va.) *Pocahontas Times*.

Photographs

The newspaper's potential as a visual medium began modestly in America on January 26, 1707, when the New York *News-Letter* printed a drawing that had been cut in wood. Other publishers did not rush to emulate the leader because they were too busy trying to get type on paper and did not have time to worry about developing the medium visually. The New York *Evening Telegram* started using cartoons regularly in 1867, even though the process of making them into woodcuts was time-consuming and cumbersome. In the 1870s and 1880s, zinc etchings (zinc plates etched with acid) were introduced, and the reproduction quality improved. There was no rush to develop a method for using halftones in newspapers because the photographic process was still in its infancy. A Frenchman had discovered a way of producing a positive from an exposure in the early 1820s, but despite further developments, the lengthy exposure time inhibited use of a camera for anything but landscapes for nearly 30 years. Matthew Brady made thousands of pictures of the Civil War; then, as for years after, "pictures" in newspapers consisted of artists' renderings of photographic images.

The first photograph, which showed some of the Shantytown dwellings in the city, appeared in the *New York Daily Graphic* on March 4, 1880. Public reaction was a resounding silence. Meanwhile, Joseph Pulitzer, who was caught up in the yellow journalism circulation battles, ordered his editors to reduce the number of woodcuts because he was afraid they hurt the dignity of his paper. Circulation fell. Pulitzer responded by reinstating pictures and increasing their size. When the halftone process was perfected in 1886, Pulitzer was one of the first to use it (Kobre 1980).

The development of the halftone process was to newspaper photography what steam-driven presses were to mass circulation. The process involves the use of a screen that breaks the image into thousands of tiny dots of varying sizes on a film. The larger the dot, the darker the tone. The dots transfer the ink to the paper as it runs through the press. The result is a picture (halftone) that has all the tones between black and white. Reproduction improves as the screen becomes finer. Newspapers today commonly use a screen of 85 to 100 lines. A 133-line screen is often used in high-quality commercial work.

Reproduction may not have been as good in the 1890s when Pulitzer finally embraced photography, but it was exciting. On May 4, 1890, Pulitzer's *World* used 39 2-column photos of a clergyman who was the subject of a 4-page supplement.

The first news photography developed during the Spanish-American War in 1898 but was still considered a curiosity. Melville Stone, a great editor of the *Chicago Daily News* said, "Newspaper pictures are just a temporary fad, but we're going to get the benefit of the fad while it lasts." The *Daily News* went out of existence in 1978, but newspaper photography is stronger than ever.

To realize photography's potential, camera size had to be reduced, film speed increased, and artificial lighting developed. Dangerous flash powder was replaced by flash bulbs, which were followed by electrically charged flashes in the late 1930s. The 4 by 5 Speed Graphic was the standard camera until the 1950s, even though the smaller and faster 35-mm camera had been introduced by Leica in 1924.

The impact of news photography was stunning. It brought home the Spanish-American War (even promoted it), proved that the Wright brothers had invented the airplane, and complemented the works of the muckrakers. Slums were shown to people who did not know they existed, and child labor laws were enacted after stories and pictures appeared of little children working in the coal mines and fields.

Picture syndication began in the early 1900s, and by 1927 the Associated Press News Photo Service was inaugurated.

On June 7, 1939, the Associated Press distributed the first spot news color picture (President Roosevelt welcoming King George VI in Washington, D.C.) for the daily press. Because of the time needed to process the film and make separations and the extra press capacity required, color photographs did not commonly appear in American newspapers until the 1960s, although they were frequently used on special occasions and in special sections before that. In the 1970s, laser scanners were introduced to make the separations, and computers were used to enhance the color. By 1980, the technical problems were being solved rapidly.

In less than a century, the industry had advanced from illustrations to color photography. The next technological advance is expected to be a startling new development—a filmless camera that stores images digitally in a waferlike sensor and then transmits them to a computer where they can be examined, enhanced, and cropped. The Associated Press and United Press International already handle most of their photographs in a computer. Development of the filmless camera will speed processing time, cut development costs, and improve the quality of the pictures.

The continued development of photographic technology and photographic techniques has had a substantial effect on newspaper design. Better reproduction quality has brought about more frequent use and larger sizes, which in turn has encouraged horizontal formats. The increased use of pictures has had yet another benefit; communication improved as photographers and reporters learned to work together. Even Melville Stone of the *Chicago Daily News* would admit today that pictures are here to stay.

The future

Predictions for the future would be considered science fiction if it were not for the rapid advances in newspaper production technology since 1965. Developments are now occurring so rapidly that new equipment is often obsolete within a year.

In 1960, typesetters at most newspapers, as they had done for 100 years, set the copy on a metal-casting machine such as a Linotype. Headlines were set separately in the composing room and pages were made up by putting the metal type in a form. Engravings were made of the photographs and locked into the form with the type. An impression of the page was made on a metal plate, and the plate was placed on a letterpress unit to be printed.

By 1970, reporters at most newspapers typed their stories directly into video display terminals (VDTs), from which the material was sent electronically to a photocomposition machine that produced the type on paper through a photographic process. That type; the headlines, which were also produced photographically; and any prescreened pictures were pasted on the page. The completed page was photographed, and a negative was prepared. If halftone negatives were used, they were spliced into the page negative. After the page negative was transferred to an aluminum plate by exposing it to a bright light source, the plate was placed on an offset press or a letterpress converted to use offset-type plates. The introduction of cold type composition and video display terminals eliminated human typesetters and saved publishers 30 to 50 percent of previous production costs.

By 1975, newspapers were eliminating not only the typesetters but also many of the pasteup employees because the text and headlines could be set together on photocomposition machines. Because cutting and pasting was reduced, pages were produced faster. In addition, lasers were being used to burn the impressions on plates, sometimes at far-flung printing plants.

At present, the composing room is in danger of being eliminated altogether. In the 1970s, a group of 40 newspapers and IBM teamed up to produce a pagination system that would permit composition of an entire page on a video display terminal and printing by photocomposition equipment. After seven years and $25 million without success, the effort was disbanded, but similar research was continued by private companies and pagination has become a reality.

In each of these steps, the editorial department gained more control over the product because there were fewer people between the journalist and the reader. The new systems also permitted more flexibility with type and white space, better standardization, and more opportunity to experiment with design.

At present, the industry is working feverishly on a system that would take the editorial department's work directly to the platemaking stage. Instead of producing type and headlines on paper in photocomposition machines, the editors would position the elements on the page electronically, and the computer would direct a laser beam to burn a plate with that information. Such a system would improve the quality of reproduction, a necessary step considering the deteriorating quality of newsprint and news inks.

Even as this system is being developed, newspapers are investing in electronic home delivery systems. Most analysts believe that the newspaper will survive for many years to come, but the number of pages and its content will probably change as the home delivery systems siphon off the content most easily digested on a screen, such as calendar items, classified advertising, and news briefs. The newspaper of the future will continue to be an information disseminator, but the information will be distributed electronically as well as on newsprint. For both systems, the industry needs journalists who can report, edit, and bring words and visuals together to help the reader understand the message and increase the impact of the story.

Layout and design research

Legibility has been studied by researchers in several fields (see Chapter 11), but design research is rare. As a result, many journalists are looking for help in designing pages. Most of the academic research has been confined to classroom experiments, and the results may not apply to the general audience. Much of the significant research on design characteristics is being conducted by newspapers or their corporate headquarters. Even if the generalized results are made public, the methodology and specific findings are seldom revealed.

Yet by reviewing the literature that is available, we can reach some conclusions about the direction, if not the goal, toward which newspapers should be heading.

Click and Stempel (1974) reported on research based on the response of readers in four cities to different page formats. The study is significant because it was done among a general newspaper audience of men and women of various ages in cities with different characteristics (Louisville, Ky.; Loveland, Colo.; Lansing, Mich.; and Hattiesburg, Miss.). Front pages of six newspapers were selected for the study; three were traditional (Fig. 1.2), and three modern (Fig. 1:3). The modern formats had 6 columns with a low story count and were horizontal and modular (of equal depth). Two of the traditional formats had 8 columns, but all three had a high story count and were vertical, not modular. Respondents were asked to rate the pages on a scale of one to ten (semantic differential scale) using a variety of factors such as interesting, boring; fair, unfair; exciting, dull; bold, timid; and active, passive. The authors concluded, "Our respondents gave an overwhelming endorsement to modern-format pages. The exceptions to the preference for those pages are relatively minor." Even respondents who were over 40 years old preferred the modern pages. Contrary to an earlier study, the researchers also found that readers did not consider the modern formats sensational or unethical.

Fig. 1.2.

Fig. 1.3.

Siskind (1979) did a study on contemporary versus traditional designs and well-designed pages versus those of average design. The audience was college students, and the pages were designed specifically for the study; all had the same name, but each had a different style (Figs. 1.4, 1.5). Again,

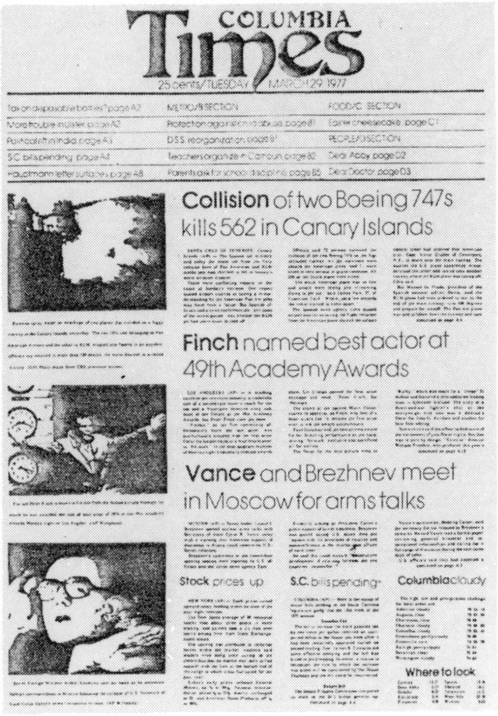
COLUMBIA Times

25 cents/TUESDAY MARCH 29 1977

Collision of two Boeing 747s kills 562 in Canary Islands

Finch named best actor at 49th Academy Awards

Vance and Brezhnev meet in Moscow for arms talks

Stock prices up

S.C. bills pending

Columbia cloudy

Where to look

Fig. 1.4.

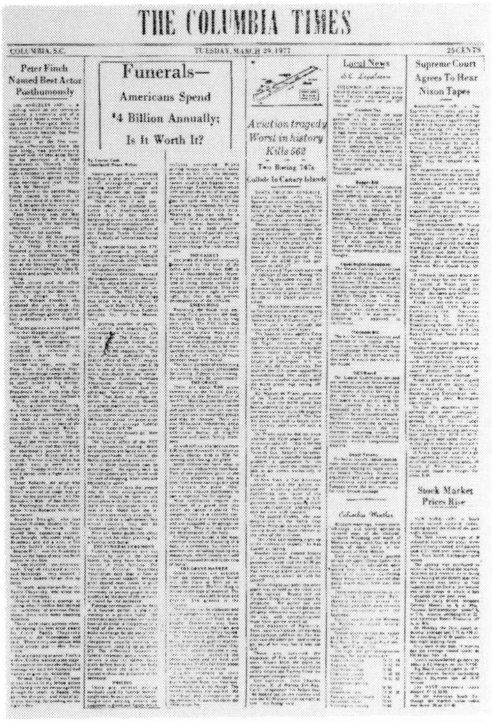
THE COLUMBIA TIMES

COLUMBIA, S.C. TUESDAY, MARCH 29, 1977 25 CENTS

Peter Finch Named Best Actor Posthumously

Funerals— Americans Spend $4 Billion Annually; Is It Worth It?

Aviation tragedy Worst in history Kills 562

Two Boeing 747s Collide In Canary Islands

Local News

Columbia Weather

Supreme Court Agrees To Hear Nixon Tapes

Stock Market Prices Rise

Fig. 1.5.

a semantic differential scale was used to test the same kind of factors Click and Stempel had measured. Siskind found that the respondents rated the contemporary well-designed page and the contemporary page of average design as more informative and interesting than either of the traditional models, even though they did not appear to define the designs in the same way as the researcher.

Another design study using college students for respondents was conducted at Indiana University (Bain 1980). Two versions of the November 13, 1978, student newspaper were printed and Bain listed these findings:

1. More readers finish a story if it is all on the same page. If the story

jumps, readership falls off considerably after the midpoint. Content, however, makes a difference.

2. More of the story is read if it does not jump.

3. Readers do not necessarily drop off in increasing numbers on longer stories. About the same number of readers complete the story as those who stop after the lead paragraphs. The pattern is even more pronounced if the story does not jump.

4. Most readers say they read jumps; in actuality, most did not.

5. Readers liked headlines that had bold and light type or a variety of type sizes better than roman-italic combinations.

6. Large pictures attract readers to an accompanying story better than small pictures and also hold the readers' attention deeper into the tie-in story.

7. Type is readable whether it is presented in columns of equal depth or in irregular wraps, but readers prefer the modular format.

In 1979, using focus-group sessions in which researchers lead respondents through an in-depth discussion of newspapers, Clark (1979) of Yankelovich, Skelly & White produced a wide-ranging report for the American Society of Newspaper Editors. Because her study was qualitative rather than quantitative, the findings were not given in percentages and cannot be generalized for all audiences. However, she did find a strong preference for well-organized newspapers. Said one reader, "I wonder what the editors would think if they could see me reading the paper. . . . I'm dropping it all over. The pages fall out. It's hard to fold. Either the baby is on my lap or I'm drinking coffee — and sitting there hunting and searching." The respondents also objected to blurred pictures, poor color reproduction, graphs that were difficult to read, and maps that did not show what was beyond the boundary.

In 1978, the Gannett Company interviewed 5,000 readers in four cities (Curley 1979) and found that:

1. Production, packaging, graphics, and appearance are important in determining satisfaction with the newspaper in general.

2. Graphics and packaging are especially important to younger and occasional readers.

3. A significant minority of readers, especially younger ones, want color pictures.

4. Type should be larger or more readable.

Speaking through the researchers, readers have made a strong plea for newspapers to improve graphically. That means change. Although some newspapers are anxious to change, others resist stubbornly. All ask how.

The role of design

Look at your local newspaper and ask yourself, "If this were a car, what year and make would it be?" The answers, depending on where you live, would range from a 1920 Ford to the latest Mercedes-Benz (Figs. 1.6, 1.7).

Fig. 1.6.   *Fig. 1.7.*

Old does not necessarily mean bad; newspapers are institutions of tradition. Some communities value tradition more than contemporaneity, but most of us do not like to think we live in the past. If we can afford it, we wear modern clothes, hairstyles, and glasses; buy new cars; and watch movies on video disks at home. Why, then, should we subscribe to a newspaper that has not changed significantly since our grandparents' day, unless, of course, the content is superior to all competition and so useful that we cannot do without it.

Some newspapers have changed dramatically but not necessarily for the better. Big pictures and big type do not necessarily make a better product.

There must also be a clear understanding that the purpose of design is to help the reader understand the information. Design is not something added; it is part of the message. Good design can be achieved by following two axioms: (1) simpler is better and (2) form follows function.

Newspaper readers spend only a few minutes with the product daily. If the paper is well organized and the individual stories and pictures are presented without clutter, readers will find the product useful and informative. If readers are given an opportunity to make a mistake (such as going back up to the second column of type because a blurb extends beyond one column of the setting), some probably will (Fig. 1.8). Stripping away the clutter means

,ew York gets 22 inches

,h, humbug! Christmas was too white

ational	Airline flights were cancelled and airports throughout New York were closed.	"This is the most severe ice and snow storm since 1974," groaned a spokesman for Pennsylvania Electric Co.	Christmas are happy."	busiest — for a third many "red-eye" speci. early morning hours.
painted New York hiter-than-necessary y and weighty ice and ower blackouts in es in western Penn- alt headaches to	Workmen on holiday vacation were		Travelers advisories for blowing and drifting snow were posted from New England into Ohio and from the Nebraska Panhandle through south- western North Dakota. Gusts of up to 56 mph (88.5 kph) whipped up snow in Rapid City, S.D.	The fog drifted in from. ocean, decreasing visibili, runways and closing dow began to disperse with the sur the airport resumed full oper long after sunrise.
Weather Service : in upstate New nder 22 inches (55 now. Utica had 15 eters) and Albany (30 centimeters). ed Buffalo got off v 5 inches.	'Forgive me for my cynicism, but I hope those of you who asked for a white Christmas are happy.'		Sub-zero morning temperatures of northern Minnesota. Readings in the 40s F (4 C) were reported across the California coast, while Floridians basked in 70 degree F (21 C) tem- peratures.	Mid-Missouri may get s white stuff too. The Nation Service is predicting partly · cold weather for the next few a chance of snow on Thurs
	among those called in to deal with the massive blackout in western Penn- sylvania that left holiday cheer as the only source of warmth. The blackout was triggered by heavy ice and snow that snapped power lines.	Attendance at holiday church ser- vices dropped throughout the snowbelt, prompting one Scranton, Pa., priest to begin his sermon with humbug: "Forgive me for my cynicism, but I hope those of you who asked for a white	Fog hampered operations at the Los Angeles airport — the nation's third	more weather details, see Pa[

Fig. 1.8.

eliminating cutesy drawings of ribbon around wedding pictures and foot-prints around pictures of a tour of homes (Fig. 1.9). If the temptation to use such devices ever looms, lie down until it goes away.

"Form follows function" is a basic theorem of design in many fields, notably architecture. In a way, newspaper designers are also architects. They build a basic format for the newspaper. Each day, they arrange the elements so that readers know where to find them and can read them quickly with understanding. The function of news is to communicate information, but the function of news design is to help the reader absorb the message in the presentation. If a president resigns, the story should be clear and simple with a photograph that captures the emotion of the moment. When a president is elected, the story requires charts, maps, graphs, pictures, headlines, and text. When the Environmental Protection Agency releases car mileage ratings, the story *is* a chart. When a city council meets, the story usually demands a summary to report the variety of actions.

Because the function of feature design is to inform and entertain, the pace is more relaxed. The stories are written and displayed differently than news stories. For instance, fashion, especially high fashion, is often splashy. Perhaps the design should incorporate this feeling (Fig. 1.10). As a rule, the design should be simplified as the message becomes more complicated.

Fig. 1.9.   Fig. 1.10.

Most of all, design is a planning process (see Chapter 8) in which creative minds decide how to cover various events or conduct investigations. Just as good writing needs good reporting, good design needs good stories, charts, and photographs that are planned, not ordered as an afterthought. The tyranny of deadlines can be eased by good planning and scheduling.

Finally, design is an attempt to achieve the newspaper's potential as the visual medium. People do not listen to it; they look at it, scan it, and read it. When editors use the range of available elements—text, display type, photographs, illustrations, maps, charts, graphs, and white space—with strength and simplicity, the readers will find their newspapers more informative, entertaining, and useful. That is what the following chapters are all about.

Newspaper

II

Layout

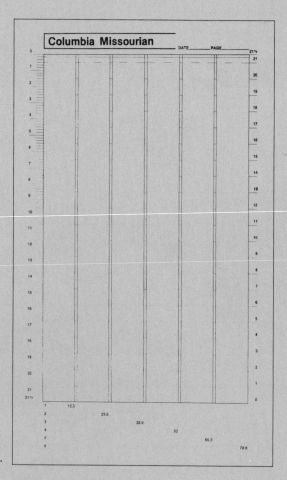

Fig. 2.1.

The language of layout and design

THE main purpose of newspaper design is, of course, to improve communication — to get more people to read more of the newspaper.

Wallace Allen
ASSOCIATE EDITOR
Minneapolis Tribune

"GIVE ME CUTLINES for these pix, Crocker."

"I need a 3-36-2 jump head."

"That boxed copy is three points too wide. Should we eliminate the box or reset it?"

"Get that Oxford rule out of there and set those heds flush left."

"This story's a couple of inches long, but we can get it all in if we change the leading from ten to nine."

Sound Greek to you? If it does, you are not alone. This jargon is a shorthand version of the vocabulary of layout and design editors. It is sometimes logical, sometimes illogical, and often inconsistent from newspaper to newspaper. You too must become fluent in the language. When you are familiar with the vocabulary, you will be ready to begin transferring stories, illustrations, and headlines to the dummy or grid, a blueprint for the newspaper page. The dummy used by layout editors is usually half the size of the actual page (Fig. 2.1). A good dummy sheet should show the number of column inches along the margins and pica breakdowns within the columns. Some designers prefer to work with a full page to get a better picture of how the finished product will look. After the dummy is completed, it is sent to the composing room where employees paste up the page. At a plant using cold type, a wax coating is used to affix the type and headlines to the full-sized page, according to the directions on the dummy. At the few newspapers still using hot type, the compositors place the elements into a chase, a steel rectangle.

This chapter explains the basic layout and design vocabulary. Other terms are defined throughout the book, and all appear in the glossary.

Measurements

Although feet — and soon, perhaps, metres — are the basis for most measurements in the United States, editors work with picas and points. The pica, ⅙ inch, is the basic measurement and is divided into points. There are 12 points per pica and 72 points per inch. The width of copy is expressed in picas and points. A typical measurement is 1306 or 13½ picas. The "06" refers to the number of points. The designation 1312 would never be used because there are 12 points per pica; 1312 would be 14 picas. The zero before the 6 eliminates the confusion that would arise if it were written 136, which could mean either 136 picas or 13 picas and 60 points. The zero is used for measurements less than 10 points. Decimal points are not used because they could also be confusing. For example, 13.6 could mean 13⁶⁄₁₀ picas or 13 picas and approximately 7 points.

Prior to computerized typesetting, editors were not concerned about points. Old production methods restricted settings to even and half-pica widths, but computerized typesetting, now common throughout the industry, offers more flexibility. Editors, who can designate exact widths in fractions of picas and points, have more control over the final product.

Picas and points are also used to measure the gutters, the white space between columns of type and between pages. The gutters between columns usually range from 1 to 2 picas. The vertical measurement of type columns is usually expressed in inches. Newspaper pages range in size from approximately 20 to 22½ inches in height. Widths usually are expressed in picas and range from approximately 80 to 90 picas. Tabloids are approximately half the size of a full or broadsheet newspaper page.

In layout and design, the editor must determine horizontal widths exactly. Elements that do not fit horizontally must be corrected; copy must be reset, and illustrations must be trimmed or resized. Such corrections take too much time. When fitting items vertically, however, the editor has more flexibility. Copy that is too long can be trimmed quickly, so vertical problems are solved more easily.

Ems, ens, and quads used to be familiar terms in newspaper offices. Now, outside the composing room where the pages are pasted up, the terms are not common. Some VDT systems still have ems, ens, and quad spaces designated on the keyboards; others have translated them into more common terms. An em is equal to the space occupied by the capital *M* in whatever type size is being used. An en is equal to half an em. In hot-metal production systems, a quad referred to a piece of metal less than type high and used for spacing. An em quad is the square of the type size.

The basic measurements at a newspaper, then, are picas, points, ems, ens, and quads. Picas and points are the most important.

The elements

The five basic tools that editors use are text, headlines, rules, photographs, and artwork. Each has its special vocabulary.

TEXT. Text is another term for the type that is used to set the stories and editorials. It is measured in points, and most newspapers use sizes of 8½ to 10 points. By comparison, books are often set in 10- to 12-pt. type. This book is set in 10-pt. type. Variations in size and legibility are discussed in more detail in Chapter 11.

The space or leading (sometimes spelled ledding) between the lines of textual type is important to the legibility of the copy. Some newspapers set the copy with minus leading (less than the size of the type being used). For example, the Baltimore *News American* uses 10-pt. type with 9¾ points of leading, as below:

This is possible because type is measured from the top of the ascender (the upper parts of letters such as the *d* and *b*) to the bottom of the descender (the lower parts of letters such as *p* or *y*). Even when a descender is aligned directly over an ascender, the two do not touch at that leading, as this example set in 10-pt. type with 9¾-points of leading, illustrates.

Most newspapers, however, have ½ to 1 full point of leading between lines. The type size and amount of leading affects the number of lines that can be printed in a newspaper column. Legibility is also affected by how these factors are manipulated. When metal type is used, a slug is the combination of the type size and the leading.

Most text copy is set flush left and flush right. That is, the copy lines up evenly on both the left and right margins. To accomplish this, the type is justified by placing extra space between words and hyphenating words at the end of a line when necessary. When newspaper type was set by hand on Linotypes, the operator had to justify each line of type. Now the computer does it much more quickly.

Type can also be set ragged right, and this style is becoming fashionable in newspapers. Instead of hyphenating words, the computer leaves white space at the end of the line and starts a new one. Despite the irregular space at the end of the lines, ragged right does not take up more room. Some newspapers, such as the New Haven (Conn.) *Journal-Courier* and the Allentown (Pa.) *Morning Call,* set all their text type ragged right.

Computers can also be programmed to set type in a modified ragged right. That is, the computer will hyphenate words to ensure a minimum width. An editor might want to program the computer to hyphenate only when a line of type would not exceed 50 or 60 percent of the potential line length. This eliminates inordinately short lines.

Newspaper text is set in columns or wraps of type. A story that extends across five columns of a newspaper page is said to have five wraps.

HEADLINES. Headlines, or heds as they are sometimes spelled, are the larger version of text type. They too are measured vertically in points. Headline type starts at 14 points and extends over 100 points. Normal headline schedules, a list of type sizes available to the editor, include 14-, 18-, 24-, 30-, 36-, 42-, 48-, 54-, 60-, 72-, and 84-pt. type. Some head schedules go even larger. Because of technological developments in computerized typesetting systems, the sizes available are now endless. Early models of phototypesetters restricted editors to the traditional headline sizes because lenses were used to magnify the type to specified sizes.

Later models, which have digitized type on computer chips, permit the editor to set type in any size desired. If a headline written to be 60 points is a letter too long, the computer can be directed to set the type in 59 points. If the headline is too short, the editor can instruct the computer to set it at 63 points. Even at plants where earlier phototypesetting machines are used, editors can have a headline photoenlarged or reduced in the camera room to any size desired.

The shorthand for headline instructions varies from newspaper to newspaper. One of the common systems is to designate width, size, and number of lines by writing 2-36-3. This means the headline is 2 columns wide, 36 points, and 3 lines.

Various newspapers use different rules of capitalization in headlines. The least legible (see Chapter 11) is all caps, headlines written with all the letters capitalized. Many newspapers still use the traditional or uppercase style of capitalizing the first letter of every word except articles and prepositions. The lowercase style capitalizes only the first letter of the first word of the headline and proper nouns.

Most newspapers position the headlines flush left; that is, the headline begins at the left edge of the copy. Other styles include (1) flush right, the end of the headlines is aligned with the right-hand edge of the copy and white space appears to the left of the headline; (2) centered, the headline is centered above the story; and (3) stepped down, the second and all subsequent lines of a head are written shorter than the preceding one and indented under the one above it. The stepped-down style is archaic. Although few newspapers center all heads, most use centered and flush right heads for special display packages.

Not all the vocabulary that refers to special uses of headline type is standardized. However, the following terms are common (Fig. 2.2):

The headline story
When headlines are titles or labels
they need elaboration. One way to do this
is through a readout or a dropout

Kicker head
This line is usually indented

This format can be used
to sell the story. It is
called a
Readin

Hammer head
These attract attention

This is a sidesaddle headline
DENVER (UPI) — It would be easier for prosecutors to use illegally seized evidence in certain cases if Attorney General William French Smith had his way.

Smith Saturday told UPI's 23rd annual EDICON conference of editors and publishers that law enforcement has been handicapped by a legal doctrine known as the exclusionary rule, which bars the use of illegally obtained evidence in criminal cases.

Fig. 2.2.

Banner — a large headline that extends across the top of the front page above the most important story of the day.

Deck — one or more lines that are subordinate to the main headline and give the reader additional information about the story.

Kicker — three or four words that are set half the size of the main headline and usually appear flush left above the main headline. Generally, the main head is indented under the kicker, which should not be smaller than 24 points.

Hammer — a one- or two-word headline in large type. It is effective in attracting attention and adding white space to the page but needs a deck to further explain the story. The hammer usually is twice the size of the deck.

Sidesaddle — also called a side head, the type is placed at the left of the copy rather than over it.

Readin — similar to the kicker in size and placement, the readin is a conversational approach to headline writing and needs the main headline to complete the sentence. The main head, a label or title, should be able to stand alone.

Readout (dropout) — a deck, but reads directly out of the main head. The readout is more conversational than the traditional deck and is not written to a specific count.

Blurb — a quote or short piece of interesting or alluring information pulled from the body of the story and set in larger type, such as 18 points. It is either tucked under the headline or placed somewhere in the body of the copy.

Headlines, regardless of where they are placed or their format, must fit. The writers usually count the letters, but more and more, computers are doing that work quickly and accurately. However, at offices where letters must still be counted, a standardized method is needed. There are several formulas, each equally good if used consistently. In a typical formula, all lowercase letters are counted 1 except *f, i, l, t,* and sometimes *j,* which are counted ½, and *m* and *w,* which are counted 1½. All capital letters are counted 1½ except *M* and *W,* which are counted 2. Punctuation marks are usually counted 1, and the space between words is assigned a value of either ½ or 1.

A headline schedule is then established. The easiest, though not the most exact, way of making a chart is to set the headlines, using the same wording, in all the sizes you will be using. Lay the headline across a full newspaper page marked off by columns. Determine the number of counts that will fit in each column width or establish the number of counts per pica. You can check this schedule by setting another headline using different words. Sometimes a headline will count shorter because it has an unusual number of *l*'s, *t*'s, or *f*'s. The following headline is marked using 1 as one count and - as a ½ count:

1- - - - 1- 1-1 1 1 - 1-1 1-1 - - -1 - -1 1
St. Helens blows its top

There are 20 counts in this headline, which was run as a 72-pt. banner in the *San Francisco Examiner* on May 19, 1980.

BORDERS AND RULES. Sometimes borders and rules are used to set off headlines and are also used around illustrations and copy. A rule usually refers to a simple, plain line. Borders are more ornamental in design. The terms are often used interchangeably. A selection of both is shown in Figure 2.3. When a rule or border is used around copy, it is called a box. Different newspapers use different-sized rules for boxes, and sometimes the same newspaper uses more than one size. Most, however, use rules rather than borders to box stories. In earlier times, rules were used in the gutters to separate columns; now white space is commonly used to perform this function. A 2-pt. rule is usually used, but 4-, 6-, 8-, 10-, and even 12-pt. rules are appearing more often. Cutoff rules, lines below or alongside an illustration to separate it from unrelated copy, used to be 1 point. Now, to emphasize the cutoff and add weight to the page, 4- and 6-pt. rules are often used instead. Among the many ornamental borders available, the two most common are the Oxford and Ben Day rules. Most of the others are used only on special features on a seasonal basis or by the advertising department.

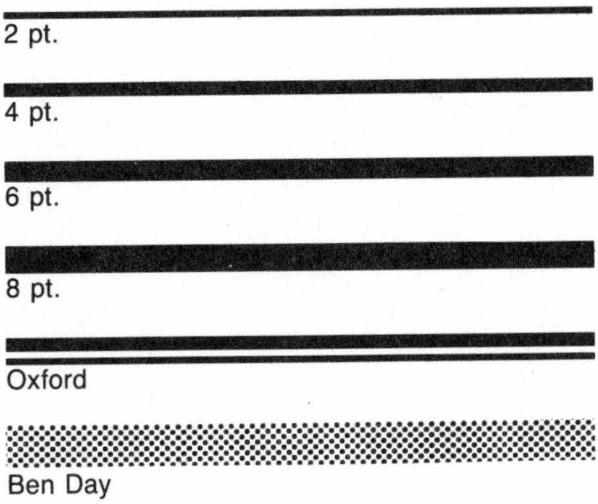

2 pt.

4 pt.

6 pt.

8 pt.

Oxford

Ben Day

Fig. 2.3.

PHOTOGRAPHS. Photographs are also called cuts, pic (singular) or pix, and sometimes, mistakenly, art. Photographs come from staff photographers, wire services, and free-lancers (persons who sell individual pictures to a publication). Staff photographers and free-lancers provide glossies, pictures printed with a shiny surface. Photographs transmitted by the Associated Press, which has a laserphoto transmission system, are also glossy. United Press International calls its system Unifax. Regardless of the source, all have tones ranging from black to white. The text that accompanies a photograph is variously called a cutline, caption, or legend.

ARTWORK. Artwork is any illustration other than a photograph and includes serious or humorous illustrations, maps, graphs, and charts. Photographs used for special effects, such as silhouetting or screening to produce a different image (Fig. 2.4), are properly classified as art. Art that is black and white, such as a chart or simple line drawing, is shot without a screen and is called line art. If it is the correct size, it can be affixed directly to the page from which the plate is to be burned. If it has gray tones, it must be screened (shot as a halftone).

Fig. 2.4.   Halftones can be shot with special-effects screens such as this one, which produces a mottled or overexposed effect.

Almost all photographs and artwork need to be reduced or enlarged before they are printed. The proportions are established by the layout editor and designer. A proportion wheel is usually used to determine the proper percentage of enlargement or reduction. Artwork shot at 100 percent will produce a duplicate the same size as the original. Anything shot at larger than 100 percent results in an enlargement; less than 100 percent provides a reduction. To size illustrations with a proportion wheel:

1. Measure the original illustration. In our example (Fig. 2.5A), the photograph is 45 by 30 picas after cropping. Always express the width first.

Fig. 2.5A.

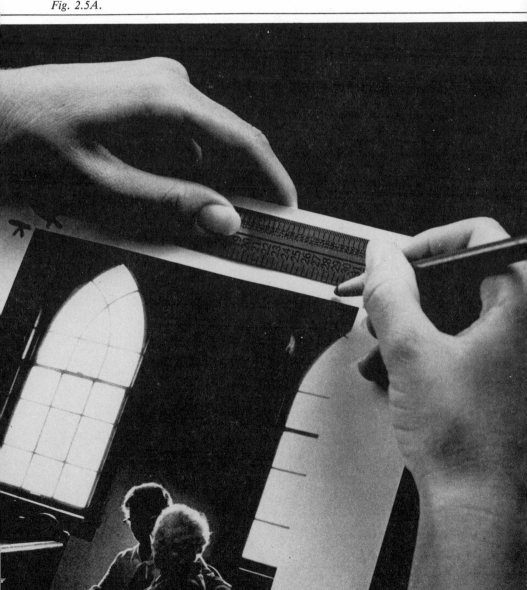

2. Determine the most important measurement needed to fit your dummy. Usually that is the width. In the example, the known measurement of the reproduction is 3 columns wide (42 picas in this case).

3. On the proportion wheel, place the number showing the original size (45) under the reproduction size (42) (Fig. 2.5B). Without moving the wheel, look at the arrows showing the reduction ratio. The arrow points to 94 (Fig. 2.5C), which means that the photograph will be shot at 94 percent and will be reduced 6 percent from its original size. When an illustration is enlarged or reduced, its size is changed proportionally in all directions. Consequently, while the width is decreasing 6 percent, from 45 to 42 picas, the depth will be shrinking by the same percentage.

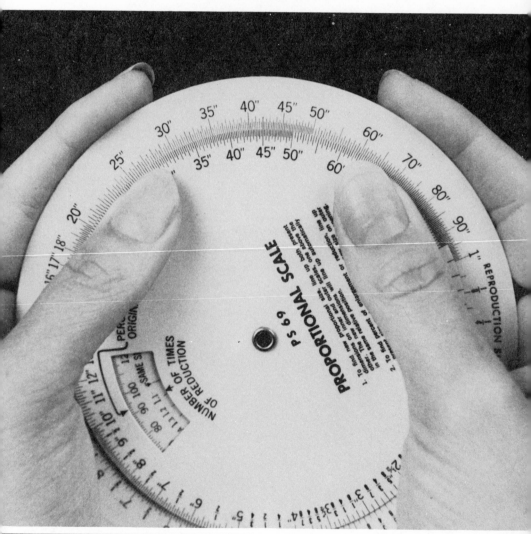

Fig. 2.5B.

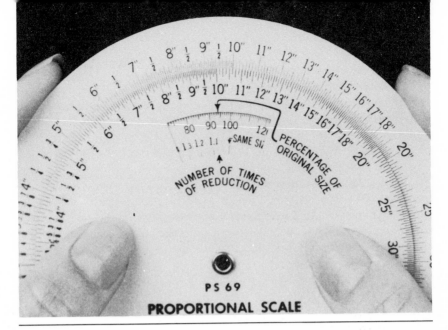

Fig. 2.5C.

4. Again, without moving the wheel, look at the 30 (depth of the present photograph) on the inside wheel, which is marked original size (Fig. 2.5D). The number above 30 is 28, the depth of the reproduced picture. In every case, you have three known measurements and one unknown. In this example, you knew the original width and depth as well as the new width. The unknown was the new depth. The same result can be achieved by working

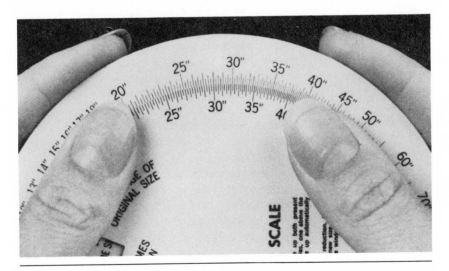

Fig. 2.5D.

the standard proportion formula, 45:30::42:x. The original width (45) is to the original depth (30) as the new width (42) is to the new depth (x). Multiply the extremes (45 $\times$ x) and the means (30 $\times$ 42) and complete the calculation as shown.

$$45x = 30 \times 42 = 1260$$
$$x = 1260 \div 45 = 28$$

With minicalculators common at many desks, the proportion wheel may soon become a thing of the past. There are other ways to size illustrations, but the wheel and the proportion formula are the quickest and easiest.

Structures

The structure of a newspaper is its basic architecture. While there are many varieties of architecture, there are only three basic newspaper structures: vertical, horizontal, and a combination of the two. Each has its advantages and disadvantages.

The *Wall Street Journal,* which has the largest circulation of any newspaper in the United States, is structured vertically. A vertical newspaper runs few headlines more than 2 columns wide. Stories start at the top of the page, and many run all the way to the bottom. On the inside, the vertical structure is not so pronounced because the vertical copy flow is interrupted by ads. A newspaper using a vertical structure has a personality that is conservative, reliable, and traditional. The structure of the *Wall Street Journal* contributes to its image and coincides with its content. In that sense, the *Journal* is a well-designed newspaper. Vertically structured newspapers are also quicker to lay out and compose. There is little for the layout editor to do but fit the stories in the holes vertically. The composing room employees can put the page together quickly because they do not have to divide columns of type. Most of them simply run down the page.

Since 1- and 2-column headlines take up less space than larger, multicolumn headlines, it is possible to get more stories on a vertically structured page. Consequently, the vertical format is the best choice for newspapers seeking a high story count on Page 1.

For some newspapers, however, the advantages of the vertical structure are also disadvantages. Newspapers that do not want a conservative, traditional image or are more concerned with the quality and length of the stories than the count on Page 1, see the vertical structure as a disadvantage. This structure also works against a page design that attempts to move the reader around the page. Vertical papers usually are top-heavy; the bottom half has little or nothing to attract the reader's attention, and it is difficult to keep the page from getting gray and dull. The *Wall Street Journal* is a special-interest publication with an unusual consumer profile. What works for it may not work for others. Some newspapers have tried to capitalize on the reliability aspects of vertical makeup while introducing a more modern look. The *Chicago Tribune*'s "Business" section (Fig. 2.6) is a good example.

Fig. 2.6.

Few newspapers have either a pure vertical or pure horizontal structure. There are several advantages to the horizontal structure, the most prominent being that the majority of readers perceive it as more modern and pleasing (Siskind 1979). Stories laid out horizontally take advantage of the reader's inclination to read from left to right. The horizontal structure also permits the layout editor and designer to be more flexible when balancing the page. The larger, multicolumn headlines used in horizontal makeup not only attract attention but also add color and weight to the page (Click and Stempel 1974).

Another important advantage is the optical illusion that results when a story is laid out horizontally. A 20-inch vertical story would extend from the top of a page to the bottom. It would look long, and because of the limited number of things a designer can do in one column, it probably would look dull. Readers who wear bifocals have difficulty reading a vertical story because they must fold or raise the paper as they proceed down the column. The same 20-inch story run horizontally across 6 columns would be 3⅓ inches deep. Consequently, it would look shorter, and the designer or layout editor can use more graphic devices to relieve the grayness. Not many readers want to spend the time required to read a 20-inch story, but it is the designer's job to stimulate their interest.

One of the few disadvantages of the horizontal structure is the additional time required for layout or design. Also, papers can easily become sensational in appearance with overly large headlines and cluttered graphic elements such as stars and arrows; this can affect the public's perception of the newspaper's reliability. A purely horizontal page (Fig. 2.7), however, is as dull as purely vertical makeup. What is needed is a combination of the two. A good horizontal structure needs strong vertical elements to provide contrast. Monotony is the enemy of any structure. To the editor working on a horizontal page, nothing is more welcome than a strong vertical photograph. Copy run more than the standard column width can perform the same optical function. One newspaper format features a wide column on the front page every day.

Fig. 2.7.

Newspaper formats

The *W*-format, so-named because one wide column is run down the left side of the front page, has a built-in vertical element. Newspapers most commonly use it to run news summaries or feature a popular local columnist. It is the page anchor. Used every day, it gives the page a familiar look no matter how much the rest of the page changes. The setting for the wide column is determined by the number of other columns and their width. For example, on a page 85 picas wide, the editors may decide to run 4 regular columns and 1 wide column. Using a rule of thumb that the wide column ought to be approximately one and one-half times larger than the regular columns, the editors could have 4 columns 14½ picas wide and 1 column 21 picas wide. Enough flexibility should be provided so that the wide column can start at the top left or sit at the bottom left. Such flexibility permits the use of a banner headline for important news. It also permits the editor to run copy all the way across the bottom on occasion, a pleasant variation from the usual use of space to the right of the wide column.

The *W*-format is one of four basic formats in use today. The others are the 8-column, optimum (6-column), and 6-on-9 columns. The 8-column format was standard in the industry for years but rapidly went out of favor in the mid 1960s when newsprint prices increased rapidly. Publishers tried to cut costs by decreasing the size of the paper. The new narrower width, in turn, forced a change in the number of columns. Legibility researchers had already suggested that newspapers should use wider columns of type for ease of reading. The 6-column width, which has come to be called optimum format because the type is within the optimum ease-of-reading range, was the logical choice of many newspapers because of the new page width and size of text type. The newsprint crunch, coupled with the examples provided by the now-defunct *National Observer* and the *Christian Science Monitor* (then a broadsheet), convinced many editors to try the optimum format. For many, the change to 6 columns was a headache because advertising was still being sold on an 8-column basis. Although specifications could be changed locally, it was more difficult to sell national advertisers on the new widths. The destandardization of newspaper formats had begun, and even today national advertising agencies complain that it is impossible for them to prepare ads in all the sizes required by newspapers across the country. Now that newspaper pages are becoming narrower, optimum line length is closer to 5 columns.

Some newspapers chose the 6-on-9 format. The page was divided into 9 columns for advertising and 6 columns for editorials. That made the editorial and advertising material compatible in some combinations, but it produced some news columns that were 8 and 9 picas wide on inside pages. As a result, many newspapers have gone to 6 columns throughout.

Design philosophies

Within these formats, the only design philosophy still in wide use is the contrast-and-balance or informal balance approach. Editors balance the top and bottom of the page by using the contrasting weights provided by headlines, text, white space, and illustrations. Within the contrast and balance approach, copy can be laid out in rectangular blocks (modular), or stories can be tucked into each other in irregular shapes (brace). Almost all newspapers use contrast-and-balance because it provides unlimited flexibility in layout and design. Other design philosophies have more or less been discarded.

Formal balance was popular in the late 1800s and early 1900s, but the necessity of having two of nearly everything made the approach impractical. In formal balance, it was necessary to balance one headline with another in terms of size, column width, and weight. If there was a 1-column picture in the upper right, there had to be a 1-column picture in the upper left. In formal balance, form overrode content.

Circus makeup enjoyed a spectacular but relatively brief reign, particularly among the Hearst and Pulitzer papers that were competing for circulation. Big headlines; plenty of typographical ornaments such as bullets and stars; large pictures, often in irregular shapes; and copy set in various sizes and widths were features of circus makeup. It was exciting but hard to read. It is still practiced by grocery store tabloids such as the *National Star* and *National Enquirer.*

CHAPTER THREE

Laying out pages

I THINK (pagination) is going to be just horrible. I think we are going to be locked into formatting, and you can't have an infinite number of formats. I have a bad feeling that pages are going to be very, very humdrum.

Edmund C. Arnold
AUTHOR AND EDUCATOR

IN TRIBAL TIMES, witch doctors protected their position in the community by hoarding knowledge. In our time, many beginning journalists in newspaper offices think there is some magical process for laying out pages that involves potions and secret formulas. Its not that experienced journalists are hoarding knowledge; its just that most young journalists never take the time to learn the rather simple process of dummying newspaper pages.

Dummying is the technique of producing a blueprint for page makeup by placing elements on a page. Normally, it is done under deadline pressure. A designer might do one page in two or three hours, but a layout editor may need to do several. Journalism, as it refers to the reporting and writing process, has been described as literature in a hurry. Layout is design in a hurry. Journalists doing layout need to know how to work in modules, show relationships, and display photographs. They must also understand the basic principles of contrast and balance. Because speed is essential for the majority of pages in a newspaper, there is and will continue to be a need for people who know the basics of layout. Newspapers can neither afford to have an entire staff of newspaper designers nor give them the time to do the work. Designers may work on Page 1, sectional fronts, and special projects, but the majority of pages will continue to be drawn by layout editors.

Prior to preparing the dummy, some decisions must be made.

Predummy decisions

Before your pencil touches a dummy sheet (or your video cursor touches the grid) the following decisions must be made within the philosophy of the publication on which you are working:

1. Determine the number and size of the various stories, pictures, and pieces of art that will be placed on the page.
2. Decide which elements are related and how to group them.
3. Select the major display element or elements for the page.
4. Select the second major display element or elements for the page.

The number of elements goes a long way toward determining the looks of the page. Traditionally, that decision has been made by managing editors, and the layout editors were left to find a way to make all the pieces fit. However, this method is increasingly recognized as being unsatisfactory. The problem and a proposed solution are discussed further in Chapters 8 and 9. Regardless of who makes the decisions, story count is critical to what can be done with the page.

The newspaper's jump policy is also critical. If the paper is willing to continue stories from Page 1 or from one inside page to the next, as the *Los Angeles Times* does, the layout editor has one set of options. If the paper does not jump stories or sets a maximum number of stories that can be continued, the layout editor has another set of options. Within the confines of the newspaper's policy, then, you determine the number of elements that must appear on the page and their size or length.

The second decision involves related elements. Which picture or pictures go with which story? Do any of the stories have sidebars? Is there more than one story on the same general topic, such as health or education? The process of grouping related elements forces the editor to think in terms of packages rather than individual elements. Sometimes this can result in elevating two or more less important stories to a larger package that is more significant because of its combined message, makes more sense to the reader, and is easier to handle graphically. For instance, the Allentown *Morning Call* found that it had several stories related to the then-developing crisis in Iran. Handled separately, they all would have been on inside pages. Grouped, with a map of the world pinpointing the trouble spots, the package became the lead story (Fig. 3.1). Grouping related stories helps the reader make sense from the news. Packaging is good journalism.

The next step is to determine which element or elements will be the major display item. This is not always the same as selecting the most important story. The major display element consists of the dominant visual element. If the lead story does not have any photographs or artwork with it, the major display element may consist of a secondary story that has visuals. However, even if the most important story does not have any visuals, it still can be the major display element. The editor can use type and other graphic

Fig. 3.1.

devices to create a package that adds to the information in the story and attracts attention to it. This is discussed further in Chapter 12.

Usually, the major display package consists of text and illustrations. If the major display element is also the most important story, the editor's job is simplified. If it is not, the editor must lay out the page so that the most important story attracts the attention it deserves even though the page is built around the visual elements.

The final decision is identification of the second major display element, which will anchor the bottom of the page. That package, which usually includes illustrations, is needed to balance the weight at the top of the page and attract the reader's eye. This creates motion on the page. The reader's eye will move from the major display elements at the top to those at the bottom. In the process, most readers scan the headlines on the page as they go. If the stories are interesting and the headlines are well written, they may stop or return after reading other stories. If no major display element is placed at the bottom, the editors have conceded that half of the page to dullness.

Basic principles

The following basic principles should always be kept in mind when dummying a page (note exceptions):

1. Avoid tombstoning, the practice of bumping headlines against each other. You should not bump heads because the consumer might read from one head into the next. This practice also concentrates type in one area and can upset the balance of the page. When neither of these conditions exist, tombstoning is acceptable in moderation. For instance, bumping is permissible with a large, multicolumn head and a small, 1-column head. It is reasonable to assume that a consumer would not read from a 4-column, 48-pt. headline into a 1-column, 24-pt. headline. However, do not bump 2 multicolumn heads. Some editors alternate regular and italic headlines to keep the reader from going from one tombstoned head to the other. That is not a good use of italic type and does not alleviate the problem of massing type in one area of the page. Photographs, artwork, and boxes should be used to separate headlines.

2. Do not tombstone unrelated photographs or artwork. Again, there are two reasons: bumping photos or artwork concentrates too much weight in one place on the page, and the reader may think the photographs or artwork are related because they are adjacent to one another.

3. On inside pages, avoid placing art, photographs, or boxes next to advertisements because they usually have a high "noise level"; that is, they contain their own large type, photographs, or artwork. Similar editorial material placed next to ads also results in an unbalanced page. Because many inside pages have little news space, it is not always possible to avoid bumping editorial art against advertising art. As a general practice, however, it is better to speak with a softer voice on inside pages dominated by ads. The contrast is likely to attract more attention than if both the news and advertising are competing with the same type of materials. Boxed news stories on top of ads, which also are boxed, look like advertising copy (Fig. 3.2). If it is necessary to box a story adjacent to an ad, the box should extend into the news space instead of running flush with the advertising.

4. Do not Dutch-wrap copy. A Dutch wrap, or raw wrap, occurs when copy extends beyond a headline. Readers are not accustomed to having the text width exceed that of the headline. However, if there is no possibility that the reader will become confused by the layout, it is permissible to wrap the copy from underneath the head. This most often occurs on inside pages where advertising takes up all but the top few inches of the page. If there is only one story, the reader can easily follow the path of the copy (Fig. 3.3). If there are two or more stories above each other, the material must be separated. Sometimes this is done with a heavy rule such as 4 or 6 points or by wrapping copy underneath a related photograph (Fig. 3.4). This technique must be done carefully to avoid confusing the reader.

Fig. 3.2.

Fig. 3.3.

Fig. 3.4.

Two design principles

The principles of design are discussed in detail in Chapter 9. Only two, contrast and balance, are dealt with here.

Contrast refers to the technique of using different typographical elements — text type, headline type, white space, photographs, and artwork — and different shapes to relieve dullness, provide visual excitement, and balance the page. Balance refers to the distribution of weights on the page. Formal balance, as practiced by newspapers years ago, meant balancing a 2-column, 48-pt, 3-line head in the upper right with the same headline specification in the upper left. This principle produced a symmetrical page. However, artists have known for centuries that symmetry is not pleasing because it is dull. For example, a square is symmetrical and is the least attractive shape to work with. Editors gradually realized that balance could be produced by contrasting different elements with similar weights. The weight of a headline is determined by its design, size, width, and number of lines. The weight of a photograph is determined by its size and tones. A photograph can be used to balance the weight of a headline mass. White space that is used properly around headlines and between other elements on the page also helps balance the page.

Both designers and layout editors try to balance their pages. Placing the second major display element at the bottom of the page helps balance the weight at the top. Depending on the other elements, the second element usually is placed at the corner opposite the lead visual element. Balance, then, is achieved by using contrasting elements to distribute the weights. When properly done, this draws the reader's eye around the page.

Dummying the page

Inside pages arrive at the layout desk with the advertising space already indicated on the dummy sheet. In Figure 3.5, the dummy shows five ads on the page. At some newspapers, the name of the advertiser may be shown on the dummy. Even though editors know the name, they seldom know the content of the ads. Consequently, it is best to avoid placing illustrations adjacent to the ads because there might be too much competition for the reader's attention. With the ads stacked to eliminate uneven edges, the editor already has a good modular space to work with. The 1980 campaign was chosen as the major display package. Because the only photographs available were from the newspaper library, the editor chose to use type and rules to show relationships and attract attention. Besides the three spot-news campaign stories, the editor selected a White House staff reorganization story and a national story on the 55-mile-an-hour speed limit. Figure 3.6 shows the dummy that went to the composing room, and Figure 3.7 shows the final product.

Fig. 3.5.

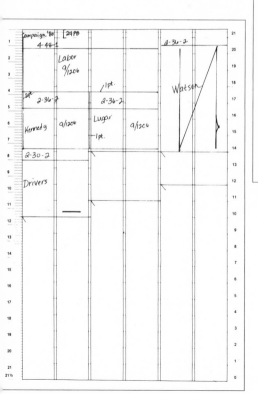

Fig. 3.6.

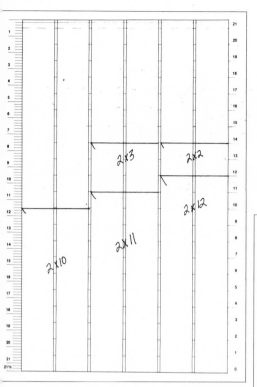

Fig. 3.7.

The editor grouped the three campaign stories under the "Campaign '80" label. The headlines on the Kennedy and Lugar stories are both 2 columns wide, 36 points high, and 2 lines deep. Ordinarily that would be tombstoning, but the 1-pt. rule solves the problem.

Figure 3.6 shows how the material is indicated on the dummy. Each story has a slug, the identifying name. That slug also appears at the top of the copy. At newspapers where the headline is set with the story, the slug usually appears over the headline in small type so that it can be trimmed easily. The paste-up person matches the slug on the story with that on the dummy to ensure proper placement.

The story slugged "Labor" has a 4-48-1 headline. That means the headline is 4 columns wide, 48 points high, and has 1 line. The headline over "Watson" is 2-36-2, that is, 2 columns wide, 36 points high, and 2 lines. Such a designation is common, but many newspapers do it differently. Some use numbers. A #4 head, for example, might mean a 36-pt. head over 2 columns. Others give headline directions by writing only 6-48, which indicates the number of columns and the point size. At some papers, the number of lines in the headline is indicated by marking X's on the dummy. At others, the number of vertical lines underneath the type size indicates the number of lines.

Regardless of how headlines are marked on the dummy, size selection is important. For the experienced editor, this task is second nature. For the beginner, it is more difficult. The best way to get a feel for it is to learn to recognize headline sizes. Go through a newspaper and try to identify the size of the type in the heads. Then take a pica ruler and measure the heads from the top of the ascender to the bottom of the descender (see Chapter 10). The headlines may not come out in traditional sizes because of the variety of type designs, because some phototypesetters can produce type in 1-pt increments, and because some newspapers reduce their pages slightly before printing them, but you should be within 1 or 2 points.

The proper size for the headline depends on the type design and column width. The bolder the headline, the less size is needed. At newspapers that use the regular weight as the standard head and have column widths of 12 to 14 picas, Table 3.1 can be used as a guide.

The X's indicate, for instance, that you can use a 30-pt. headline for 1- and 2-column stories, but not for 3 and larger. The chart is based on the number of characters it takes to fill the space in a given column width. Type set at 36 points in 1-column width looks large; but spread over 4 or 5 columns, it looks smaller and is difficult to read. Type set at 48 points in 2 or 3 columns looks large and makes the story look more important; however, used across 6 columns, it looks smaller and is used for softer or feature stories. Type set at 24 points looks small over 25 to 29 picas, but it will work on a 2-column news summary or as a conversational readout headline over a story that is 2 columns or wider. Even then, however, the type is usually set

Type	Column Width					
Size	1	2	3	4	5	6
18	x					
24	x					
30	x	x				
36	x	x	x			
42	x	x	x	x		
48		x	x	x	x	x
60		x	x	x	x	x
72		x	x	x	x	x

Table 3.1.   Guide for sizing headlines

narrower than the copy underneath and is indented under the main head.

At newspapers where headlines are set separately from the copy, it is important to mark the depths of the headlines on the dummy. This permits the composing room employees to paste in the copy even before the headline arrives. This is not necessary, however, where the newspaper is produced on video display systems connected to photocomposition machines, because the headlines and copy are produced together.

At the top of the campaign box (Fig. 3.6), which is indicated by drawing a line around the stories, there is a designation "24 PB." This indicates that a 24-pt. Poster Bold headline should be used. Poster Bold is one of the weights available in Compugraphic's version of the Bodoni family. The 2-pt. designation under the "Labor" slug indicates that a 2-pt. rule is desired; a 1-pt. rule has been ordered for the interior lines.

The setting in the boxed material is 9/1206, which means 9-pt. type, 12½ picas wide. Normal setting for this newspaper is 13 picas. Any copy set other than the normal setting is indicated on the dummy.

Copy flow indications on the dummy sheet vary widely among newspapers. Some depend on the dummy to indicate where the copy begins and ends. The "Campaign '80" package does not have any copy flow marks, but the person doing pasteup probably will have no trouble determining how to place the copy on the page. Other newspapers use a line as illustrated in the "Watson" story (Fig. 3.7). Still others show the end of the story by drawing a horizontal line, as shown in the story slugged "Drivers." Each newspaper has its own set of easily learned symbols. As the industry moves toward dummying pages electronically, those symbols will be relegated to history books.

On June 7, 1980, the editors of the *Boston Globe* decided that their lead story was the economy (Fig. 3.8). They coupled it with a sidebar that was the first of a four-part series on the unemployed in Massachusetts. The most

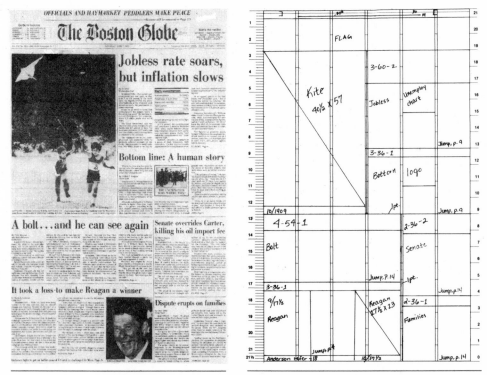

Fig. 3.8.   *Fig. 3.9.*

important story did not relate to the major display element, however, which was a picture of boys flying a kite. Such a picture, because it does not have a related story, is variously called a stand-alone picture or wild art. The second major display element was the Reagan package. The extra sizing on the photo of Reagan, 17½ picas instead of the normal 13 picas, gave the picture more punch.

Unlike the inside page dummied earlier, this page included photographs. Again, newspapers mark them in various ways, but one of the best is to indicate the size of the photograph in picas (Fig. 3.9). The kite, for instance, is 40½ by 57 picas, a more exact measurement than 6¾ by 9½ inches. If pictures are cropped and sized correctly, a pica can make a difference. Pictures are often indicated on a dummy either by a diagonal line or by crossing out the area. Space must be left for the cutline and varies according to the cutline required. Some pictures need a lot of text; others need hardly any. The kite cutline is set in 10-pt. type and is 19¾ picas wide (shown as 1909 on the dummy).

Every story on this page jumps. The dummy indicates where the story continues, but it does not indicate the key word, usually the first word of the headline, over the continued story. At newspapers where the continued head is written before the dummy goes to the composing room, the key word can be indicated on the dummy. At other papers where jump heads are written later, it is sufficient to indicate that the story jumps to another page.

Interior rules are built into the Boston *Globe*'s format. Sizes would not have to be indicated on the dummy unless they were a departure from the norm. There are two "refer" or reference lines on the page. One is the all-cap headline at the top of the page; the other is the 14-pt. line referring to the story about John Anderson on Page 6. The index at the upper left and the weather at the upper right are called ears, and they appear every day as part of the flag, or nameplate. They do not have to be shown on the dummy.

Special layout problems

In Figures 3.7 and 3.8, some copy was set in a width other than the newspaper's standard format. This occurred on the inside page example (Fig. 3.7) because the copy is boxed; on the front page example, the use of a photograph larger than the standard column required the accompanying copy to change accordingly. How are the correct settings determined in cases like these?

You must know three measurements of your newspaper: the column width, the gutter width, and the space being used by your stories or package of stories. With these measurements, you can determine the correct copy settings for a boxed story by:

1. Subtracting a set amount of space for the box. In Figure 3.7, the box is a 2-pt. rule. That newspaper subtracts 2 picas to accommodate the rule and to leave a sufficient and standardized amount of space between the rule and the copy. The space between the rule and the first column, and between the rule and the last column on the right, is provided for in the two picas deducted for the box.

2. Subtracting the space for gutters.

3. Dividing by the number of columns or wraps of type. The result should be a copy setting adjusted for the box.

The package in Figure 3.7 occupies four columns. In that newspaper, the columns are 13 picas and the gutters are 1½ picas. Four columns, therefore, occupy 56½ picas of space [(4 × 13) + (3 × 1½)]. Following the steps listed above, subtract 2, the space occupied by the rule and the white space adjacent to it, from 56½, leaving 54½ picas. Then subtract the gutter space. With four columns of copy, there are three gutters. Completing the steps above: $56\frac{1}{2} - 2$ (box) $= 54\frac{1}{2} - 4\frac{1}{2}$ (gutters) $= 50 \div 4$ (number of columns of type) $= 12\frac{1}{2}$ or 1206 (copy setting).

If only three columns were set in the same amount of space, the computation would be changed as follows: $56\frac{1}{2} - 2$ (box) $= 54\frac{1}{2} - 3$ (gutters) $= 51\frac{1}{2} \div 3$ (number of columns of type) $= 17\frac{1}{2}$ or 1706 (copy setting).

This method of determining the correct setting for bastard copy (set in a different width from the standard setting) assures uniformity in the amount of white space between the type and border and between columns of type.

Selecting the setting for copy that accompanies a picture that is not a standard column width requires determination of the size of the picture. In the Reagan example from the *Boston Globe,* the picture was sized to $17\frac{1}{2}$ picas and the two wraps of copy came out to the same width. Often, however, the picture is a different width than the copy. The editor who enlarges the picture to 19 picas and still wants two wraps of copy would have to follow this formula (the columns are still 13 picas, but the gutters are 1 pica in this example):

1. Total space for the package: $54\frac{1}{2}$ picas.
2. Subtract space for the photograph: 19 picas.
3. Space remaining for the copy: $35\frac{1}{2}$ picas.
4. Subtract space for gutters (2 picas): $33\frac{1}{2}$ picas.
5. Divide by number of wraps desired (2): 1609 or 16 picas, 9 points.

In this case, the size of the photograph determines the space left for the type. In another situation, the photograph must accommodate itself somewhat to the needs of type. This occurs when a package is boxed and copy runs alongside and under the photograph as it does in Figure 3.10. The process is the same as determining the setting for boxed copy. The editor must first determine the setting for the copy just as if there were no pictures in the box. The difference between this example and the Reagan example, in which the picture size was determined first, is that the Reagan picture and copy were not boxed.

Electronic dummying

Pagination is a production system in which editors lay out pages on a video display terminal (VDT), and the full page is produced from a photocomposition machine. Because of the potential cost savings of reducing the composing room work force, publishers have eagerly awaited the arrival of this new production system. After several false starts, pagination systems appeared early in the 1980s. The most advanced was produced by Hastech, a subsidiary of Hendrix electronics. The first installation was at Gannett's Westchester-Rockland Newspapers. The system was able to do most of the editorial func-

Fig. 3.10.

tions required to successfully produce a page and drastically reduced the number of composing room employees.

Hastech's Pagepro system consists of two VDT terminals, one a 12-inch screen on which copy is edited and the other a 15-inch screen on which the page is laid out (Fig. 3.11). The board has two sets of keys, one for editing and one for layout. The editor inserts instructions for size, shape, and position of the elements on the page by using the typing keys, a tablet, or a crosshair cursor controlled by what is called a joy stick, a leverlike rod at the right of the keyboard. The editor can move headlines, bylines, pictures, and copy. The screen shows the headlines in simulated type, but copy is shown only by straight lines when the full page is on the screen. However, the editor can zoom in on a portion of the page and see the actual copy. Using commands such as right-fill, left-fill, square-off, even-leg, uneven-leg, and box, the editor directs the copy flow as desired.

Photographs did not appear on the screen of the earlier systems, but the newer systems have that added capacity. Other companies have successfully produced pagination systems. Although editors appreciate the advantages of pagination, they are concerned that certain editorial functions be protected. Some believe it is important that they see the entire page, including text, on the screen. The traditional method permits some adjustments as the pages are being pasted up, but that opportunity might not exist in pagination systems after the page is sent to the photocomposition machine. Hastech and some other systems have the ability to insert rules and boxes, but special effects such as decorative borders still have to be added in the composing room. Whether this new system will inhibit the fledgling newspaper design movement is not known, but if editors do not retain the option to make some changes, it is clear that design will suffer. Looking at a page electronically on a 15-inch screen is not the same as examining the full page in paste-up form.

Pagination systems also permit editors to program a number of preset page layouts. The material for a page will be entered and the computer will be told to select an appropriate layout. If the editor cannot override the computer, there will be problems. Undoubtedly, some newspapers will use such computer functions to do inside pages. That will be an advantage if it permits editors to spend more time on open pages. If newspaper layout becomes strictly a machine function, journalism will not be served.

Fig. 3.11.

(1) An editor electronically strips a headline onto the page.

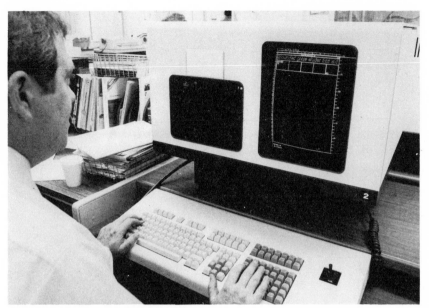

(2) Rectangles appear when the editor specifies a story shape.

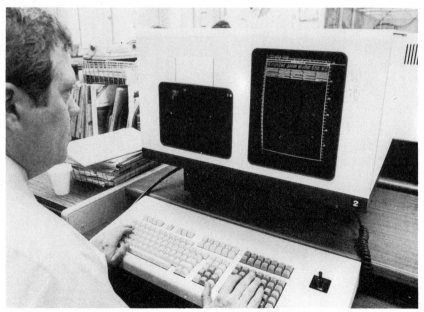

(3) Satisfied with the shape, he hyphenates and justifies the text.

(4) The page continues with space reserved for the photograph and stories.

(5) Completed, the page can be enlarged for a final check.

(6) In less than five minutes, the full page is in the composing room.

At newspapers where quality has never been a concern, pagination is likely to hurt the design of the paper. If the paper is concerned with quality, some changes must be made. For example, it may be necessary to move light tables into the newsroom so editors can make adjustments to pages, especially sectional pages that are not being produced against a daily deadline.

At the same time, pagination systems will permit designers to experiment with type placement and sizing in ways not previously possible. For instance, if an editor had 48-pt. type and wanted to see how 60-pt. type would look, the new size would have to be set, a time-consuming process. With pagination, however, the editor simply types in a new command and the desired type size appears on the screen.

Any new technology creates problems. The first VDT systems, for instance, were difficult for editors to use because the keys were all labeled with printer's terms. Eventually, the names were translated to more familiar terms. VDT functions that originally required two or three commands now require only one. If history is a guide, pagination systems will be refined and become more useful as an editorial tool.

Because the technology is so new, publishers eager to lower production costs should guard against going too far too fast. When optical character readers or scanners were introduced, they were marketed with the idea that publishers could eliminate costly and duplicative typesetting personnel. The reporter's typed copy was fed into a scanner that read the copy and put it directly into a typesetting system. Publishers were expected to replace typesetting personnel with less expensive clerical people who would retype stories so they would be clean enough to feed into the scanner. Unfortunately, few publishers hired typists. As a result, reporters, who should have been reporting, spent extra time typing to prepare their own copy for the scanner. The introduction of VDTs solved that problem. Similarly, the initial stages of pagination may be a setback for designers if publishers take immediate steps to eliminate the entire composing room without making provision for page adjustments. In the long run, however, pagination is another step in the evolution of complete editorial control over the product.

Fig. 4.1.

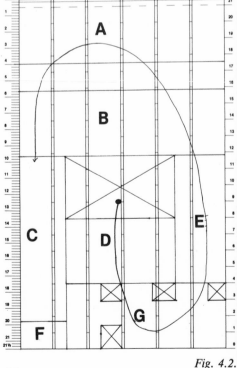

Fig. 4.2.

Working in modules

EVEN the ads in many papers make the news design look shabby. But sometimes newspapers stack up ads for a dreadful appearance.

Frank Ariss
DESIGNER

THIS IS THE AGE of modules—modular homes, modular schools, modular furniture, modular electronics, and modular clothes. This too is the age of modular page design.

A module is a unit, a subdivision of the whole. As applied to page design, it is a square or, preferably, rectangular unit. It contains anything from a single story to a package that includes a story, sidebar, and illustrations. Pages are formed by assembling modules. If they are put together in a pleasing arrangement, the page is well-designed.

The *Miami News* is one of many newspapers whose editors work in modules. On the front page, shown in Figure 4.1, there are seven modular units. The lead photograph, which is the focal point of the page, is in module D (Fig. 4.2), the same module as the related story underneath. The page is clean, orderly, and balanced and has a natural flow in the classic reverse-six pattern. The dominant photograph attracts the reader's attention first. Most readers will continue to the information below the photograph and then travel through the rest of the page on a shopping trip. The quality of the headlines and the reader's interest in the subject matter determine which, if any, of the other modules receive attention.

An alternative to the modular page is one in which copy wraps irregularly around related or nonrelated stories and pictures. This type of layout is supported by the principle that readers can be led from one story to another by interlocking them like a puzzle. Many newspapers, including the *Daily Oklahoman* (Fig. 4.3), still subscribe to this theory. The *Oklahoman*'s front page contains nine units. Two stories are in modules, but the other five wrap around another story or picture. Story B (Fig. 4.4) wraps around C, C and E wrap around the unrelated picture D, and H wraps around G. It is probable that most readers will start with photograph I, but the rest of their reading pattern is difficult to anticipate.

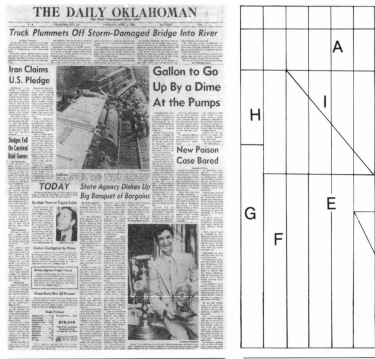

Fig. 4.3.   *Fig. 4.4.*

There are other differences between the pages of the *Miami News* and the *Daily Oklahoman* that do not relate to the use or absence of modules. The *Oklahoman* has 9 columns; the *News* has six. The *Oklahoman* is vertical; the *News* is horizontal. These and other factors create differing personalities for the two publications. The *Oklahoman* subscribes to the philosophy that a newspaper should appear busy. Thus it has a higher story count and more activity on the page. The *News* has chosen a contemporary look that features fewer stories and fewer jumps from Page 1. What the *News* loses in story count, it gains in readability.

Neither the *News* nor the *Oklahoman* is printed on an offset press, and type for both papers is set with photocomposition equipment (cold type). The introduction of photocomposition and offset printing stimulated wholesale changes in the face of U.S. newspapers during the 1960s and 1970s. Better reproduction led to a desire for more attractive newspapers that were easier to read. Beginning in the early 1960s, many newspapers went to the simplified modular style and eliminated column rules, fancy borders, and decorative type. By 1974, when the *Louisville Times* sponsored the watershed experimental newspaper design seminar, nearly all the proposed redesigns were modular. Newspapers did not suddenly invent the concept of working in modules. Magazines had been doing it for years with good reason. Most of them sold advertising in quarter, half, and full pages. The result was an editorial space blocked off in squares or rectangles. Most newspapers still do not have that advantage.

Advantages of modular layout

In addition to its clean, simple look, modular layout saves time in the production process, adapts quickly to technological changes, permits better packaging of related elements, provides the opportunity for contrast on the page, and has the ability to cater to reader preferences.

A pasteup person working on copy that wraps unevenly across two or more columns needs more time to measure, cut, and position columns of type than the person who is able to measure the depth of one wrap and cut the column of type into equal parts. Corrections are also quicker on modular layouts because lines can be added or subtracted more easily than on irregular wraps.

Production time is also saved when editors have to substitute stories on a modular page. A pasteup person can easily pull out a modular story and substitute another in its place without disturbing the entire page or a large section of it. Such changes are more difficult on a page with several uneven wraps. If the new story is shorter, the editor can insert two stories; if it is longer, the editor can eliminate two or more modules. In either case, the editor does not have to disturb a substantial portion of the page to make a change. This flexibility is especially attractive to papers with multiple editions.

People who are accustomed to working in modules will be able to adapt more quickly to pagination systems. Editors already are laying out pages on video display terminals, which permit them to move copy around the screen in modular blocks. Although it is possible to wrap copy unevenly when using a pagination terminal, it takes more time.

Working in modules also forces the layout editor to group related stories, pictures, and artwork for the reader's benefit. (More will be said about proper packaging in Chapter 6.) The basic principle is that all related material should be in the same module. Readers want to know which stories are related and prefer to have similar stories grouped by subject matter (Clark 1979, p. 30). Proper use of modules accomplishes this in a strong visual message.

Modules also make it easier for the editor to provide balance and break up the grayness that results from unrelieved areas of textual matter. Dividing the page into modular units forces the editor to work in specified subdivisions of the page, and the final product usually has better contrast throughout. Paul Back (1980), *Newsday*'s director of design, says that breaking up the broadsheet into smaller, more manageable areas allows the reader's eye to deal more effectively with the space.

The last and most important advantage of the modular format is the favorable reaction of the readers. Respondents to a survey in the early 1970s told researchers they preferred newspapers with a modern design, which is characterized by modules, optimum 6-column format, and horizontal layout. In fact, the authors concluded that the findings were a "ringing endorsement" for such newspapers (Click and Stempel 1974).

Sissors (1974) sampled young college-educated readers to determine format preferences. Reactions to the four front pages were mixed; and even though a traditional page edged out a more modern design, the clearest finding was the extremely low rating given to the only page not done in a modular format.

Until research is done using modules as the only variable, it is impossible to say flatly that modular layout is preferred over irregular wraps. It is unlikely that people in all communities will prefer one over the other. Readers on Long Island and in Miami, Minneapolis, and San Francisco may prefer newspapers with a modern appearance, but readers in other cities may like a more traditional approach. In fact, at least one of the papers in Little Rock and in Omaha use the traditional approach. Most of the research, however, lends support to modern formats. Designers who are trying to achieve a clean, uncluttered appearance and are conscious of legibility research prefer to use the modern formats.

Advertising arrangements

It is a challenge for editors to accommodate the reader's desire for uncluttered design on pages that contain both news and advertising because some advertising formats work against good design. There are three basic advertising configurations — the well, or U-shaped layout; the pyramid layout; and the modular layout.

From the readers' standpoint, the well advertising arrangement is the most annoying because news copy is stuck between overpowering advertisements. In Figure 4.5, Bob Hope and Helen Hayes are sandwiched be-

Fig. 4.5.   Fig. 4.6.

tween advertisements for a furniture store and a dishwasher. Because the well layout uses advertisements in both the upper left and upper right, it is impossible to design a page with a strong editorial focus. Seldom is there enough room to display photographs or artwork adequately. In fact, it often is preferable to use only headlines and text. Advertisements often have such large headlines and artwork that the editor may attract more attention to the stories on the page with a scaled-down design that offers a contrast.

Few newspapers still use the well arrangement; most use the pyramid layout in which ads are stacked left or right (Fig. 4.6). This permits the news department to use either the top right or left of the page for a package that will attract readers as they look through the publication.

The well and pyramid arrangements both are designed to place news copy adjacent to the advertisements. Newspaper advertising departments have long sold the idea that editorial copy that touches the advertisements brings readers into contact with the advertisements and thus increases exposure. While the intent is to serve the advertiser, the arrangement of the news and advertisements may be counterproductive. As one reader told a researcher, "I was reading this story and it was interesting, but then I turned to where it was continued and all I could find was a big ad for discount drugs or liquor or something which occupied most of the page" (Clark 1979, p. 29).

From both an economic and readership standpoint, advertisements are

important. A newspaper without advertising sells far fewer copies than a
newspaper with ads. Papers that do not have a good selection of grocery
ads, for instance, are harder to sell than papers that do. Classified ads attract strong readership because advertisements carry information that readers
want. Consequently, it is important from a design standpoint that advertisements and editorial copy work together. While readers object to searching
for copy buried among the ads, they also object to editors using space
alongside large ads for uninteresting stories. A well-designed advertisement
can attract readership on its own, and does not need the perfume of news
copy.

A modular advertising arrangement improves the looks of the paper,
provides better compartmentalization, and puts fewer roadblocks before the
reader. Because this arrangement requires that advertisements be stacked upon
each other (Fig. 4.7), some ads will be buried, in the sense that no editorial
copy will touch them. Shoppers should still be able to find them, however,
when only large ads are buried and smaller ads appear at the top of the page
or when several smaller ads are grouped by subject matter, such as dining
guides or movie listings (Fig. 4.8). Readers who want to dine out or know

Fig. 4.7.   Fig. 4.8.

what movie is playing are likely to read all the ads on that topic anyway.

In the 1970s, modular advertising formats were adopted by many newspapers including *Newsday* (a tabloid), the *Chicago Tribune,* and the *Los Angeles Times.* Smaller newspapers may have trouble selling the concept to local advertisers because a pure modular advertising system restricts ad sizes to eighth, quarter, half, or full pages. However, smaller papers can adopt a modified modular system by selling all the traditional sizes and stacking the ads so that they are blocked off. The publisher of a small Nebraska daily reported that he adopted a modified modular system in 1978 without telling his advertisers. None of them noticed. The readers, however, appreciated the more orderly inside pages, and as a result, the advertisers benefited too.

Working with advertisements

Editors of newspapers that do not use modular advertising stacks must learn to work *with* advertisements instead of *against* them. The pyramid stack poses problems, but they are not insurmountable. The editor can create modular units with the space remaining on the page by working off the corners of the ads. In Figure 4.9, lines are extended from the corner of the stacked ads. The letters A through D indicate the modular units created. Each of these units can be subdivided into more modules.

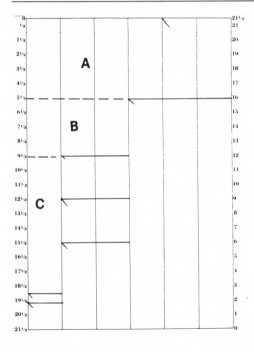

Fig. 4.9.

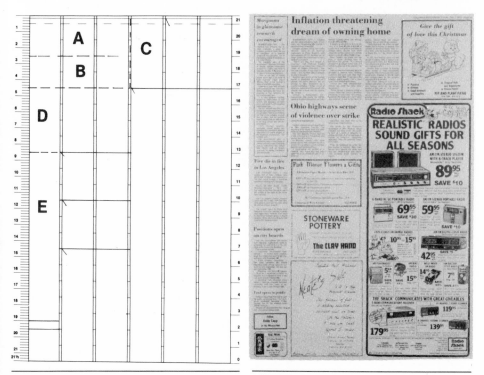

Fig. 4.10.   Fig. 4.11.

The lines represent either headlines or the edges of photographs or artwork. The number and shape of possible modules are limited only by the
editor's imagination. Figure 4.10 shows a different modular arrangement with
the same ad stack, and Figure 4.11 shows how one newspaper actually handled
the problem and produced a clean, orderly page. The contrast between an
inside modular page and one that has wraps around the corner of the ads
is illustrated by Figures 4.12 and 4.13. The ads in the first illustration are
pyramided right. Both the music and dance columns wrap around the corners
of ads instead of breaking neatly off them, and the book column wraps around
the dance column. In the second illustration, the ads are stacked in a module.
No copy touches the ad at the upper right, yet it has a good display space.
The space remaining for news copy has been used simply and effectively.

Every reasonable designer and editor would be quick to acknowledge
that the content cannot always be accommodated in a modular unit on an
inside page. Often this is not possible because there is room for only one
story, and the editor cannot break off the ad stack with headlines for secondary stories. In all cases, logic must temper layout decisions.

Fig. 4.12.

Fig. 4.13.

Modular open pages

Although it is much simpler to work in modules on pages with no advertisements, editors are obligated to arrange the elements on these open pages in a pattern that enhances readability.

The editors at the Lewiston (Idaho) *Tribune* achieve this goal consistently. The page in Figure 4.14 is typically modular, horizontal, and clean. There are eight modular units. The dominant focal point is in module C, and the layout takes advantage of the reverse-six flow pattern (Fig. 4.15). The story count, size and weight of the type, and lack of promotion for inside material gives the paper a "cool" or low-key personality. The modular format contributes to, but is not the exclusive reason for, the personality. Modules can bring order to disorder. However, editors can also put more action into their pages than that illustrated by the *Tribune*. The *Shreveport Journal* (Fig. 4.16) and the Baltimore *News American* (Fig. 4.17) show increasing degrees of activity. The *Shreveport Journal* has a 6-column color promotional block at the top of the page. The word "Friday" in the box to the left of the nameplate

Fig. 4.14.

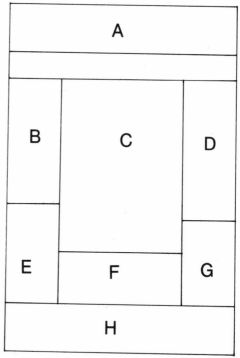

Fig. 4.15.

Fig. 4.16.

Fig. 4.17.

or flag, the date to the right, and the rose by Shreveport are also in red. Color increases the tempo of the page. Each of the modules is boxed with a 1-pt. rule to emphasize the unit approach. Although the combination of the promo, the large flag, and the heavy banner headline makes the page unusually top-heavy, the bottom has not been neglected.

USA Today, serving a different market, produces a "hot" paper, one that is modern in format and high in activity. *USA Today* combines the modular look with a high story count. The result is less simplicity and focus but more activity. There are twelve modular units on the page, which includes five pictures and two graphics.

All three papers are modular and horizontal, but each has a distinct personality. The modular format does not dictate uniformity.

Working with a modular layout is relatively easy, but using modules to communicate relationships can be complicated. The effort is necessary, however, if publications are to serve the best interests of readers. Grouping stories in an orderly fashion adjacent to each other or to accompanying pictures helps the reader understand the relationships, but putting all the elements into a single module makes it easier for the reader to actually see the relationships. When related elements are not in the same module, the reader may still make the connection, but not without some effort. In Figure 4.18, the story stripped across the top has a sidebar at the lower right. The editor is depending on the content of the headline to make the connection. Sometimes that works; sometimes it does not. In Figure 4.19, the two bridal pictures at the top of the page are not packaged in the same module with the related stories to the right and left of the pictures. Unfortunately, this layout gives the visual message that the pictures go with the child-abuse story directly below them. The content and the layout are in conflict.

Fig. 4.18.

Fig. 4.19.

When multiple elements are put into the same module, a relationship is established. In Figure 4.20, two stories and four pictures dealing with the potential baseball strike are packaged into a single module. Clutter is eliminated because each element within the larger module is a module itself, and the larger module fits into the overall page design.

Fig. 4.20.   Fig. 4.21.

Because copy laid out in a module is easier to read than columns of type that jump irregularly, it follows that an L-shaped copy block is the next best alternative to columns of equal height. Modular copy gives the reader a fixed focal point, a principle long prized by legibility experts. In Figure 4.21, even though there are four wraps of copy, readers return to the same height or focal point each time they finish a column of type. Little is lost with an L-shaped copy wrap (Fig. 4.22) where the jumps from the end of each column are the same. The L-shaped wrap also requires that the reader make less of

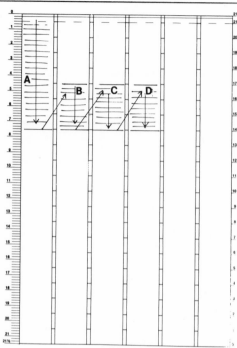

Fig. 4.22.

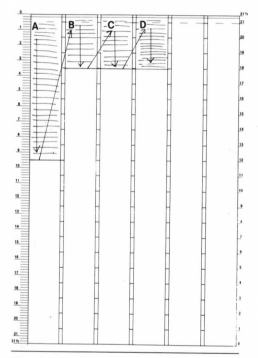

Fig. 4.23.

Fig. 4.24.

a jump to columns B, C, and D than many other alternatives, such as a reverse L (Fig. 4.23). The jump from column A to column B is longer, more difficult, and more time consuming. The L-shaped wrap is particularly effective when the copy adjoins a related photograph (Fig. 4.24). The traffic flow pattern is easy to follow, and the layout has the advantage of creating a strong visual relationship between the copy and the picture.

Putting copy in a module eliminates the problems illustrated in Figures 4.25 and 4.26 in which the reader is required to make progressively higher jumps from each column. The eye flow required looks like the sales chart of a successful company. The layout, however, is not successful.

Fig. 4.25.

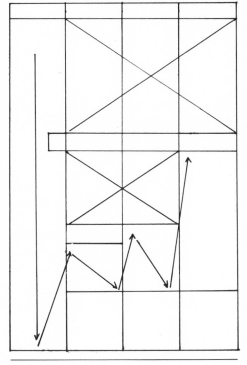

Fig. 4.26.

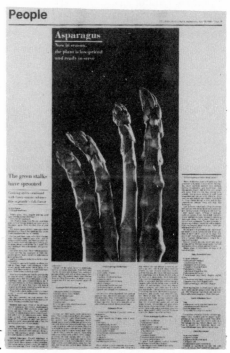

Fig. 4.27.

Many newspapers use the U-shaped format illustrated in Figure 4.27, even though the reader must make a long journey to the last column of type. By moving the picture to the right, the editor could relieve the monotony of the formal balance inherent in a U-shaped layout and improve the copy flow.

Editors must constantly be aware of the traffic pattern they are mapping on a page. Modular layout makes the paper easier to read, and both the reader and the publication benefit. Readers have told researchers, however, that too many newspapers are still hard to read.

Using photographs and artwork

NEWSPAPERS belong to you, as photographers, fully as much as to anyone. They are in trouble. They need your minds in all of their dimensions. So make the entire newsroom, not just the photography department, your home. And get involved.

Eugene Roberts
EDITOR
Philadelphia Inquirer

THE POTENTIAL of the photograph to attract the reader's attention, report the news, and dramatically improve the looks of our newspapers is the great untapped resource of journalism. Successful use of photographs and words in tandem is realization of the powerful potential of the newspaper as a visual medium. Photographs are the stop signs in the designer's traffic pattern. Stories with pictures command better readership and hold the reader's attention longer than stories without pictures (Bain and Weaver 1979).

We have come a long way since 1893 when the editor of the respected magazine *Nation* asserted that pictures appealed chiefly to children and were beneath the dignity of good newspapers. Even though *Look* and *Life* magazines pushed the still photograph to new limits and *National Geographic* dramatized its potential as a reporting tool, it was not until the 1960s that a significant number of newspapers integrated the photograph into the news product instead of using it only as a decoration or to break up type.

Many editors still consider the photograph a supplement to words rather than a form of reportage. That is not surprising because most newspaper managers were trained to use words. Consequently, photographers have been second-class citizens in the newsrooms. This management structure (see Chapter 8) has stunted the growth of the newspaper as a true visual medium. As a result, a significant number of newspapers are just beginning to use photographs for their informational as well as design value.

Once there is a willingness to use photographs, staff members must be trained to use them correctly. At large newspapers, a photo editor, usually a photographer by training, is responsible for the selection and display of all photographs and artwork. At small and medium papers, that job usually is done by the layout editor, who was trained as a copy editor. Editors who would be aghast at having a photographer run the copy desk think nothing of having copy editors serve as photo editors. Photographers need training to be copy editors; copy editors need training to be photo editors. Both need training to make words and pictures work together. This chapter is a start in that direction. The first step is learning the function of a photograph.

Integrity of the photograph

Some of us treat computer cards with more care than we do photographs. We do not bend, fold, staple, or multilate the cards; the photographs we do. We cut them in circles and triangles, mortise them, silhouette them, flop them, and print type over them. Most of the time this is done for the sake of art, not communication. Artists use photographs for their shapes and tones. Editors use them to inform. If you can cut a picture into circles or stars, mortise its corner, or run type over it indiscriminately without interfering with the message, the picture probably is not worth publishing in the first place.

Photographs, like stories, have an integrity. Just as the substance of a story should not be changed in the editing process, the substance of a photograph should not be changed either. Do not tamper with facts. Removing someone essential from a picture, for instance, is not unlike leaving an important name out of a story.

Ironically, it takes more time and effort to ruin a photograph than to handle it properly. It takes time to cut pictures to fit into snowflakes and holiday ornaments, as one newspaper did on a page devoted to women's Christmas fashions. All the pictures were cut into circles, and snowflake and tree ornament decorations were drawn around them. The page successfully presented the idea of Christmas, but the purpose of communicating fashion was lost. A picture of a woman modeling a dress became a head-and-shoulders shot stuck inside a snowflake. A picture of another woman modeling slacks was trimmed below the knees. The message in the photographs was ruined.

By contrast, Alan Berner, who shot and designed the page on winter hay (Fig. 5.1), used his photographs to their potential. The rectangular photographs communicate their content with a simple, strong statement. Decorations are used to cover flaws or weaknesses.

Although snowflake flourishes are extraneous, some photographic alteration is permissible and even encouraged in some instances. Retouching can remove wires, trees, and poles that appear to stick out of heads or can shade

Bringing in the winter hay

The big doors of the country barn stand
open and ready,
The dried grass of the harvest-time loads
the slow-drawn wagon,
The clear light plays on the brown gray
and green intertinged,
The armfuls are pack'd to the sagging
mow.

I am there, I help, I came stretch'd atop
of the load,
I felt its soft jolts, one leg reclined on the
other,
I jump from the cross-beams and seize
the clover and timothy,
And roll head over heels and tangle my
hair full of wisps.

From Walt Whitman's "Leaves of Grass"

MIDSUMMER'S HEAT is hay hauling time; hard work for four cents a bale.

Worn denim patches above the right knee mark where hay haulers give each 27 kilogram (60 lb.) bale a boost to the wagon. They call it "buck'n" hay." On a good day a four-man crew will pick up and store 1200 bales.

The work is satisfying — friends working together outdoors with the aroma of new-mown hay. This crew hauls part-time in Boone County and includes Rick Goodman, Gary Moss, Donald Duncan, Jamie Duncan and Kevin O'Brien.

PHOTO ESSAY
BY ALAN BERNER

Fig. 5.1.

Fig. 5.2.   The street light in the distance distracts from the flow of this picture. (Bill Sikes photo)

a peripheral light source that detracts from the photo's message. Sometimes photographers can change the setting or angle to remove these distractions; at other times, they cannot. Occasionally, the offending element can be removed by cropping. The difference between photographic fakery and legitimate alteration is clear. When retouching is used to remove distracting elements that are not part of the center of interest, it is used correctly and ethically (Figs. 5.2, 5.3). When it is used to alter the essential content, it is fakery.

Retouching is not the only way to fake a photograph. Printing two pictures as one is unethical. A photograph pulled from the newspaper library files and published as though it were current can be at best misleading and

Fig. 5.3. Taking out the street light is a legitimate use of retouching. (Bill Sikes photo)

at worst unethical. Editors who would never consider tampering with the facts in a story have been known to stretch the bounds of propriety to illustrate it. Resist the temptation.

There is a difference between innovation and fakery. When a photographer for a Texas newspaper was assigned to cover a men's body-building competition, the result was a dramatic play of light and darkness combined in a well-handled montage (Fig. 5.4). No damage was done to the credibility of the event by this technique.

Other alterations can also be made. Mortising, which is the overlapping of two or more photographs or a headline and a photograph, is rarely effective (Fig. 5.5). Poor placement of the close-up head shot interferes with both

Fig. 5.4.

Children enlist in war on cancer

By KAY SIMPSON

LAB TECHNICIAN Delcye White gives test to young cancer patient; inset, Dr. Paul Zeltzer.

Fig. 5.5.

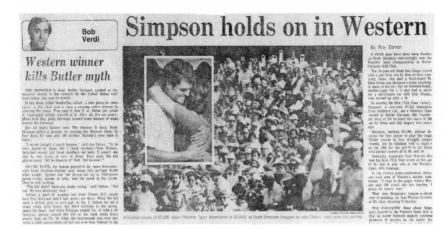

Fig. 5.6.

the copy and the dominant picture. The unequal gutters to the left and right of the head shot emphasize the misplacement. Another possibility is an inset that is placed in an empty portion of the photograph. This technique is successful only when the inset adds information to the dominant photo and is effective in a small size. The inset does not work in Figure 5.6 because the background is too busy. The intention was to show the crowd watching the victory hug for golfer Scott Simpson, but the result was a cluttered background of heads sliced by the inset. This space-saving effort was not successful. In Figure 5.7, the insets and type work together but the mortise detracts from the package. This could be corrected by running the roller skater as an inset at the lower left and moving the copy underneath the picture or by eliminating the skater.

Fig. 5.7.

Fig. 5.8.

The use of insets in Figure 5.8 illustrates the potential and dangers of this technique. The winners of the races are set into an excellent cross-country shot that was enlarged to 9 by 14 inches. By shooting when the runners were turning and descending a hill, the photographer was able to get a flow and feeling of motion. But do the insets work? The inset in the upper left cuts off a head and obviously interferes with the content of the photograph. Although the inset at the lower right may be in an empty space, there might have been a sign there indicating location. Even if the space was left empty, it could serve a purpose. Photographs with motion need space for the action to flow into. The space may be empty, but it serves a function. Remember this when cropping. The winner's photographs would have been more effective if they had been run next to each other at the bottom right at no more than half the size shown or taken out of the larger photo.

The guidelines for overprinting headlines or occasionally text on a photograph are similar to insetting. Type should be used only if there is an empty portion of the photograph that has a continuous tone. Black type can be printed against a light area such as the sky, or type can be reversed to run against a black background. In the photo illustration on math anxiety (Fig. 5.9), the editor combined the type with the photograph without interfering with either message. However, the Saturn package (Fig. 5.10), while dramatic, is too difficult to read because there is so much small text type.

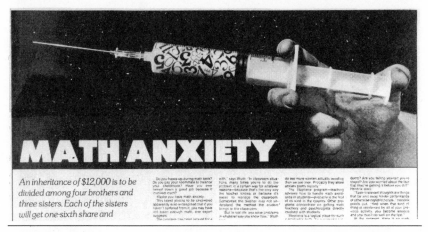

Fig. 5.9.

Fig. 5.10.

(See Chapter 11 for legibility considerations.) Reversed display type works when there are few words and the type is large. Text type should be larger than normal (14 to 18 points) and used in small amounts (Fig. 5.11).

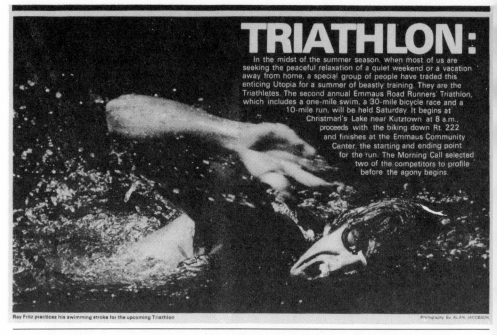

Ray Fritz practices his swimming stroke for the upcoming Triathlon   Photography By ALAN JACOBSON

Fig. 5.11.

Silhouettes are only effective when the contrast between the silhouetted object and the background is substantial. A person wearing light clothes should never be silhouetted against a light background. Silhouettes also need an expert artist with the skill of a surgeon to cut them out and lift them off the print. Otherwise, they may have square shoulders, nicked legs, and blocked chins. A better production method is to have the photographer shoot for the silhouette and then drop out the background when the picture is printed.

Editors who appreciate photographs for their informational content are not likely to destroy them with artistry. Those are some of the potential pitfalls. Some solutions come next.

How to use two or more photographs

The one-frame mentality that dominates the thinking of many editors inhibits good photo selection and use. While a reporter can cover several disparate topics in a single story, a photographer can usually capture only one segment of a story in a single frame. Much of the drama is left in the photographer's discarded contact sheets when the editor says, "Give me your best picture to go with this story." However, the best picture may be a two-picture package. Here are some common situations:

1. Contrast. Look for dissimilarities in like subjects and subtle similarities in unlike subjects (Hurley and McDougall 1971, p. 5).

2. Close-up and context. When the photographer has to back up to show where the action is taking place, the picture makes a general statement. A second shot can give a close-up look at a small portion of the overall scene.

3. Sequence. One frame captures just one moment in the series; two or more frames permit the action to unfold.

In photography, one and one makes three. Although each photo has its own story, the message can be intensified by pairing. For instance, when Pope John Paul visited Brazil, the wire services sent hundreds of pictures. In their first edition, the editors of a South Carolina paper selected one showing police trying to hold back the crowds. It was so tightly cropped that it failed to show either the pope or the immenseness of the audience. In the third edition, the editors paired this same photograph with a context shot showing the pope surrounded by hundreds of thousands of people. Together, the pictures communicated the dimension of the crowd and the difficulty of protecting the pope.

One and one will not equal three, however, when the pictures are not next to each other. When Rumanian gymnast Nadia Comaneci took a fall during the 1980 Moscow Olympics, it was big news in America where she had become a television personality. UPI sent pictures showing her about to fall from the uneven bars, hitting the mat, and with a dejected look on her face. The sequence was a natural. One newspaper, however, chose to use the picture of the fall on the front page as a teaser (Fig. 5.12). Besides

Fig. 5.12.

separating an obvious sequence, the editors had the photo outlined. Because Nadia was dressed in white, the outline was so noticeable that it was distracting. Because the sequence was broken, the reader had no idea why the gymnast was on her back. On the sports page (Fig. 5.13), the moment before the fall was played with dramatic sizing, and the inset showed her disappointment. The inset sizing and the plain background were good. The use of the second picture in the sequence on Page 1 and pictures one and three in the sports section destroyed the impact and the message.

Fig. 5.13.

Properly employed, the pairing principle tells a story quickly and dramatically. When law officers searched a field for murder clues (Fig. 5.14), they were looking for a needle in a haystack. Two pictures tell what one never could: they were looking in a weed-choked field for something small. The top photo, which shows the officers carefully picking up a piece of evidence, does not show the environment. The bottom picture shows the environment but does not indicate the size of the object they were looking for. Together, the pictures tell more of the story.

Murder suspect is sought

By Jim Snell
Missourian staff writer

Boone County Sheriff's deputies and Jefferson City police questioned the ex-husband of murder victim Leigh Ann Wilson, 38, for more than an hour Friday night in an effort to turn up information regarding the slaying. Ms. Wilson was found eight miles (12.8 kilometers) south of Columbia Friday morning with her throat slashed.

Capt. Frank Fiske of the Jefferson City police said the questioning was just to gather information. "No one is being held at the present time. We don't have any suspects," he said.

Late Friday night Fiske said several more people still had to be questioned in an effort to find out about the slain woman. "We're still gathering up the information," he said.

Ms. Wilson's partially-clad body was found about 7:30 a.m. Friday just off an access road on U.S. 63 just south of the Columbia Regional Airport turnoff. Her throat had been slit, and Boone County Sheriff Charlie Foster said she also had a knife wound in her back and she had been beaten.

Foster said the time of death has been placed at close to 1 a.m. Friday, "but it's very possible it could have been 11" Thursday night.

Ms. Wilson was last seen about 10 p.m. Thursday when she left her Jefferson City apartment. A neighbor was leaving at the same time and they had a short conversation, Foster said. "She said she was going to pick up cigarettes and Pepsi-Cola," Foster said.

She should have returned in a few minutes, and when she was going to be gone for any length of time "she would always tell the people next door to watch her kid 'her 9-year-old daughter'," Foster said. "But she didn't do that."

The body was discovered by Wesley Offringa, Route 1, as he was going to work. His son had driven the same road a few minutes earlier, but hadn't seen the body.

Offringa spotted the body only because he stopped his truck, got out and tried to make his dog return home. As he stepped out of the truck and turned, he noticed the body.

The joint communications center log shows Offringa's call to the sheriff's department at 7:33 a.m. By 7:45, two deputies were on the scene. Soon numerous law enforcement officers joined them. "We grabbed everybody we could grab 'to work'," Foster said. Columbia police and Highway Patrol troopers joined the search for evidence.

Because the murder could have taken place in Cole,

(See DEPUTIES, Page 16)

Boone County Sheriff's Deputies Robert Knapp, left, and Gary Voss examine a sweater that may have belonged to a Jefferson City woman found murdered Friday morning on an access road to U.S. 63 a few miles north of Ashland. Deputies also searched along the highway for the knife used to commit the murder. The weapon was not located but deputies found other evidence including articles of clothing and bloodstained paper towels. The victim's purse and its contents also were recovered. Jefferson City police questioned several of the woman's acquaintances Friday night in an attempt to uncover information that might aid in the investigation.

Fig. 5.14.

A feature story on a rail bum is told through an environmental shot of the subject far down the tracks and a close-up that shows him smoking a cigarette (Fig. 5.15). The top picture communicates the loneliness and solitary nature of his life. The close-up permits readers to see him. Together, they work.

The pictures in both examples are adjacent, not redundant, and dominant-subordinate. Those three points are important to remember whether two or five pictures are being used. The adjacency guideline ensures that the

Lindy Burdick smokes a cigarette after a long walk down his favorite road — the railroad   Nick Lammers

Transient finds life on the move remedy for mental breakdown

By Nick Lammers
Missourian staff writer

Springfield, Ill., Memphis, Tenn., Jackson, Miss., Birmingham, Ala. — you name it, Lindy Burdick has been there by train or foot.

Lindy hops trains and rides wherever they take him. He has done so since a mental collapse he suffered in the Korean War 25 years ago.

When I met Lindy at 8 a.m. Sunday, he was near Merna, Mo., about six miles (9.6 kilometers) east of Boonville. He described how he got there.

After serving three years in World War II and enlisting to serve in the Korean War, military life inflicted unbearable pressures on Lindy.

"I had a mental breakdown in Japan," Lindy said. "Hallucinations, beating my head on walls —" His voice broke and he shook his head.

"I've got a cure for insanity in my head," Lindy said. "But beer and cigarettes don't help it any." Staying on the move helps.

"Those boxcars are hard on you," Lindy admitted. "If I keep hopping from car to car I'll become physically wrecked." That's why Lindy walks some of the distance.

"I got this cold or something," Lindy said after wiping his nose with a hand-

kerchief. "I'm out getting some exercise today. That helps strengthen the blood," he said.

Lindy tries to average 30 miles (48 kilometers) a day to keep in shape. Sometimes he does more. Leaving Marshall, early Saturday morning, Lindy walked about 40 miles (64 kilometers) to Boonville, where he spent the night in a boxcar.

When Lindy resumed his travels eastward from Merna on the Missouri-Pacific line, I wanted to learn more about him. I drove about six miles (9.6 kilometers) to Wooldridge, Mo., where I waited for him to arrive.

After walking a half mile (0.8 kilometers) with him, he opened up.

Lindy acknowledged that the World War II was not the only cause of his depression. His family life had added to it.

Born in Utica, N.Y., Dec. 29, 1927, he lived for a while without a name until his neighbor named him "Lindy" after Charles Lindberg, the famous aviator. His father left the family when Lindy was only 4 months old.

During winter Lindy travels the southern states. He says he'll probably never stop traveling. "Gee, I've been doing this for 25 years, what else would I do. I couldn't stand myself sitting in a room with nothing to do."

Nick Lammers

Fig. 5.15.

relationship between the pictures is immediately grasped by the reader. The redundancy guideline ensures that the pictures complement each other and do not communicate the same message in two ways. The dominancy guideline ensures that there is focus to the package in the same way that a writer must focus on one aspect of the story.

If a package contains three or more pictures, there are three additional guidelines: Interior margins should be consistent, excess white space should bleed to the outside of the package, and sizing should be proportionate. The use of these guidelines is shown in Figure 5.16 where four pictures are displayed in a space not much larger than that occupied by the dominant photo. The dominant context shot shows the outside of a remodeled house, and three interior shots complement it. The sizing is large enough to communicate the detail of the light fixture and brass doorknobs but is no larger than necessary. The interior margins are consistent, the extra white space bleeds off the top right-hand corner of the package, and the four photos are proportionate in size. The context picture is large enough to dominate the page, and the others are sized proportionately to their informational value and importance to the total package. To be dominant, a picture must be large

Fig. 5.16.

Above, Scott Hilderbrand, 5 years old, sits in front of the recent addition to his family's 50-year-old home. Right, from the top, are a light fixture from the living room, the master bedroom in the new addition and double doorknobs on a closet on the second floor which they got from older homes.

An older home keeps on growing

By Marcia Koenig
Missourian staff writer

Remodeling is a way of life for the Hilderbrand family. In a 50-year-old house it has to be, says Pat Hilderbrand. There are so many things to be done, it's easiest for us to tackle one item or a few at a time," she says.

Originally, she and her husband thought they'd want to move when they had children. They knew their five-room house was not big enough for a family. But instead of moving when their son, Scott, arrived, they decided to build an addition. The addition they are currently finishing includes two bedrooms, one bathroom, a garage and a shop.

Before deciding to remodel, they considered moving, even building a house, but found many drawbacks. Other houses in the same area needed work. The Hilderbrands had already replastered, patched and painted walls and woodwork in their own home, laid new subflooring, added wall-to-wall carpeting and updated wiring and plumbing. "We didn't want to do it all over again," Mrs. Hilderbrand says.

Lots for new houses were expensive and not to their liking. Mrs. Hilderbrand and her husband have both lived on farms and enjoy large yards. She says the lots they saw either had limited yard space or they limited square footage in their home.

Location was also important to them. They currently live near a private park which they

enjoy. Living close to downtown Columbia and the University is convenient for the Hilderbrands, who work at the University.

"Adding on had been in the back of our minds all along," Mrs. Hilderbrand says. The people living in the house before them had an architect draw plans for adding a bedroom over the original garage. The Hilderbrands found the garage had poor footings and would be unable to hold the extra weight. They also considered adding two bedrooms in the large attic space, but the original construction might not have supported the extra weight.

Positioning an addition without eliminating too much back yard space was a problem. The Hilderbrands decided to replace the original single-car garage with a larger addition on that side of the house.

Mrs. Hilderbrand says another consideration in adding to their house was the value of other houses in the area compared to their own. "We didn't want to put more money into our house than the rest of the houses in the neighborhood were worth."

One year after they began constructing the addition, Mrs. Hilderbrand says it turned out better than she thought it would. The addition is dark brown brick and brown trim, just like their English-looking house. "I'm not in favor of alteration without blending with the old," Mrs. Hilderbrand says. They had to add items like a false dormer in order to make the plan work. She says the construction crew kept telling her she really did not want the dormer. She agreed but said the addition would not

look right without it.

Inside the addition, the door and window trim matches the second story of the main house, as do the glass doorknobs. Mrs. Hilderbrand says they found the glass knobs in another older house in town. They bought and installed new knobs to replace those they took, and then washed and polished the old knobs. She says the exchange process was quite a chore.

Mrs. Hilderbrand also incorporated modern elements into her addition. Track lighting and a molded fiberglass bathtub with ceiling are visible examples.

Mrs. Hilderbrand creates a clean, modern appearance throughout the house with white walls, plants, and narrow blinds at windows rather than drapery.

They have not spent a lot of time decorating the interior, Mrs. Hilderbrand says. "No room is completely finished." She says they'll enjoy gradually changing furnishings when the major remodeling is finished.

In six and one-half years, they have refinished the wood banister in the entry, installed a tub and double sink in the old bath upstairs, laid burnt-orange wall-to-wall carpet in the living room and green wall-to-wall carpet upstairs and painted throughout the house. Their current project is renovating the kitchen.

She and her husband have done much work on the house themselves. When they moved in, the hardwood floor under the old carpet was too thin to refinish and had a large poorly

"etched hole in the entry hall. The square terra-cotta tile they selected for the first floor required firmer subflooring. The Hilderbrands had to lay new subflooring before they could lay the tile.

"The overall plan of the house was pretty good, so we did not have to move walls around," Mrs. Hilderbrand says.

However, some compromises are still necessary, even with the addition. Because of the small living room, the second-floor master bedroom formerly doubled as a family room. Since the addition, the two are now separate, but the family room remains on the second floor. Mrs. Hilderbrand says some people would consider this a disadvantage. For them it is a necessity.

One of the other major compromises is the location of bedrooms. As a designer and mother, Mrs. Hilderbrand would prefer her son's bedroom closer to his parents'. But since this was not possible, they installed an intercom system between the bedrooms, family room, and kitchen. She says the system works well.

"The house now suits most of our needs," Mrs. Hilderbrand says. "We could stay here for a long time."

This is the last in a three-part series on how interior designers satisfy their own housing needs.

Designer makes Winter-proof clothes

Fig. 5.17.

in proportion to the page or portion of the page it occupies. For instance, in *National Geographic,* a picture 20 picas wide will dominate the page. In a tabloid newspaper, however, a dominant picture needs to be 40 picas wide, and in a broadsheet newspaper, 50 picas wide. The size of the dominant picture should be proportionate to the total space available, but the size of the subordinate pictures should be proportionate to the dominant picture. The difference in size between the dominant and subordinate pictures should be obvious to the general reader.

Experience in the use of photos permits possibilities beyond these guidelines. Some situations require two large photos of equal size. A sequence or story about a man who is a banker by day and a farmer by night might have more impact with two equal pictures. Knowing how to handle these exceptions comes with experience. For instance, an editor at the *Detroit News* paired a silhouette picture of a designer with an inset of one of her creations against a screen (Fig. 5.17). It worked.

The picture page

A page of pictures does not make a story, but a page of pictures with continuity does.

Selecting and displaying a group of photographs is similar to writing a major story. When the material is selected and arranged in a coherent and entertaining manner, it has impact (Fig. 5.19). If poorly done, the information is submerged in the resulting clutter (Fig. 5.18).

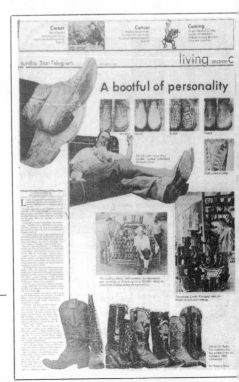

Fig. 5.18.

Lifestyle

Fig. 5.19.

Chris Bryant, a student at North Texas State University, doesn't let his handicap get in the way of swimming. He works out every Wednesday afternoon at NTSU's indoor pool, which is accessible to the handicapped. A friend, far right, holds his wheelchair as he gets in and out of the pool.

For Chris Bryant, swimming is

One More Challenge

By ELIZABETH CLARK
Lifestyle Editor

The water waits, tranquil in the midday lull as it mirrors the swimmer. He waits, too, breathing deeply as he sits at the edge, sets the brakes on his wheelchair and removes his eyeglasses. He closes his eyes, lunges forward — and he's free.

Buoyed by the water, he's unencumbered now by his long, useless legs. He takes the laps — all 10 of them — with the elementary backstroke and the back crawl.

"It's like climbing Mount Everest," he says afterwards. "Every time I jump in the water, it's a thrill in itself."

Chris Bryant, 26, is the swimmer. Handicapped five years ago by a motorcycle accident, he has been testing the waters since June for other handicapped students at North Texas State University's new indoor pool. He's a self-proclaimed "guinea pig," here being the "someone who's got to do it" in the school's experimental water therapy program. The pool, unlike the school's outdoor one, is accessible to the handicapped. And the new program is reducing the number of excuses the disabled have for not going into the water, said Pam Erwin, pool supervisor. It attracted nine students and 12 volunteer instructors, she said.

Ms. Erwin has been consulting with Chris ever since she found him swimming on his own last summer. Together they drew up a list of equipment needed to continue the program: padded tables for dressing, a manual hydraulic lift, a ramp to wheel a chair into the water, walkers to use in the water and shower chairs so students don't use their own chairs wet.

An NTSU's new pool supervisor, part of Ms. Erwin's job is to set up a program for the disabled. The water

therapy program, which will be offered to the handicapped next semester on a credit basis, is an example of NTSU's gradual compliance with a federal phase-in program that considers the vital rights of the handicapped.

The program is not the first of its kind in Denton. Texas Woman's University has a large adaptive aquatics program that teaches physically handicapped and emotionally disturbed students from Denton State School and Denton Independent School District. But the NTSU program will cater specifically to its own handicapped college students, said Ms. Erwin, who is working on her doctorate at TWU. "They have really been neglected ... at least I feel they have."

Like other schools, agencies and programs that receive federal funds, NTSU was required to create access for the handicapped by the federal Rehabilitation Act of 1973. Chris has served on committees since enrolling in 1977, and has been instrumental in helping pinpoint areas that needed to be adapted for the handicapped.

"Chris is one of the few people you'll find who's disabled and is vocal enough to get things going," Ms. Erwin said. "Because of being so vocal, he has certainly made people aware, and caused them to get on the ball and do more than they normally would."

Chris doesn't seem to feel hampered by his handicap, and last summer he lived on his own to see if he could do it. He did. He's planning to build a water-ski device for himself, and eventually wants to get out his deer rifle and go hunting again. His attitude is that everyone is handicapped in some way. "My handicap you can see; other people's handicap, you

See CHALLENGE, Page 5D

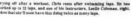

Drying off after a workout, Chris rests after swimming laps. He has worked up to 32 laps, and one of his instructors, Leslie Coleman, right, jokes that she'll soon have him doing twice as many laps.

Photography by DOUG MILNER

The difference between a picture story and a picture essay is like the difference between a news article and interpretive reporting (Hurley and McDougall, p. 69). The picture story is a narrative. The essay expresses a point of view. Both require focus, a strong opening, and a strong closing. Unfortunately, too many groupings of pictures are just collections of related events. Such groupings are similar to stories that ramble, and they should be rejected.

When doing picture pages, remember that:

1. The telling of a story through pictures begins before the shooting when the photographer and reporter plan the project. Even if the photographer is doing both pictures and text, planning is important. It makes the difference between a story and a collection of facts.

2. The pictures and text must work together. If the text is going to tell a story by focusing on one person, the photos should too.

3. The title of the page must capture the essence of the story. The display type is essential to the success of the page because the title is the quick explanation of all the pictures and text. The title and dominant picture should hook the reader.

When selecting and displaying pictures, include these steps:

1. Select as few pictures as possible (most picture pages have too many pictures), so that the ones that survive can be sized adequately. Do not use a full page if the material is not worth it. Good photo editing saves space.

2. Edit redundancies. If the story is told with as few pictures as possible, redundancy will not be a problem. Unfortunately, there is a temptation to repeat ourselves photographically, both in full pages and lesser packages.

3. Select a dominant photo. That photo should be the dramatic moment or emotion, the essence of the story.

4. Maintain consistent interior margins. White space is trapped when the margins are not consistent, and the reader notices it for itself rather than as a feeling of airiness. Let the extra white space bleed to the outside of the package.

5. Provide enough space for the cutlines to avoid grouping. Asking readers to match information in a cutline with two or more photos is inviting them to leave the page.

6. After you have selected the pictures and determined the length of the text, set the photos before you. The story line and the flow of action should determine the arrangement of the pictures on the page.

7. Place the copy in a modular block. The title does not necessarily have to go directly over the copy, but if it does not, a subhead over the copy is useful.

The comparison of a page that does not work with one that does illustrates the importance of following the suggested guidelines. The page about children in Figure 5.20 has several problems. In one part of the two-part program, children dressed up to reflect the kind of work they would like to do as adults; in the other, they acted out nursery rhymes. The headline refers only to nursery rhymes. There is no dominant picture, and the use of nine pictures produces clutter. Because the interior margins are not consistent, white space is trapped in the middle of the page. The pictures of Little Bo Peep and the three kittens should be moved to within one pica of the pictures on the left to permit the extra white space to bleed into the right-

Fig. 5.20.

hand margin. Such a correction, however, is similar to giving a pint of blood to a patient who is hemorrhaging. The cure requires reshooting of the pictures. Rather than six children in the same pose, the photographer could have arranged for a group shot of all the children. The contrast within a single frame would have been interesting and, considering what usually happens when several children are in one place, probably humorous. Paired with the photo of the youngster interviewing the scuba diver, that portion of the program could have been told in two frames and still satisfied both children and parents. The nursery tale portion should have a separate but connected headline or title. Figure 5.21 represents an alternative layout. The dominant photo could be the group shot, and the bottom of the page could be devoted to the nursery tales.

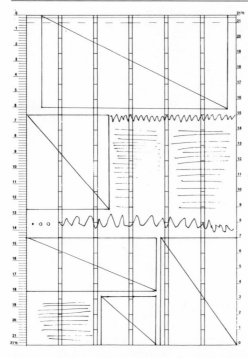

Fig. 5.21.

By contrast, "His Brothers' Keeper" (Fig. 5.22) has a story line that runs from the management of household chores to relaxation in the shade. The title is a nice play on a well-known line and also tells how an old man cares for his two brothers. The gutters or interior margins are consistent; additional white space bleeds to the outside at the lower left corner. The dominant picture concludes the story. The page successfully combines words and pictures in a pleasing display.

Lewis cooks Sunday noon dinner on an old wood and coal stove.

Earl and Owen relax outside while Lewis, who will join shortly, finishes washing and drying the dishes on the kitchen table.

Since inside plumbing is nonexistent, Lewis draws water from an outside pump and later pours it out behind the house.

His Brothers' Keeper

Just beyond Nichols Grocery several miles southeast of Harrisburg a gravel road branches off Route 124 and begins to wind through the countryside. About 2½ miles it kilometers) down the road the Shelton homestead overlooks 120 acres of evergreen farmland.

On a site that once housed a family of 14 live three bachelor brothers: Owen, 72; Earl, 80; and Lewis, 82. Older, but in better health than his brothers, Lewis performs most of the household chores.

A clue to Lewis's responsibilities is the location of his bed, which is in the kitchen. The bed is cornered by a washing machine, an old stove and a cabinet full of clean dishes.

The stove is fueled by coal, which at one time was mined on the farm, and wood, which Lewis splits from a pile of logs in the back yard.

Lewis spends most of the morning preparing lunch which is the big meal of the day. After the midday meal is over, he washes and stacks the dishes neatly in the corner cabinet.

Clothes are washed on the basis of need. When the pile of clothes on top of the washing machine begins to overflow onto his bed, Lewis decides the need has become great enough and does the laundry, a task made more difficult by the lack of inside plumbing.

The other more immediate concern is Earl. Last winter he caught pneumonia, from which he is still recovering. At first he refused to see a doctor, and then he wouldn't eat. Earl seldom bothered to go to bed, preferring instead to curl up with a quilt in a lounge chair by the pot belly stove.

"Half the time Earl didn't know what he was doing," Owen recalls. "We'd have to stay up with him all night because we didn't know what he was going to do next. He damn near drove me crazy."

Owen acts as the mobile man. Healthier than Earl, but still weakened from a runner operation 18 years ago, he sweeps the two room downstairs, cooks breakfast and takes care of most of Earl's wants and needs.

Hard of hearing, but never at a loss for words, Owen has slowed down of many things, but conversation is not one of them.

"There was this one fellow in Harrisburg who was about as hard of hearing as I am," he says. "One day we met downtown and got to talking, and people clear on the other side of town could hear us trying to talk to each other."

Alone with two sisters, Mary and Lena, both of whom married and moved off the farm many years ago, the brothers are the only surviving members of the family. After their parents died, Owen, Lewis and Earl lived on the farm with two other brothers. Owen and Lewis occasionally worked for construction companies in Columbia, while Earl has always managed the farm.

Hay, tobacco and milk were grown, and cattle, sheep and hogs were raised on the Shelton farm. The farm gradually reached its present size of inexpensive living as set age and chore forced retirement upon the three brothers.

An diligent as Earl is careful and clever gardening, Lewis is the cement that holds the family together. It unselfishly takes care of his brothers and as far as he's concerned, even for a Shelton.

Photos and text
by Jack Glasscock

Since he lost his false teeth last winter, Earl's usual lunch consists of hot dogs, mashed potatoes and angel food cake

After lunch is over and the daily chores are done, the Shelton brothers spend the rest of the day outside in the shade of several large oak trees.

Fig. 5.22.

No list of guidelines can prescribe the proper way to produce a successful page. Such guidelines can only steer the beginner away from pitfalls that others have experienced.

Editing photos

Designers seldom get involved in the editing of a story, but they often make decisions about the selection and cropping of photographs. However, the best photo editors have a sense of news as well as balance and flow. Designers who try to be photo editors without the proper training will do no better than an untrained city editor trying to work with reporters. The best results occur when the photographer is involved in the decisions. Like reporters, photographers often are the best judges of their own work. They do some physical editing while shooting and some mental editing on the way back to the office. However, also like reporters, they occasionally are too close to the story to see the significant or the unusual. Sometimes a second editor can catch the overlooked frame.

Picture selection depends on the space available and whether there is an accompanying story. Photos that stand alone must capture the essence of the story; photos with text can concentrate on a part of the story. The successful wedding of pictures and words sometimes requires that photos be selected to follow the text or that the text be written to focus on the dramatic angle developed by the photographers. Consequently, it is important that the photographer and reporter work together on assignments. Such teamwork can produce startlingly good journalism. For instance, consider the photographer and reporter who had been working on a story about the disagreements within an agency that repaired homes for low-income persons. The journalistic team knew there was going to be a showdown at the board meeting over money for the program, and the photographer was ready. The result was a package in which editors were able to show the two principals squaring off. The pictures as well as the "Confrontation" type focused on the disagreement (Fig. 5.23).

Sometimes photo editing can be an enormous job. Two photographers can shoot hundreds of frames at a football game. Normally only two or three would be used, and they must be selected in minutes. Skeeter Hagler of the *Dallas Times Herald* shot 70 rolls of black and white and 12 rolls of color on Texas cowboys. Editing reduced the number of photos actually used to 37, and the result won a Pulitzer Prize in 1980.

A former photo editor for *National Geographic* compiled the following list of questions to ask yourself when selecting a photograph (Terry 1980):

1. Can you justify your selection on a sound editorial basis?
2. Are you looking for a record or snapshot of the event, or do you want the pictures to add depth to the story?

Fig. 5.23.

3. Is the photograph more than just technically acceptable and editorially useful?

4. Does the photograph have a mood?

5. Does the picture have photographic qualities that make it appealing, such as strong graphics, interesting light, and forceful composition?

6. Does the photograph tie into and reinforce the text?

7. If the photograph is unusually good, have you reconsidered the space allotted to it?

A good photo editor is like a strong city editor who can find the story line in a reporter's notes and help the reporter organize the story. A good photo editor recognizes possibilities in the photo that others may not see. Photo editors can turn tepid shots into red-hot drama by cropping tight for impact and backing off for content and form or by cropping to eliminate distractions in order to focus attention on the point of the picture. Such techniques may sometimes require close-ups; other times, context photos are needed (Figs. 5.24, 5.25).

Fig. 5.24. A loose crop fails to emphasize the key subject in the photograph. (Bill Sikes photo)

Fig. 5.25. A tight crop emphasizes both the subject of the photograph and the intensity of the discussion. (Bill Sikes photo)

Cutlines

Newspapers should have two basic cutline formats: text and one-liners. A text cutline is used when a photograph needs a longer explanation. When a picture stands alone, it often has a catchline or headline over it. Depending on the newspaper's headline style, the catchline is either flush left or centered. Cutline text type should be 10 or 11 points and should contrast with the text type. Sans serif works well, but italic and boldface are also available. The designer can use all caps or all caps boldface for the first two or three words if such a style matches that of the copy.

The newspaper should have standardized text cutline settings for each width of picture. Text cutlines generally should not exceed 25 picas in width. Gutters should be the same as those used elsewhere in the paper. If the paper is gray, the designer may want to specify that cutlines be set 2 picas less than the width of the picture. This permits 1 extra pica of white space at either side of the text.

A one-line format should be a larger version of the cutline text face; 13- or 14-pt. type works well. The cutline should be written so that there is only one line of type under the picture. With this format, there are no gutters; the cutline can extend the width of the picture.

Although cutlines should appear underneath the related photo, occasionally they are placed to the right or left. In such a case, they should line up with the bottom of the photo. Cutlines set to the right can be set ragged right; cutlines set to the left should be justified left and right. If the cutline to the left is one short sentence, ragged left may be permissible. Cutlines generally should be placed underneath photographs because readers read out of the bottom of the photograph. Grouped cutlines irritate readers because they have to work much harder to match the text information with the appropriate photograph.

Credit lines can appear at the end of the text cutline, but they usually look better when they are anchored at the lower right corner of the photo. When they appear at the end of a text cutline, they often dangle on an extra line. In addition, they do not fit neatly into a one-line format. Credit lines that appear at the right-hand corner of the picture should be set in type smaller than the cutline and can even be in agate type.

One-column head shots usually have only a name line, a name line with a descriptive underline, or a name with a short phrase on a single line. Whichever style is chosen, there should be a contrast between the name and the description. This can be achieved by varying the type size, boldness, or form (such as italic).

Photo illustrations

When a photographer cannot get a literal representation to accompany a story, a decision must be made whether to order an artist's drawing or a photo illustration. For instance, a photographer cannot always be at an undercover investigation, but an artist can effectively recreate a scene such as an exchange of drugs or money in the shadow of a doorway. Stories that discuss ideas may lend themselves to photographic illustrations, which are pictures staged with people and/or props that represent ideas rather than literal scenes.

To produce an illustration, a photographer needs time, props, facilities, and a thorough understanding of the story being illustrated. Ideas for illustrations are often produced in conferences involving the reporter, story editor, design editor, and photographer. It is a time-consuming process, but it pays visual dividends. The photographer who received the assignment to illustrate an article on junk food (Fig. 5.26) brought two important elements to the job: a lively imagination and a casket, which she just happened to have in her van. The result was a page-stopper.

The illustration should not be used as a substitute for traditional

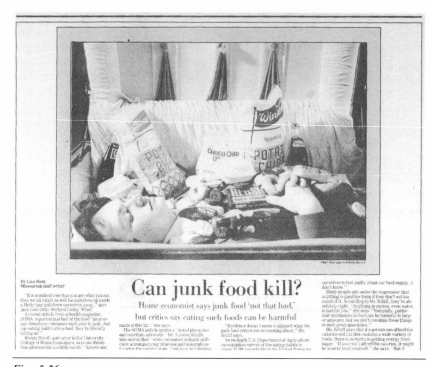

Fig. 5.26.

photography because it lacks immediacy, spontaneity, and to some extent, credibility. It is, after all, a made-up situation. On the other hand, photographic illustrations can communicate ideas quickly, effectively, and with more impact than pencil and ink.

Working with art

The artist was the first visual communicator in U.S. newsrooms, but it was not until the weekly newsmagazines started showing the potential of news graphics that artists became an important part of the news process. Publisher Nelson Poynter of the *St. Petersburg Times* was not satisfied to let *Time* magazine have an exclusive franchise on color graphics. He asked why newspapers were not doing it and was told his staff did not know how. He suggested they learn and learn they did. That was 30 years ago. Now the *St. Petersburg Times* frequently uses colorful news graphics. In 1980, they had one part-time and five full-time artists with a budget of $132,000, all but $4,000 of which was used for salaries. "A good artist costs no more than a good reporter," according to Robert Haiman, executive editor. "And the impact you get is well worth it."

The *St. Petersburg Times* and many other newspapers are now producing quality news graphics on a timely basis just as Poynter wanted. When an airplane missed its landing and 14 crewmen were killed aboard the U.S.S. *Nimitz,* the *St. Petersburg Times* published a color graphic showing where the plane was supposed to land as well as where it crashed (Fig. 5.27). Eleven days later, *Time* magazine published a color graphic illustrating the same point (Fig. 5.28). *Time* magazine's graphic was better, but it was also old news. *Time* though, pioneered the concept of combining charts and illustra-

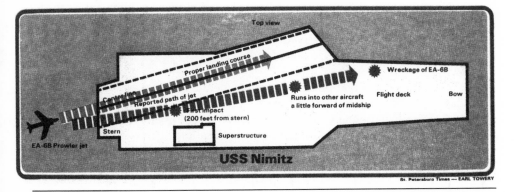

Fig. 5.27.

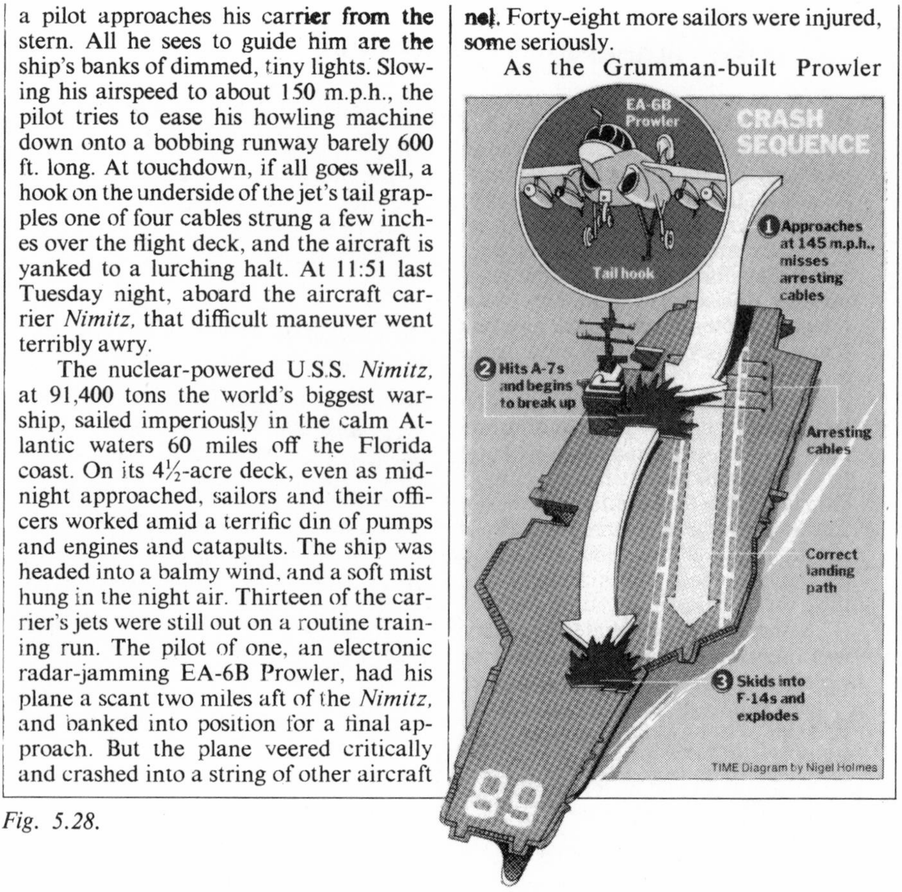

a pilot approaches his carrier from the stern. All he sees to guide him are the ship's banks of dimmed, tiny lights. Slowing his airspeed to about 150 m.p.h., the pilot tries to ease his howling machine down onto a bobbing runway barely 600 ft. long. At touchdown, if all goes well, a hook on the underside of the jet's tail grapples one of four cables strung a few inches over the flight deck, and the aircraft is yanked to a lurching halt. At 11:51 last Tuesday night, aboard the aircraft carrier *Nimitz*, that difficult maneuver went terribly awry.

The nuclear-powered U.S.S. *Nimitz*, at 91,400 tons the world's biggest warship, sailed imperiously in the calm Atlantic waters 60 miles off the Florida coast. On its 4½-acre deck, even as midnight approached, sailors and their officers worked amid a terrific din of pumps and engines and catapults. The ship was headed into a balmy wind, and a soft mist hung in the night air. Thirteen of the carrier's jets were still out on a routine training run. The pilot of one, an electronic radar-jamming EA-6B Prowler, had his plane a scant two miles aft of the *Nimitz*, and banked into position for a final approach. But the plane veered critically and crashed into a string of other aircraft

net. Forty-eight more sailors were injured, some seriously.

As the Grumman-built Prowler

EA-6B Prowler

CRASH SEQUENCE

Tail hook

1 Approaches at 145 m.p.h., misses arresting cables

2 Hits A-7s and begins to break up

Arresting cables

Correct landing path

3 Skids into F-14s and explodes

TIME Diagram by Nigel Holmes

Fig. 5.28.

tions. When done well, this technique is both informative and entertaining. It is just beginning to show up in newspapers. *USA Today* has dozens in each issue.

Poynter was also an internationalist who believed that it was the newspaper's fault if foreign stories were foreign to readers. Not content to leave maps to *Time* magazine, Poynter ordered his editors to do whatever was necessary to be sure their readers understood the geography of the world. That commitment has been admired and copied, but not as much as it should be.

"Many editors and publishers appreciate the effective use of news art they see in newspapers that do it well," says Frank Peters, who does most of the Page 1 charts and maps for the *St. Petersburg Times*. "But [they] don't seem to take it as seriously for their own publication." Peters also says that news artists must be good journalists as well as good illustrators: "How can news artists expect to interpret the news properly through their work if they neither understand nor are aware of current events?" A good news artist is one who is able to read a story, understand its thrust and meaning, and convey it visually to a reader. Peters strives to make the graphic informative, attractive, imaginative, and simple. Graphics that are crammed with information are generally not effective.

Artists can also use color to attract attention and help tell the story. Even if only one color is available, the use of screens can give the effect of more than one color, and the artist can always use the range of shades from black to white. With or without color, graphics look better if they are run just large enough for the type to be read comfortably. Unlike photos, graphics generally do not improve with increased size.

Not every newspaper will rush out and hire a news artist for the newsroom, but any newspaper, even the smallest weekly, can find someone who has the ability and willingness to draw on a per piece basis. The smallest papers might run only a dozen drawings a year, while small dailies might use one or two a week from a free-lance artist. Syndicated news illustrations are also available on a timely basis. The Chicago Tribune Syndicate pioneered in this area (Fig. 5.29). Both the Associated Press and United Press International are now sending maps and charts to their clients.

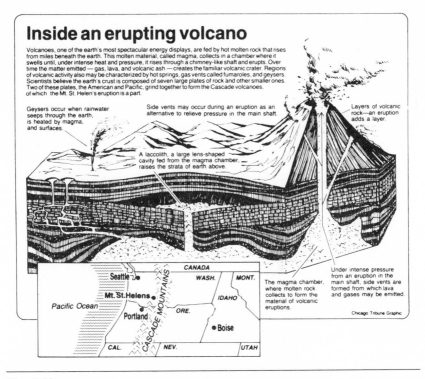

Fig. 5.29.

Some art directors prefer free-lance illustrations because of the variety of styles available. The *New York Times,* for example, has no illustrators on the staff. More and more graphs and maps are being programmed into newspaper computer systems. However, chart art, in which information on a chart is combined with a symbolic representation of the message, requires a skilled artist.

Source material

An Associated Press Managing Editor's Committee compiled the following source list of drawings and materials that are useful to a newspaper art department:

1. *Art Direction* magazine
2. *Bettman Portable Archive,* a graphic history with 3,369 illustrations
3. *Communication Arts* magazine
4. *Creativity Annual*
5. Dynamic Graphics Clip Service
6. *Graphics Annual*
7. *Hart Picture Archives*
8. *Henry Dreyfuss Symbol Source-book*
9. *Illustrators Annual*
10. *Handbook of Pictorial Symbols* by Rudolf Modley and William R. Myers
11. Used set of *Encyclopaedia Britannica*

In addition, every newspaper art department should add local, state, national, and international maps; a free membership in the National Geographic News Service; and a good filing system.

Packaging sections and stories

I'D PROBABLY read the paper more often if I knew where to find what interests me. Some days sports are mixed up with classified, sometimes they are in the B section. I want to reach in and find it right away.

An occasional reader

"THIS IS MY IDEA OF A GOOD NEWSPAPER," the reader said. "I could go right to sports and business and get rid of everything else except the front news section" (Clark 1979, p. 30).

That bittersweet assessment by an out-of-towner seeing the *Chicago Tribune* for the first time strikes at the heart of traditional newspaper philosophy. Newspapers give readers the information they *need* and the information they *want*. If the newspaper is properly departmentalized, it is easier for readers to find what they want regardless of whether it is important, trivial, or both. Departmentalization also helps many readers tune out the unpleasant. Former Chief Justice Earl Warren once remarked that he turned to the sports pages, which chronicled man's achievements, before turning to the news, which chronicled man's defeats.

At least he knew where to turn. When you pick up some newspapers, you never know where the daily sections, if they even exist, will be. As a typical occasional reader told a researcher, "I'd probably read the paper more often if I knew where to find what interests me. Some days sports are mixed up with classified, sometimes they are in the B section. I want to reach in and find it right away." And a typical regular reader said, "I find it frustrating to look through stem to stern to find all the international or all the local news" (Clark 1979, p. 31).

Readers are also frustrated when they are confused by the arrangement of elements on the page. When related stories are separated by unrelated stories or unrelated stories and pictures are positioned so that they appear to be related, confusion often results. One critic commented about a front page: "Once I'd worked out that the fine rule over the picture was probably meant to set it off from the headline, I then had to decide which story—the one to the left or to the right of the picture—actually went with the headline" (Pitnoff 1980).

Readers are often jerked through the publication by jumps and reference lines. Readership surveys, such as those by Clark (1979) for the American Society of Newspaper Editors and the News Research Reports for the American Newspaper Publishers Association, remind editors that readers want their papers properly organized and easy to read.

Departmentalization

Readers buy newspapers out of habit and for enjoyment. Unfortunately, many of them find frustration instead of gratification. Better packaging will lower the frustration level; better writing, news judgment, and reporting can reach those readers who feel alienated by the content. The designer must take the best the reporters, photographers, and artists have to offer and arrange it in a manner that will attract attention, be readable, and add to the message. Two reader characteristics must be foremost in the designer's mind: daily readership is a habit, and readers want the newspaper to be useful and enjoyable (Tipton 1978). A newspaper designer should organize the product before dealing with its aesthetic aspects.

Readers want to be as comfortable with their newspaper as they are with their slippers. Editors who pay no attention to the organization of their newspapers are likely to find that their readers soon will pay no attention to them. Editors should not irritate readers by making them search every day for the sports, features, or national news. We all are more comfortable with the familiar; the more familiar we can make our publications, the more secure our readers will feel with them. Robert Haiman, executive editor of the *St. Petersburg Times,* wants his readers to feel comfortable. He says, "I believe in the notion that there is a place for everything and everything in its place and in the same place *every* day."

If a newspaper is properly departmentalized and clearly labeled, readers are likely to find it useful and gratifying. They also will recognize and appreciate what the newspaper carries every day. When the editors of Gannett's Reno, Nev., newspaper learned that readers thought they did not have as much national and international news as the competing San Francisco paper, they started measuring. They found that the Reno papers had as much coverage or more, but it was scattered throughout. The solution was to group the news by categories and label them clearly. Publisher Warren Lerude (1979) described the change as going "high profile" with the news.

The size and production facilities of the newspaper dictate how easily departmentalization can be achieved and how many sections there will be. Some newspapers do not have the press capacity to divide their product into all the sections they would like. For those who do have the capacity, typical departments are "General News," "Business," "Sports," "Features," "Food," "Travel," and "Religion." Each department may be broken down into subsections. General news often is divided into city, region, state, national, and international. The sports section is often split into spectator and participant events. The newsmagazines are strictly sectionalized, and even though the sections expand and contract, they do not move. By contrast, many newspaper readers often find their favorite subject matter rotating from section A to section B to section C. "Dear Abby" may appear in the news section one day and the feature section the next. When Randy Miller began work on a redesign of the *St. Louis Post Dispatch* in 1980, one of the first things he did was anchor the newspaper's sections.

Newspapers need to look carefully at the electronic news delivery systems that will offer subscribers the opportunity to request not only sports but also numerous subdivisions within sports. Football, for example, might be divided into high school, college, and professional. High school football might be further divided by city, county, region, or leagues. Subscribers will be able to move quickly from the general to the specific. When electronic news becomes reality, newspapers will be competing with more than the skin-deep news of television and radio. Instead, they will be competing with an in-depth version of themselves. Perhaps such competition will stimulate improvements in newspaper packaging.

While many newspapers have been quick to embrace departmentalization by content, they have done little to correlate the advertisements. A few sections, such as fashion and food, have compatible advertising and editorial content and are popular with readers. Unfortunately, they are the exceptions. A consumer who wants to buy a lawnmower has to search all the sections from news to sports to find the department and hardware advertisements. Similarly, advertisements for such products and services as snow tires and tune-ups are likely to be scattered throughout the newspaper.

Although it is possible to group one-subject ads such as food, fashion, movies, and automobiles, it is more difficult to group all the ads for lawnmowers because they often are just one part of an advertisement containing many other items. However, if those ads were grouped by the type of store (discount or department, for instance), both the consumer and the advertiser would benefit. As computers take over the job of dummying advertisements, the ability to improve their organization increases. Locating advertising indexes in the same place in the front section would also help the consumer. Such organization is where design starts.

Secondary packaging

Packaging should not be confined to sections. Readers want organization by subject matter, but they also want organization and labeling of the content within a section. The editor's skill in packaging the material and communicating relationships visually determines how useful the publication is to the reader.

We communicate with our readers both explicitly (through the headlines, text, and pictures) and implicitly (through arrangement of material on the pages). Because the arrangement can say as much as the content, it is mandatory that we be careful not only about page balance but also about the relationships among the elements on the page. Being careful means never having to apologize for unwittingly saying something visually that was not intended. Such situations can be embarrassing. For instance, it was not the intent of a New Mexico editor to juxtapose a bridal picture and a story on birth control, but it happened. Neither did the editor intend to imply that the well-known poet Nikki Giovanni was a gay soldier but, typographically, that was the message (Fig. 6.1).

Nikki Giovanni

Poet moves audience with verse and insight

by Anne Loecher
associate editor

Everybody had been waiting for what seemed like hours.

Marcella Curry of the LBC Gospel Choir nervously reapplied her lipstick, and the 80-year-old Reverend Leon Frank Hannah of the Emmanuel Baptist Church of Columbia clung to his favorite Bible waiting in the wings to introduce the choir who would introduce black poetess Nikki Giovanni.

Then suddenly, Giovanni appeared onstage at Jesse last night.

Giovanni, who has written volumes of poetry and essays and children's story books, drew Gospel members and their friends, and grandmothers in their Sunday clothes, simply to hear her read – even if she was a bit late. "I have hay fever," she excused herself and laughed. The audience of about 800 laughed in response.

She had heard about the black students, about what she calls their fear of commitment and their attrition rate – "87 percent? My God." Before she read her poetry, she wanted to talk to them about that. So, for an hour, the tiny woman with the dark eyes and the business-like manner from Tennessee, New York and Cincinnati did just that.

"You're not dumb and you're not asleep," she said. "You've got to do everything that has to be done when it has to be done. I think you'll find that usually when things have to be done, that somebody that usually has to do it is you. You should study yourselves; learn to

Pond;" and she read her son's favorite, "Ego Tripping" to which all the choir girls in the front row recited in unison the last line.

So it was to be expected that after the standing ovation and after the Omega Psi Phis had presented her with a plaque and the Delta Sigma Thetas gave her a single rose in a silver vase,her audience would follow her to the Black Culture Center for a casual discussion and some potato chips.

Planting herself in a big white armchair with a microphone looming in front of her, she pressed a few more cigarettes into a big, glass ashtray and waited for the people to crowd in.

One woman, sitting up close, wanted Giovanni to talk about black men and women. "The black woman," she said, leaning into a cloud of smoke and crossing her legs, "is very, very important. Her choices are no longer only the black man, she has more, and she will compete for it. And I think most of the time she will win."

Attrition rates were discussed again, along with who might or might not be running for president in 1980 (Giovanni is going with a Carter-Kennedy Democratic team) and the "culture shock" of students coming from a black, urban community to GPA's and socializing in Columbia, Mo.

"There's culture shock coming out of your mama, but you get used to it. You are here. You are not incapable and I don't care if you like it or not. The fact that you're here says you're interested. A lot of dumb crackers come here, to. You know them–they're in your classes, asking the dumbest questions. And they graduate. So hang on for awhile."

Gay soldier speaks at week

Leonard Matlovich, an Air Force sergeant who publicly challenged the military's ban on homosexuality, will be featured speaker at the second annual Gay Pride Weekend Sept. 28-30 at UMC.

Matlovich, whose case is still in the courts, will speak on "The Right to be Gay" at 7:30 p.m. Friday in Ellis Auditorium. The speech will be followed by a reception and the showing of a film on homosexuality, "A Very Natural Thing," presented again at 2 p.m. Saturday.

will be held at 9 p.m. on the Bengal Lair deck.

Sunday, Sept. 30 will begin with a 9 a.m. meeting of the Missouri Coalition for Human Rights in Memorial Union, followed by services in the A.P. Green chapel at 11 a.m. The weekend will conclude with a picnic at 1 p.m. Sunday in Rock Bridge State Park.

Tickets for the entire weekend are $8. Tickets for individual events–the film, the dance, and the Pinkham show–are $2 each. UMC students will receive a 25

Fig. 6.1.

If you give readers an opportunity to make a mistake, many of them will. It is important to convey the correct relationships of elements on the page to help the reader avoid making a mistake. For the same reason, typographical devices should be used to show when units on the page are *not* related. Editors have not always been careful in this regard. Until recently, many newspapers used 1-pt. cutoff rules whenever two unrelated elements came in contact. It was thought this thin rule would show the reader that the elements were not related. However, this technique was not always successful. When the *Albuquerque Journal* reported the death of former Vice President Nelson Rockefeller (Fig. 6.2), his photograph faced away from the story of his death and was placed in a different module. The normal eye flow would be from the picture to the story below, which could be mistaken for a story about Rockefeller the banker. Furthermore, many readers would go from the mortgage bond headline to the train fire picture, then to the headlines on the left, and finally to the upper right where they would discover that Rockefeller had died. When a photograph competes with a headline, the photograph will win almost every time. The 1-pt. cutoff rule under Rockefeller's picture is the editor's way of disassociating the picture from the story below, but its effectiveness is questionable.

It is common to place unrelated stories under pictures, but it is always a visual mistake unless special precautions are taken. In Figure 6.3, a continued story with the label ". . . Energy" opens directly below the picture of a woman who is the subject of the story across the top of the page. Although the headline at the top runs over the story and related picture, the reader is given conflicting visual messages about the proper relationships on the page. Even so, it could have been worse—the editors could have continued the ". . . Waste" story under the woman's picture.

For years, editors used the cutoff rule, usually 1-pt., to disassociate elements on the page. When newspapers adopted a more open look, most editors eliminated both column and cutoff rules. Many editors were puzzled about how to disassociate unrelated elements. Some editors never did solve the problem, and 4- or 6-pt. cutoff rules have made a reappearance in some publications. The heavier rules are more effective cutoffs than the 1-pt. rule and are also an integral part of the format because they add color and weight to a page.

Showing relationships

Through habit, readers have learned that the normal pattern for a related picture and story is a vertical package that starts with a photograph and continues down through the cutline, headline, and text. That flow pattern is based on the sound principle that the reader's eye is attracted by the photograph first and then travels out of the bottom of the picture. The cutline explains

The Weather
ALBUQUERQUE — Partly cloudy and continued cold today. High mid to upper 30s and lows tonight near 15. Details on C-12.

ALBUQUERQUE JOURNAL

NEW MEXICO LEADING NEWSPAPER

Good Morning
The Midwest Is Starting To Think Of Snow As A Four Letter Word With Every Letter A Capital.

98th Year No. 26   76 Pages in Eight Sections   Saturday Morning, January 27, 1979   Price: Daily 20c; Sunday 35c   ★ ★ ★ ★

Journal Photo
Nelson Rockefeller Shown During Albuquerque Visit
Former Vice President Died Friday of Heart Attack

Heart Attack Kills Nelson Rockefeller

NEW YORK (AP) — Former Vice President Nelson A. Rockefeller died at his office in Rockefeller Center Friday, Hugh Morrow, his spokesman, said.

Rockefeller, 70, was rushed to Lenox Hill Hospital in Manhattan about 11:45 p.m. EST after suffering an apparent heart attack.

Morrow said Rockefeller was working on a book featuring his extensive modern art collection when he slumped over his desk.

Rockefeller spent a "normal day at

his office today" before the incident, said Morrow. He added that Rockefeller's health had been excellent.

Rockefeller's wife, Margaretta, was at the hospital, Morrow described her as "composed."

Rockefeller was elected four times as governor of New York and tried three times to gain the presidency. He had no previous history of serious illness during his lengthy political career.

He was sworn in as vice president on Dec. 19, 1974, and served under

Gerald Ford, who completed the term of Richard Nixon.

Since leaving public life after the Republicans lost the White House in 1976, Rockefeller has concentrated his energy on his considerable art collection.

His latest venture was the retail sale of reproductions of art works he owns.

Rockefeller had been scheduled to speak to the Fifth World Antiques Market Conference today, and has planned to announce plans to make his retail art store in Manhattan a permanent operation.

Storm Forces Food Airlifts In Nebraska

By the Associated Press

A widespread winter storm dumped more snow on Western rangelands Friday, and officials said the situation is "extremely critical" in Nebraska where cattle are dying and food is being airlifted to stranded farmers.

Snowbound Midwesterners battered down for another ordeal as the storm pushed eastward, dropping snow from Utah and Arizona into Minnesota and Missouri.

Freezing drizzle mixed with snow fell from northeast Ohio into New England, causing at least one death in Vermont and knocking down power lines and trees.

Maureen T. Corrow, 70, of East Arlington, Vt., playing at home because
Continued on A-2

Sandoval Board Weighs Grader Return Offer

By TOMAS U. MARTINEZ
Assistant State Editor

BERNALILLO — The Sandoval County Commission will decide Feb. 6 whether to accept a heavy equipment dealer's offer to return two road graders the county sold during a controversial December auction.

A spokesman for the county said the decision will be based on whether the transaction benefits the county financially.

Louis Valencia, chief deputy district attorney said the proposal was made to the county by Santa Fe attorney Fred Standley in behalf of the buyer, Iron Mac, Inc. of Albuquerque.

State Corporation Commission reports for Standley as registered agent for the firm. Albuquerque heavy equipment dealer, H.K. "Fats" Leon-

ard, is shown as incorporator and director of Iron Mac, Inc.

The Dec. 9, 1978 auction of surplus county equipment angered some Sandoval County residents. Sale opponents claimed the equipment sold could have been repaired for less money than it would take to replace it.

The central issue of the sale is that county records fail to show authorization by the County Commission to sell the equipment. The only authorization is reflected in a contract between the county and Hensel-King Associates of Corrales, the firm that conducted the sale for the county.

One of the principals in Hensel-King Associates is David Hensel, a Corrales resident who served as auctioneer during the sale. Hensel is also Sandoval County Democratic Party chairman.

At the sale, Iron Mac, Inc. bought
Continued on A-2

City's Mortgage Bonds May Total $61 Million

By SUSANNE BURKS
Journal Staff Writer

The amount of mortgage revenue bonds to be sold by the city to help prospective and current homeowners has been set tentatively at $61 million, city officials said Friday.

City Councilor Alan Reed said the council approved a proposed ordinance Monday authorizing sale of the bonds, and approving a two-inch thick package of legal documents.

He said the $61 million is tentative pending settlement of some questions and that any necessary change can be made by the council's Finance Committee when it hears the bill.

Eighteen mortgage lenders had asked for $128 million in discussions with the city.

Moneystar Simms, assistant director of the Department of Finance and Management and the city's bonding authority, estimated 1,500 Albuquerque families could receive loans if the average loan were $40,000.

He said the money will be available to lenders March 26 through the trustee and program administrator, Albuquerque National Bank, if the council approves the ordinance.

Purpose of the program announced several months ago by Mayor David Rusk, is to aid low and middle income prospective and current homeowners and improve availability of housing.

The concept is that the city uses its tax-exempt status to borrow money at lower interest rates than borrowers could obtain otherwise.

The program will not cost the city and its taxpayers any money because Albuquerque National Bank will administer it, Simms said.

Simms said there will be no risk to the city because if borrowers default the property itself serves as security. Diminished portion of the loans will be covered by mortgage insurance, he said.

Simms said the ordinance will go to the council for final action Feb. 20 and
Continued on A-2

CETA Subcontractor Says Probe Is Reprisal

By BRUCE CAMPBELL
Journal Staff Writer

A CETA subcontractor under investigation for alleged misuse of CETA employees for political and other non-job-related activities charged Friday the city probe is an act of reprisal for a suit filed in 1977.

Gene R. Bobeen, head of Las Lumiñarias of the New Mexico Council of the Blind, said said the city investigation was over part of his plot.

In a press release, Bobeen alleged that city Chief Administrative Officer James Jaramillo's "outrage that the blind dare sue for their civil rights comes as no burden Las Lumiñarias' error puts to burden of a Lumiñarias' error gets to survive as an organization and land agency" for CETA public service employees.

City officials confirmed Wednesday that Bobeen's organization has been investigated by the city county Office of Comprehensive Employment and

Training Administration, and is now under review by Assistant City Attorneys William Tryon and Lauren Mahler.

City officials said the investigation concerns allegations that Bobeen used CETA employees in his unsuccessful June Democratic primary campaign.

Another source, who asked not to be identified, said the investigation also concerns allegations that the personnel hired some of the other tasks outside their job descriptions — including operating a concession stand at the state fair, trying to sell peanuts to concessionaires, chauffeuring agency personnel and looking into the business possibilities of raising rabbits, establishing a private club with a liquor license and setting up a bow and arrow factory.

Bobeen in October 1977 sued the city, naming Jaramillo and former
Continued on A-3

Iran Troops Kill at Least 15 Protesters

Los Angeles Times
Washington Post Service

TEHRAN, Iran — Troops Friday shot and killed at least 15 demonstrators defying a renewed ban on public assembly here in a signal to Ayatollah Khomeini that the government and armed forces mean business.

As many than 100,000 Iranians demonstrated, said government sources here and other crowds followed suit in the provinces. Prime Minister Shapour Bakhtiar said in a telephone interview. "One cannot go through the apprenticeship of democracy without paying a high price."

The death toll in Tehran alone was reported to be as high as 40 by hospital sources and much higher by some demonstrators near Tehran University, where the shooting took place.
Continued on A-2

Firefighters Douse Caboose

Journal Photo by Ed Gay
Albuquerque firefighters douse a burning caboose in the Santa Fe Railway yards near Trumbull SW Friday morning. The fire was apparently caused by a defective heater in railroad car. Fire officials said a railroad spokesman said damage was estimated at $10,000 and that the caboose would be repaired in Topeka, Kan. The fire was discovered about 9:25 a.m. and took firefighters about 10 minutes to bring under control.

Life Of Today's Woman Needs Attention

By LYNNE LANGLEY
Staff Reporter

Alene H. Moris

... Waste

Continued From Page 1-F

Greenhouse Wares

Thomas W. Frank plants broccoli in a lean-to greenhouse built off the end of his home. The plants are watered by gray water — water from sinks, showers and laundry is in first run through a filter (shown in the background). (Staff Photo by Bill Murton)

... Energy

Continued From Page 1-F

Fig. 6.3.

what is not evident in the picture, and the related headline and story are right there waiting for the reader. Editors who start the story at the lower left corner of the picture are taking advantage of the reader's propensity to go to a fixed left focal point. Type lined up evenly on the left provides a standard starting place for each line and can be read faster. Headline and copy lined up at the lower left of the related picture (as in Fig. 6.4 under the picture of the man enjoying the Cinco de Mayo celebration) take advantage of a natural eye movements. The headline and copy block end at the right corner to complete the module.

Supporters of pyramid alter 'game'

3 agencies face lawsuit over PCBs

Dionicio Cerda, Nampa, appears to be enjoying Cinco de Mayo festivities Sunday in Lakeview Park

300 attend fiesta in Nampa

Fun abounds at Cinco de Mayo

Fig. 6.4.

Sometimes, however, it is not always possible or even desirable to arrange all related elements in a vertical package. If a different pattern is used, it must indicate clearly where the reader should go. There are a number of ways to do this. One technique is to use the headline as a visual cutoff rule. If the reader expects the related story to start at the lower left corner of the picture, stories that are not related should start somewhere other than that position. In Figure 6.5, the headline "A painful return to a tornado-torn city," starts one column to the left of the photograph. This arrangement tells the reader that the tornado story and the gardening picture are not related.

THE MILWAUKEE JOURNAL

338 Pages —21 Sections   Sunday, June 8, 1980   Latest Edition ()

Even a kiss hurts

Love, spunk — and Crisco — keep boy alive

Gainesville, Fla. — AP — Spunky 9-year-old Michael Ray Hammond is a prisoner of a rare skin disease that blisters his frail, pencil-thin body with purple sores. Even a kiss makes him hurt.

Vitamin E oil, whisky, hormones, wraps, aloe, lotion. All were tried, none relieved the pain. Only vegetable shortening — nine pounds of it daily — seemed to work. So twice a day, loving nurses coat Michael's body with Crisco and wrap him mummy-style in 20 yards of gauze.

"I'm not a greasy angel," Michael joked with aide Catherine Greene one day. "I'm the Crisco Kid."

And so he is, fondly dubbed by the staff at Sunland Training Center, where Michael has lived for seven years. They've planned a small sign aside his room: "The Crisco Kid — He'll Steal Your Heart."

Michael suffers from epidermolysis bullosa, an inherited, incurable disease that strikes one newborn in 50,000. Awful blisters cover his body, even his tongue. His throat bleeds. He has webbed hands and feet.

Michael's skin has no defense mechanisms and infection can be deadly. A scrape, even the bruising pressure of a simple touch, can raise infection and death.

At birth, Michael had strange sores on his ankles and thumbs. Within six days, he was covered with what looked like third-degree burns. At age 2, the state agreed to accept the chronically ill child as a state-supervised community for the retarded.

Michael was not restored. He was placed in Sunland to stay. Doctors thought he had three months to live. But he beat the odds.

"It was hard to accept," said Doris Gay, Michael's...

Turn to Boy, Page 4

Carter acts to oust criminal refugees

AP and UPI

President Carter ordered the Justice Department Saturday to try to return to Cuba any refugees known to have serious criminal backgrounds or who have violated US laws since their arrival.

"What concerns most Americans is the prospect that some of the people who have committed crimes might be relocated in American communities," White House Press Secretary Jody Powell said. "That will not happen."

Powell said the administration had evidence that Cuban President Fidel Castro dispatched "this undesirable element to the United States in a calculated effort to disguise the fact" that most of the nearly 112,000 refugees who flooded into Florida in recent weeks are law-abiding persons in quest of freedom and reunification with their families.

Abbe Lowell, an assistant to Atty. Gen. Benjamin Civiletti, estimated that no more than 750 Cubans had been detained as a result of criminal backgrounds in Cuba, and that another 100 were detained as a result of crimes committed here, primarily stemming from last weekend's riot at Fort Chaffee, Ark.

"This action by the Cuban government, in addition to its cynical and inhumane characteristics, is a direct and serious violation of international law," Powell said in a statement.

He said Cuba would be committing flagrant equally serious violations if it refuses to accept any refugees the United States tries to return.

He said the administration would attempt the return through such international organizations as the United Nations and the Organization of American States, but he would not predict the likelihood of success.

"The president has directed the...

Turn to Refugees, Page 4

Vistas of green are county's pride

By Sam Martino
Of The Journal Staff

Our parks!

They are big and small. They are used by children, teen-agers, families, senior citizens.

They are for family fun. And for singles, tots, fishermen, conservationists, senior citizens, birdwatchers, joggers, skaters, skaters, bicyclists, golfers, hikers.

Cultural events including plays

and musical extravaganzas are staged in them.

A recent film called the parks part of the area's "well-kept secret." But for the thousands who have grown up in Milwaukee County's parks, there is no secret about their diversity.

132 park areas

The Zoo, Mitchell Park Conservatory, The Stadium, McKinley Marina, Martin Luther King Community Center, The Wilson Park recreation area, Humboldt Park chalet, Washington Park Senior Center, The Pulaski, Moody, and Noyes indoor-outdoor pools. Exercise and bike trails

Beaches, Nature centers, Golf courses, Soccer fields.

Milwaukee County's system of 132 parks and parkways spans more than 14,000 acres. The parks are in the spotlight more than ever this year because of the energy crisis economic recreation and leisure.

"Our park system is going to get tremendous use," predicts County Executive O'Donnell. "People are not going to be able to afford to go 200 or 300 miles away for recreation. They are going to stay closer to home."

Milwaukee County has been chosen by the National Recreation and Park Association to take part in a national demonstration project promoting use of the parks. Called "Life is in It," the project will encourage awareness of the parks and of the value of recreation.

Executives attracted

Business and industry brag about Milwaukee County's park system and use it to attract new employees.

"I would hate to think of living in a community without parks as well kept and prominent as those in the Milwaukee area," said one businessman.

There has been an attempt in county officials to provide all areas of the county with park and recreation facilities. In 1976, for example, 21 acres of urban-renewal land became the Martin Luther King Jr. Park Center. The facility provides recreation facilities in the central city and also serves as a social-service center. Well-baby clinics, pregnancy testing, gardening programs, family-planning clinics, mental-health counseling and crime prevention...

Turn to Parks, Page 14

On, Wisconsin
An Editorial

What's a family?
Can it survive?

Where is the American family headed? Is its future sunny or dark? Should government do more — or less — for families?

We'd like to invite you to participate in The Journal's "Open Debate on the Family." It is timed to coincide with the White House Conference on Families — a nationwide series of meetings President Carter has called to examine the state of the family, increase public awareness of family issues and recommend public policies that will help families.

So far, conference delegates can't even agree on a definition of family. Must family members be "related by marriage, blood or adoption" or can they be unmarried adults, including homosexual couples? What's your view? Do you agree with the majority in a Gallup Poll who said family life is deteriorating but still is the most important part of life?

Should "family impact" studies be required before lawmakers can change tax, housing, prison, education, health or welfare policies? How can society help children whose families are torn apart by alcohol abuse, divorce and economic pressures?

Has Medicaid promoted nursing homes to the detriment of families? Should teenagers be given contraceptives without parental consent? Has welfare driven fathers from their families? Can working parents' needs for flexible hours and day care be reconciled with the needs of employers?

The Journal will publish a selection of letters and submit all comments to the White House conference. Letters must be received by June 16 and include your name and address, but not necessarily for publication. Mail to: Open Debate on the Family, Milwaukee Journal, P.O. Box 661, Milwaukee, Wis. 53201.

FLOWERING SPECTACLE AT WHITNALL — Visitors to the Boerner Botanical Gardens in Whitnall Park stopped to view the colorful array of flowering spring trees and plants lining the walkways.

A painful return to a tornado-torn city

By Nancy J. Stohs
Of The Journal Staff

Grand Island, Neb. — I never thought I'd witness hell at the least A & W or Maven bowling Alley or over the peaceful, flat farm fields near my childhood home.

But "hell" is really the only word to describe the ugly mess that has replaced these and so many other landmarks of my hometown of Grand Island.

Seven terrible tornados had crossed my city in the space of hours. By now five people have died.

After seeing the damage, it's still hard for me to grasp. And it's painful.

I had known through relatives Wednesday night 24 hours after the tornados hit, that my father and stepmother were OK and the family home and my father's chiropractic office were intact. (We have no other relatives in town.) All phone circuits in the city of 40,000 were busy, so I couldn't talk to them.

They were lucky — very lucky. I was too. Just two blocks north of our 21-year-old ranch house houses were all their foundations or were missing roofs, windows and furnishings. Their owners had lost everything. The Veterans Hospital, five blocks away, had sustained more than $1 million damage. Windows were sucked out of its high school, two blocks away.

All that my parents and their immediate neighbors suffered was tree and leaf damage and a little debris in their yards. Fortunately, the uprooted trees fell away from houses.

I was deeply thankful to get the family all okay.

Turn to Visit, Page 4

US orders formal probe of Clark trip

Ad New York Times Service

Washington, D.C. — The Justice Department said Saturday that Atty. Gen. Benjamin R. Civiletti had asked the Treasury Department to begin a formal investigation of the trip to Iran by Ramsey Clark and other Americans to determine whether they had violated American law in such travel.

Civiletti said in a prepared statement that the results of the Treasury investigation would be reviewed to determine what civil divisions of the Justice Department.

The statement did not indicate the likelihood of prosecution or other action against the 52-year-old Clark, who served as attorney general in the Johnson administration. But the statement did advance the case a step beyond the point at which it stood Friday, when Justice Department officials said only that they were...

Turn to Page 3

Reagan urges Republicans to unite, save country

By Donald Pfarrer
Journal Political Reporter

If Republicans unite and commit themselves to saving the country, their party will win the presidency this fall with the help of Democrats and independents, Ronald Reagan said in a speech here Saturday night.

Addressing about 2,000 people at a fund-raising event for the Republican Party of Wisconsin, Reagan said his party wasn't simply seeking the power of the White House but an opportunity to turn the country around.

As the overall victor in the presidential primaries Reagan, a former governor of California, is virtually certain to be nominated by the GOP national convention in August.

The trends that need to be reversed, he said, are those that have taken America away from the ideals of the Revolution.

He said that for the first 150 years of our history as a free nation, the government sought to protect the people, to preserve freedom and to assure the national defense.

But recently we have drifted to "the entirely new concept" of government intervention, redistribution of wealth, and regulation of the business and other activities of private citizens.

"I wonder if we haven't strayed down a path that was never intended?" Reagan said.

About 1,800 people in Reagan's audience had paid $100 each for a dinner held in connection with the state party's annual convention. Another $50 to $90 paid $5 for bleacher seats.

Reagan was introduced by Gov. Dreyfus, who reminded him that the Republican Party was founded in Wisconsin 126 years ago. Dreyfus, in turn, had been introduced by Green Bay Packer Coach Bart Starr, who served as master of ceremonies.

Reagan told Starr that governors down smart.

Turn to Reagan, Page 16

Inside The Journal

INSIGHT
Mission to Haiti

Spectrum
Women helping women

HOME
Gothic ghosts

TV Screen
"The Shining"

The weather
National Weather Service

Milwaukee — Partly cloudy and much cooler today with high temperatures near 80. Mostly fair and cool tonight with lows in the mid-40s.

Wisconsin — Partly cloudy and much cooler today with high temperatures in the mid-50s to mid-80s. Fair and cool tonight with lows in the mid-30s to mid-40s.

Weather map, Page 6, Part 2.

Fig. 6.5.

Another technique is the use of two headlines under the picture (Fig. 6.6). One could be a 1-column headline in a small size such as 24 points while the other is a larger, multicolumn head. Technically this is tombstoning, but there is no danger the consumer will read from one story to the other because of the disparity in sizing.

Fig. 6.6.

Headlines also can be used to connect related elements that are not in the normal vertical package. In Figure 6.7, running the headline over the story and picture of the 100-year-old woman gives a strong visual signal to the reader about the relationship of these elements. As demonstrated in Figure 6.4, the editor still must be careful about what appears under the picture.

Woman turns 100, dances

By Joanna Ramey
Missourian staff writer

Sallie Nelson had a good reason for dancing at her birthday party Friday at the Columbia House Healthcare, 1801 Towne Drive.

She turned 100 years old Saturday.

In celebration, she danced, laughed and sang along with the other residents of the center — a combination of what she says she enjoys the most.

Sallie never tells anyone her age. "I just like to walk up to people, shake their hand, tell them that I've never been married, and not to call me Miss, but to just call me Sallie," she says.

Among the many people to send her a birthday greeting were President and Mrs. Jimmy Carter. Some of the gifts she received from her friends at the center included a nightcap, a jar filled with 120 pennies and a bar of soap.

Sallie, the second of seven children and the only survivor of her immediate family, is not amazed by her age. She said she will be happy to live another year as long as it is "God's will."

Before moving to the center in March 1972, Sallie lived on a farm in Fortuna, Mo., her birthplace. Her memories of living in a rural community are many.

"I remember milking the cows when I was young," Sallie says. "I used to grab their teats and get all the milk out of them," she says.

Sallie laughs when she remembers the time a cow kicked a bucket of milk over, and her father decided that "I needed a milking lesson. As soon as my father sat down, boom. The cow kicked him and the milk over," she says.

When living in Fortuna, Sallie earned her living caring for children in her home. "All I ever did was babysit. Love those children," she says. Sallie is quick to mention that in her career as a babysitter, she never whipped a child.

To keep herself busy, Sallie spends her days reading the Bible and walking through the long hallways at the center, smiling, shaking hands and looking forward to springtime.

"I like spring when the flowers begin to bloom. It's like the world is opening up," Sallie says.

Sallie Nelson celebrates her 100th birthday   Kathy Kuper

Fig. 6.7.

Boxes also communicate relationships. All elements within a box should be related. Conversely, boxes separate the elements within the box from those outside. Many editors err when they box a sidebar or related story but do not place the main story in the same box. The box sets the sidebar apart and competes with the content by telling the reader the sidebar is not related. Boxes are visual fences. An exception would be a one-subject page with a main story and sidebars. If handled properly, a sidebar can be boxed. Often no special devices are needed to communicate relationships.

By using modules properly, editors do not need additional typographic devices to show relationships. In Figure 6.8, the *Boston Herald American* packaged three related stories with three photographs. A one-line headline pulled the three together, but each photograph had its own deck. The entire package was a module. Each story had its own message, but together they carried a greater impact. The visual package communicates the relationship as well as the content.

Fig. 6.8.

Multiple-element packages

The headline in the package in Figure 6.8 implies the relationship among the three stories, but editors can be more explicit by using labels.

Labels clearly identify a group of related elements and remind readers of what they have just read. The editor of a paper that had consistently published a good news story on Page 1 was stunned when a subscriber complained there was never any good news on the front page. The paper had been publishing a good news story on Page 1 every day for almost a year. After the initial shock, the editor concluded that readers did not recognize the effort because the stories were not labeled "Good News." Labeling can identify small groupings of news as readily as departments. Readers want complicated events explained and relationships shown. The publication that reported the historic volcanic eruption of Mount St. Helens on Page 1 but ran a story on Page 24 about the effect of the volcano-produced ash cloud on the local weather did not serve the reader. The relationship was not completed visually. Sometimes, however, it is impossible to put all the related elements in one place.

Big news produces multiple stories. In the spring of 1980, when the United States attempted a commando raid to free 53 hostages held in Iran, many newspapers ran several stories. Figures 6.9 and 6.10 show how the *Columbia Missourian* handled the news. Two major stories and two illustrations were placed on Page 1, and seven related stories and a drawing appeared on an inside page. The Page 1 package was pulled together by a box, even though the modular layout and the arrangement of the materials below made the box unnecessary. The inside package was pulled together by the reverse label running across the top of the page. The label works, but the box around the witness story tends to separate rather than unite all the elements.

Labels can be designed in several ways. The reverse label (white type against a black background) is one method. The reverse can also be screened to produce white type against a gray border. This technique permits the use of a lighter weight on the page when desired. Many newspapers also use spot color (see Chapter 14) in place of the reverse or screen.

A label may consist of one or two words of type properly placed to unite all the elements. In Figure 6.11, "The Cold War" pulls together three stories about increasing world tensions.

Logos, small graphic representations of the subject matter in which art and type are usually combined, also can be used to show relationships among either a group of stories or stories that appear over a period of time. The *Louisville Courier-Journal* combined type with small pictures of the presidents to provide an immediate identifier for running stories on the presidential campaign (Fig. 6.12).

Columbia Missourian

72nd Year — No. 192   Good Morning! It's Sunday, April 27, 1980   6 Sections — 80 Pages — 35 Cents

Iran

Militants say hostages moved, to be scattered throughout country

By John Kifner
New York Times

TEHRAN, Iran — The American hostages at the U.S. Embassy here have been removed and will be scattered in cities and towns throughout Iran to thwart any further rescue attempts, the militants holding the embassy said Saturday.

An artist sketch shows the six helicopters and a C-130 that made it to the staging area at Tabas, Iran, above. One of the copters crashes into a C-130 as the U.S. commando withdrawal begins, top left. Eight servicemen were killed in the crash.

Rescue try — a reconstruction

From our wire services

WASHINGTON — American involvement in Iran planned to fly in a secret mountain hideaway and then to Tehran for the U.S. Embassy.

Jailhouse lawyer

Inmate spends time filing legal motions

By Pat Wingquarter
Missourian staff writer

JEFFERSON CITY — A. B. Welch-Letty Tyler has filed more lawsuits than state inmates do in a lifetime.

Insight

Kennedy posts narrow win in Michigan

DETROIT UPI — Edward Kennedy captured a majority of Michigan's 141 delegates Saturday by a city-style pole barricade in a sweat-out showcases that faded to give President Carter a drive for the Democratic presidential nomination.

In the first election test since the amorphous attempt to rescue U.S. delegates it took a small edge in the state as a final American servicemen.

Studies show yearly pay loss of professors due to inflation

By Alan Wingfield
Missourian staff writer

When Hubert Rowland a professor at business came to the University in 1967, higher education was on a better financial condition. Salaries support and an entire faculty salaries were all up.

Inside today

Bogota hostages

A woman M-19 guerrilla flashes a victory sign, left, after a meeting in which negotiators may have reached an agreement to end the 69-day-old occupation of the Dominican Embassy in Bogota, Colombia. For more on the hostages, see Page 13A.

In town today

2-4 p.m. Dedication and open house, Columbia Area Career Center.
7:30 p.m. Theater, "Why Hanna's Back Won't Stay Down," University Fine Arts Building, Reynolds Theater.
1 p.m. Concert, University Jesse Auditorium.
8:15 p.m. Concert, University Hall.

Monday

8:10 a.m. Concert, Academic Meeting, University Jesse Auditorium.

Index

Background	4B
Business	5C-9C
Classified	1C
Markets	6C
Opinion	4B
People	10-11B
Real Estate	1C
Sports	1A-12A
Theaters	10A-14A

Time moves ahead

Today is the first day of Daylight-Saving Time. You should have set your clocks forward one hour.

Fig. 6.9.

116

Reaction to ill-fated rescue attempt

Aide says U.S. plan months old

From our wire services

WASHINGTON — President Carter ordered plans for a rescue mission drawn up five days after Americans were taken hostage in Iran and might have given a "go" order sooner if Iranian had not invaded Afghanistan, a White House official said Saturday.

Carter stepped decided to skip going to his Camp David retreat this weekend and stayed at the White House for reports from National Security Adviser Zbigniew Brzezinski.

The rescue mission ended in disaster. Eight American commandos died in the burning wreckage of a mega-plane and a helicopter and the hostages are still in captivity, apparently being moved by their captors to a variety of locations throughout Iran.

The commandos took in only two spare helicopters, the aide said, because a bigger fleet might have endangered the secrecy of the entire mission. "There were personal reminders ... was comfortably higher than seemed warranted from all the previous exercises that had been conducted."

The U.S. Embassy in Tehran was seized Sunday Nov. 4 while Carter was at Camp David in Maryland. By the following Friday, the official said, Carter asked Brzezinski to develop "rescue and other military courses."

The basic options were ready by Nov. 30 and were sent to Carter at Camp David. The Soviet invasion of Afghanistan in late December encouraged Carter to pursue "a negotiating track," the aide said, because Iran reacted so negatively to it.

There were no public plans at the time that Carter was considering a rescue. As late as Jan. 4, Carter told members of Congress such a mission "would almost certainly end in failure and the death of the hostages."

The aide said Brzezinski supported the mission, "absolutely, no question about it." There have been reports that the State Department, which apparently played little part in the mission, opposed it on grounds it endangered diplomatic efforts.

White House Press Secretary Jody Powell denied speculation the administration collaborated with Iranian President Abolhassan Bani-Sadr's government in the mission, and said no Iranian knew of the operation before its execution.

An artist rendition shows Iranian bus passengers being held at gunpoint by the ill-fated American rescue force. Later, Iranian eyewitnesses contradicted U.S. assertions that there was no violence. Defense Secretary Harold Brown said the the 55 Iranian passengers were later freed unharmed after the bus happened by the mission's staging area in the Great Kavir Desert.

Witnesses contradict peaceful bus seizure

TEHRAN, Iran (UPI) — Iranian newspapers Saturday carried what they called eyewitness accounts of a desert encounter between passengers of a bus and the ill-fated American rescue force that contradicted U.S. assertions there was no violence.

The report charged the soldiers on the aborted mission to rescue the American hostages from the U.S. Embassy in Tehran clubbed the bus driver. It also claimed they had shot and killed the driver of an oil tanker truck.

Defense Secretary Harold Brown, in his news conference Friday, said the U.S. force detained 55 Iranians from a bus that happened by the mission's staging area in the Great Kavir Desert.

Brown said the Iranians were later freed to a nearby plane and that the bus tires, "Pars" said.

The Iranian news reports, quoting the official Pars news agency said "armed foreigners" stopped a passenger bus about 40 miles (64.4 kilometers) south of the main town of Tabas around 1:30 a.m. Friday (4 p.m. CST Thursday).

It was at that staging site that eight Americans later lost their lives in the collision of a C-130 transport and a helicopter.

The passengers of the bus were forced to get out. Pars said, and a bus driver who resisted was struck on the head with the butt of a rifle and had his hands tied.

The foreigners "fired into the air, took the plane

When the bus passengers were boarding the plane, another aircraft caught fire. Pars said in the report.

It said the Iranians were detained on board the aircraft until dawn and released soon after the "foreigners" left, suggesting that some unidentified collaborators kept the passengers detained during the American escape.

The Pars report had no further details but Iranian officials — and other reports from Washington — asserted Saturday that Iranian dissidents elements friendly to the United States had assisted in the rescue plan.

The tension between Iran and Iraq over the plan.

Iranian turmoil feared

By Jim Anderson
United Press International

WASHINGTON — Some administration officials expressed concern Saturday that the ill-fated attempt to rescue the American hostages in Tehran may trigger another political firestorm in Iran.

The officials fear the raid, and its aftermath, will undercut any moderate elements that may be left there and possibly lead to the downfall of the shaky central government.

One immediate result of a new surge of religious or left-wing radicalism would be to thwart indefinitely any efforts to win release of the hostages.

"We see a radicalization of the situation in Iran," said one senior official.

"There seems to be some likelihood of an outbreak in a population that is as politically divided and well-armed as the Iranians, with the same chances of civil war and bloodshed.

U.S. officials estimate a million people are out of work in Tehran alone. They say that in a country of about 35 million people, at least 8 million have firearms ranging from pistols to machine-gun type weapons.

One senior U.S. official predicted before the attempted rescue that that would more benefit a more radical religious regime or internal problems mounted.

Unable to deal with those problems the religious leadership would be replaced by the only other alternative here: a radical left-wing coalition friendly to the Soviet Union.

There also is an ominous situation on Iran's border with Iraq, where there are daily armed clashes and the oil-rich search have been assigned independently as relations were attempted to be as able as we were at most it was clear the final years of the shah's reign.

Europe to keep sanctions

From our wire services

BRUSSELS, Belgium — The United States' European allies are expected to put aside their misgivings over the abortive U.S. rescue mission and stick to their diplomatic sanctions against Iran, diplomatic sources said Saturday.

The first crisis is expected to dominate discussions by the heads of government of the nine-nation European Economic Community when begin a newly summer meeting in Luxembourg Sunday.

Diplomatic sources said it was unlikely any of the EEC states would go back on the decision of their foreign ministers last Tuesday to impose sanctions at their sullenadding an economic level, blockade, unless forced actual provision by May 17 toward the release of the hostages.

But observers said the EEC might

have put pressure on Carter not to take any more unilateral measures without consulting the allies.

When they approved the plan, the EEC nations thought the move would forestall military action, but despite varying degrees of pique, because Carter went against the EEC's advice and ordered the ill-fated military force without consulting them, Britain, West Germany and other countries indicated they felt it vital to preserve the unity of the Atlantic alliance.

Diplomatic sources said that, due to pressures for European sanctions, there was virtually no chance that France would pull out of Tuesday's agreement. That country had argued that the sanctions would push the shortest move since the Suez crisis.

Japan also will stand by its sanctions policy, which parallels the EEC than Prime Minister Masayoshi Ohira told a news conference in Tokyo, Japan.

Soviets: U.S. mission may lead to 'conflict'

MOSCOW (UPI) — The Soviet Union said Saturday the American rescue mission in Iran had betrayed the U.S. and Nixon' European allies and was threatening to draw them into a larger conflict in the Middle and Near East.

Mohammad Mokri, Iranian ambassador to the Soviet Union, echoed those sentiments were as said Iran would not allow any foreign soldier to enter our territory. "He added, "If the United States wants to set the Middle East on fire, then the Soviet Union will draw 'it's own conclusions and we will draw our own conclusions."

The Soviet commentaries in response to an irresponsible action," the Communist Party daily Pravda said.

The focus of the Kremlin's press comments appeared to be concentrated Saturday on a move to divide Nixon's and its allies.

Pravda said the incident in the Iranian desert betrayed the trust of the Western European nations because they had been persuaded to take any moves and diplomatic sanctions against Iran, under Washington's strong pressure" as a demonstration of "Atlantic solidarity. Such could help keep the United States from dangerous military steps.

A separate commentary by the Tass news agency late Friday said that Western Europe and Japan might become the victims of an oil embargo if they fully support U.S. sanctions.

Cheers greet injured men

SAN ANTONIO, Texas (UPI) — A cheering crowd greeted two U.S. servicemen injured in the aborted attempt to rescue hostages in Iran as they left Saturday at Brooke Army Medical Center.

Four of the men were taken directly to the center while the fifth, Vernon (at Class William H. Terry, at Fort Walton Beach) was taken to nearby Wilford Hall Hospital.

The others were identified as Marine Majors Leslie B. Petty, 41, Jacksonville, N.C.; and James H. Schaefer Jr., 40, Los Angeles; Air Force Sgt. Joseph J. Beyers III, 27, Harrison, N; Warren Moss; and Air Force Staff Sgt. Joseph E. Beyers.

Hostages' kin get briefing

HOUSTON (UPI) — A group of relatives of the hostages held in Iran Saturday finished a two-day State Department-sponsored briefing on the Iranian situation with a renewed optimism, left about the hostages' safety and their expected eventual overturn when the ordeal is over.

The regional briefing, which occurred periodically with the aborted rescue mission, was the second of three. The first was last weekend in Chicago and the last will be next week in Washington.

"Pleased because our Friday's raid and the expected movement of the hostages out of the occupied U.S. Embassy to unknown locations around Iran.

Fig. 6.10.

Arabs greet assistance plan coolly

Zbigniew Brzezinski
Greeted coolly in Mideast

RIYADH, Saudi Arabia (UPI) — National security adviser Zbigniew Brzezinski proposed Tuesday that Arab nations lend financial assistance to Pakistan to help counter the threat posed by Soviet troops in Afghanistan, Western diplomatic sources said.

The proposal, made during two days of talks with Saudi leaders, was a new tack by Brzezinski in the face of Arab resistance to President Carter's concept of an American security umbrella for the Middle East, the sources said.

Brzezinski flew to Riyadh Monday from Pakistan and left Saudi Arabia Tuesday for the United States.

The Washington Post, in a report from Riyadh, said an Iranian jet fighter buzzed the U.S. Air Force 707 carrying Brzezinski and his party as the plane flew over the Gulf of Oman.

Details of Brzezinski's talks were not disclosed officially, and the state-run Saudi press Agency only said the discussions dealt with "the Middle East, international developments and bilateral relations."

But there were subtle indications Brzezinski's quick trip to Saudi Arabia, largest oil supplier to the United States, did not go well. While he met twice with Prince Saud and once with Saudi strongman Crown Prince Fahd, the Carter aide did not see King Khaled, for reasons that were not explained immediately.

Brzezinski was met on arrival by Foreign Minister Prince Saud Al-Faisal but was seen off by an underling, Foreign Ministry Undersecretary for Political Affairs Faisal Hojailan.

Brzezinski apparently switched the emphasis of his visit and urged Saudi Arabia and other Persian Gulf Arab states to extend assistance to Pakistan to help it meet the challenge of the Soviet invasion of neighboring Afghanistan.

The United States has proposed aid of its own totaling $400 million to Pakistan, but diplomatic sources quoted Brzezinski as saying that was not enough and that "therefore, Arab oil-producing states are urged to participate."

The reaction of the Saudi leaders was not disclosed immediately, but it was clear that Brzezinski's reception in Riyadh was cool.

His mission was made in an effort to seek ways of shoring up security over American "interests," in question since the departure of the shah of Iran and the Soviet invasion of Afghanistan.

But Washington's main push, for a U.S. security umbrella over the Middle East and the 73 per cent of the world's known oil reserves it possesses, has been greeted with mixed skepticism and suspicion by nearly all Arab Gulf states.

Saudi Arabia prefers instead a course that would see the Arab states, with outside help, build up their own armed forces to meet any threat.

U.S. rebuffs plea for detente

WASHINGTON (UPI) — Reacting coolly to Soviet calls for renewed detente, President Carter's chief spokesman Tuesday advised Americans to take a hard look at the "potential for catastrophe" in Kremlin policies.

A buildup of U.S. military power is "going to take awhile" to complete and will require an enduring consensus among Americans that such a move is needed, a White house official said.

The question of detente arose Tuesday when Soviet President Leonid Brezhnev, in his first public comments on Carter's State of the Union address, was quoted by the Communist Party newspaper Pravda as saying "our peoples have mutual concern to overcome international tension."

Brezhnev said, "Detente is a result of many efforts. It is the mutual achievement of all peace-loving states, so one can't allow unreasonable imperialistic forces to ruin its fruits."

The United States accused the Soviets of scuttling detente by sending troops into Afghanistan, a move some officials feared was just a prelude to further Russian aggression.

"It's important for the American people to take a good hard look at the potential for catastrophe in that part of the world," White House Press Secretary Jody Powell said.

"You have to give serious consideration to what it would mean if a hostile power controlled that region and the flow of oil from the region."

Paris, Bonn back U.S. boycott

PARIS (UPI) — France and West Germany Tuesday closed ranks behind President Carter's get-tough foreign policy, demanding a Soviet withdrawal from Afghanistan and warning that any further Soviet thrusts would be met by a unified Western alliance.

Though no threats of specific retaliation against the Soviet Union, such as the grain and technology export embargo, were made, diplomats said that unless Moscow withdraws from Afghanistan soon, France and West Germany would be forced to join the U.S.-initiated boycott of the summer Olympics

in Moscow and possibly take other steps.

The statement — said by officials to be the toughest condemnation on record of any Soviet military initiative by Paris and Bonn — came at the conclusion of a three-day summit meeting at Elysee Palace.

Until Tuesday, France and West Germany had responded cautiously to the Soviet invasion. The low-key approach apparently reflected hope for a promised Soviet withdrawal from Afghanistan.

The French and German leaders said the mission was unacceptable and creates grave danger

Fig. 6.11.

Labels and logos give editors the opportunity to communicate with readers explicitly. These aids should be used more often. One reader suggested that newspapers could learn from supermarkets, "They label every aisle, and it makes it easy to find things. Newspapers don't" (Clark 1979, p. 31). Defining relationships for readers, whether between two stories or within a whole category of news, is important. Newspapers have been slow to capitalize on reader habits and desires, but progress is being made. As a result of such monumental efforts as the Newspaper Readership Project, a combined research effort of several newspaper-related organizations, and studies commissioned by individual newspapers, editors are learning and publications are changing.

Kennedy barely wins caucus vote in Michigan

By ADAM CLYMER
© New York Times News Service

EAST LANSING, Mich. — Sen. Edward M. Kennedy won his second narrow victory of the week yesterday, beating President Carter in the Michigan caucuses by fewer than 300 votes and taking a 71-to-70 edge in the state's national convention delegation.

Kennedy, desperately trying to overtake Carter in the race for the Democratic presidential nomination, had sought a wider margin of victory to support his argument that he, and not the president, was the choice of Democrats in the nation's major industrial states, where a Democrat normally must be strong to win in November.

1980 PRESIDENTIAL CAMPAIGN

Fig. 6.12.

In the week's other industrial battleground, Pennsylvania, where 1.5 million people turned out to vote, Kennedy won by just 10,000 votes. In Michigan he led Carter 7,762 votes to 7,532 with 99 percent of the returns in, as less than 40 percent of the 40,635 card-carrying Democrats who were eligible to take part came out to vote.

CHAPTER SEVEN

Tabloids and Sunday magazines

PERHAPS one of the reasons that tabloids gained the reputation of being sensationalistic is because a tabloid page can carry three, maybe four news stories. If one of them happens to be about a rape, it gains more prominence than in a broadsheet. . . . It is therefore important for a serious tabloid to be careful in its type size and face design if it is to present all the news tastefully.

Paul Back
DIRECTOR OF DESIGN
Newsday

THE IDEA for an American tabloid newspaper came out of a visit between a son of a publisher of the *Chicago Tribune* and an English press baron. Joseph Medill Patterson told his cousin, Robert McCormick, of his meeting with Lord Northbrook, and in 1919 they started publishing the *Illustrated Daily News* in New York. They hoped to emulate Lord Northbrook's success with the tabloid *Daily Mirror,* which had a circulation of one million in England. Before achieving that kind of success, however, they had to slog through the yellow journalism sensationalism of the 1920s and 1930s and battle upstart competitors. The excesses committed in the name of circulation peaked in 1928 when the *News* brought in a *Chicago Tribune* staff member, Tom Howard, to surreptitiously take a picture of the execution of Ruth Synder, who had been convicted of murder. Public reaction to such sensationalism finally forced this type of newspaper to change or shutdown. The *News* changed and went on to become the largest general circulation newspaper in the United States. Unfortunately, the stigma associated with yellow journalism lingered long after the practices and slowed the acceptance of the tabloid-size paper. In 1940, Alicia Patterson, Joseph Patterson's daughter, started a tabloid on Long Island. *Newsday* has since become one of the most successful newspapers in America. Now owned by the Times Mirror Company, *Newsday* grew up with Long Island and, in content and looks, redefined the image of the tabloid. *Newsday* made the tabloid so respectable, in fact, that by 1979 even the conservative *Our Sunday Visitor,* the largest Catholic weekly in the country, had changed from broadsheet to tabloid and reported that reader reaction to the restyled paper was "overwhelmingly positive."

These days, the fear that a smaller paper will bring less advertising revenue, not the negative image of tabloids, keeps publishers from switching to the smaller size, which is widely acknowledged to be more convenient for readers. In tabloids, advertisers can buy smaller ads, usually at higher rates, and still dominate the page. Even a full page in a tabloid is only a half page in a broadsheet. Most national advertising is designed for broadsheet newspapers; tabloids often must reduce the ads to make them fit. Even if the reduction is proportionate, the reduced ads often look misshaped.

As a consequence, tabloids are seen most often where they have existed successfully for years, such as the *Rocky Mountain News* in Denver. They are also used by newspapers without much advertising (*Christian Science Monitor, Our Sunday Visitor*), the minority press (*Chicago Defender, Sacramento Observer*), and by high school and college publications (see Figs. 7.1, 7.2). Some special interest papers (*Village Voice, Rolling Stone*) are

Fig. 7.1.

Fig. 7.2.

tabloid. The grocery-store papers (*National Enquirer, National Star*) are also tabs. Many broadsheet newspapers use tabs for special theme sections, which usually revolve around an advertising promotion. Sometimes tabs are used to report the results of an in-depth investigation. Most newspapers also have Sunday magazines that are usually tabloid size or close to it. The growing number of Sunday newspapers and their corresponding Sunday magazines makes this type of tabloid an increasingly important product with a need for its own design philosophy. We will discuss the Sunday magazine later in this chapter.

Making the decision

Every successful business organization tries to maximize the strengths and minimize the weaknesses of its product. Publishers who are trying to decide whether to publish a broadsheet or tabloid must first know the advantages and disadvantages of each.

ADVANTAGES

1. Tabloids are more convenient for the reader to handle. At the breakfast table, the open broadsheet is big enough to cover three cereal bowls and the coffee; the tabloid is less intrusive. On the bus or subway, the tab does not have to be folded to be read.

2. Editors usually have more open pages. At *Newsday,* the first four pages are considered to be equivalent to the front page of a broadsheet. It is more economical for small papers with less advertising to set aside a full page for departments. An open page in a broadsheet represents twice the investment in the editorial product that the tabloid does.

3. Content, even within a section, is easier to divide in a tabloid than in a broadsheet where many stories on various subjects appear on a single page. In a typical sports section of its Saturday tabloid, the Allentown *Morning Call* labeled separate pages for "National League," "American League," "Wimbledon," "Golf," "Hockey," "Local Basketball," "Basketball," "Softball," "Horse Racing," "Auto Racing," and "Boxing." The labels were all-cap, 18-pt. heads set against a screened reverse. Figure 7.3 shows the "golf" page.

Fig. 7.3.

4. The tabloid size permits smaller papers to look and feel hefty with only half the content of the broadsheet. Falling advertising revenue and increasing newsprint costs forced the *Christian Science Monitor* to switch to tabloid. Where it only had 12 pages as a broadsheet, it has 24 pages as a tabloid.

5. Tabloids offer publishers more flexibility in the number of pages that can be added or subtracted. Depending on the press, broadsheet newspapers must go up or down in increments of two, four, or eight pages. The number of pages in a tabloid can be changed in increments of four at most plants.

6. Because of the preponderance of broadsheet newspapers, the tabloid offers publishers an opportunity to differentiate their product from others in the market. This is particularly advantageous to new publications in competitive markets.

7. The advertiser benefits by spending less money to dominate a page.

DISADVANTAGES

1. What advertisers gain, publishers lose. Although large advertisers may buy multiple pages of advertising, smaller merchants often settle for less than they would in a broadsheet. Rates can be increased to make up some of the difference, but only if the tab is operating in a noncompetitive market.

2. Advertising and circulation success breed problems. *Newsday* and the *New York Daily News* are too bulky. Successful broadsheet newspapers usually have problems with heft on Sunday, but tabs often face this problem several days of the week.

3. A smaller front page limits the number of elements tabloid editors can use to attract the same variety of readers obtained by the broadsheet. And when the big event occurs, such as a presidential assassination or man's first walk on the moon, the broadsheet can use multiple pictures and stories on the front page. The tabloid cannot do this without sacrificing impact. This limitation was very evident on January 21, 1981, the day editors dealt with two big stories — release of the hostages from Iran and the inauguration of Ronald Reagan. *Newsday* was already locked into its first color cover (Fig. 7.4), and the hostages rated only minimal play at the bottom of the page.

Fig. 7.4.

4. The tabloid cannot be sectionalized as easily as a broadsheet. The tab has only one section even though it may have pullouts. The broadsheet, however, can be divided into numerous sections, depending on press facilities. A family of readers can easily distribute the broadsheet newspaper according to interest; this is much more difficult with a tab.

5. Tabloids still suffer from a lingering image problem. Present generations are not influenced by memories of yellow journalism, but some of them associate tabloids with sensational papers such as the *National Enquirer* and *National Star.* Even people who buy those tabloids do not necessarily want their news presented in the same format. The four most successful daily tabloid newspapers, the *Daily News, Newsday,* Chicago *Sun-Times,* and *Rocky Mountain News* try to maximize the advantages of their size. All are published in communities where mass transportation is available, yet all sell thousands of copies to homes also. If mass transportation were better developed in other large cities, the tabloid might be more popular because of ease of reading while riding. San Francisco and, to a lesser degree, Washington, D.C., have decent mass transportation systems. In those two cities, the second newspapers, the *Examiner* and the *Times,* might be candidates for tabloids, but both are established as broadsheets, and the disadvantages of a change in size probably outweigh the advantages.

Differentiating the tabloid

Beyond recognizing the advantages and disadvantages, editors must also identify the unique problems and possibilities that a tabloid presents, or it will be treated merely as a small-sized newspaper. The tabloid is different from a broadsheet newspaper in the following six areas: Page 1 philosophy, sectionalizing, spreads, sizing, headlines, and jumps.

DEVELOPING A PAGE 1 PHILOSOPHY. Editors of broadsheets must decide whether they want a high or low story count, but tabloid editors must decide whether they want a low story count or no stories at all. On Page 1, tabloids have more in common with newsmagazines than with broadsheets. Both must concentrate on one or two elements because of size restrictions. Like the news weeklies, newspaper tabloids must retain immediacy while providing focus. That means stripping away the clutter. *Newsday* uses its front page as a poster; except for unusual circumstances, no stories start on Page 1 (Fig. 7.5). Instead, two to four stories are promoted with display type. Usually, though not always, there is an illustration with a reference line to an inside story. The *Sun-Times* normally starts two stories on Page 1 and jumps both of them (Fig. 7.6). Other stories are teased with lines at the top or bottom of the page. The *Daily News,* like the *Sun-Times,* uses the front to sell its best story with display type and text and promote other inside elements of interest. The *Rocky Mountain News* (Fig. 7.7) and the *Christian Science Monitor* (Fig. 7.8) treat Page 1 as a small-sized broadsheet. There are as many as four stories, all jumped, and a photograph.

Fig. 7.5.

Fig. 7.6.

Fig. 7.7.

Fig. 7.8.

There are five alternative ways to present the tabloid cover:

1. Use it as a poster to sell several stories inside. Both display type and illustrations can be used, but even one decently sized illustration will substantially restrict the number of items that can be teased.

2. Use it as a mininewspaper page. With a story count of two or possibly even three, start the best stories on the front and jump them inside. This does not rule out teasers for other stories but greatly restricts them.

3. Emphasize illustrations. Instead of display type, use one, two, or even three photographs to sell the paper. The image would be more visual than that of a traditional newspaper.

4. Use a single cover illustration in the tradition of the newsmagazines. Overprinting permits giving the illustration a title and promoting other stories inside.

5. All of the above. An editor may feel that the flexibility to choose any of the approaches on consecutive days is more important than being consistent. Any publication will discard a standard format to handle the big event; extraordinary news requires extraordinary handling.

It does not matter whether the cover contains news, display type, or illustrations because readers do not spend much time on Page 1 of a tabloid. That is why it is even more important for tabloid editors to lure the reader inside and provide a wealth of material there. Most of the major news tabloids open up the first four or more pages, but this varies with the size of the publication. The metros need several. Smaller publications, which may have only 24 to 28 pages, may need to open only the first three. The third page is an excellent place to sell the rest of the product. Most readers will go from Page 1 to Page 3 to Page 2. An editor may want to use the third page for an interesting story, news summary, or index. Page 2 is also a good location for items that appear every day, such as news summaries, indexes, and in-depth weather reports. Wherever these items are located up front, the first few pages are essential for creating reader traffic throughout the publication. Separate sections relieve broadsheet editors of some of that burden.

SECTIONALIZING. None of the successful tabs can adequately overcome the problem of size. In 1980, *Newsday* was publishing an average of 168 pages an issue. Some issues were as large as 250 pages.

To create internal departments, most tabs start sectionalized interest areas on the right-hand page so that readers can pull out the entire section. Unfortunately, unless readers work from the middle out, they will probably pull out several other sections too. *Newsday* developed a thumb index punch on the side of the paper to help readers find sections. *Newsday* runs some sections upside down to show readers where a new section starts. Three of the four tabs mentioned earlier start the sports section on the back page. The *Sun-Times* runs a broadsheet food section tucked sideways into the tab. That section, which takes advantage of the full-page grocery advertisements, can easily be pulled out.

Even though pullout sections can be useful, they can also be confusing. The *Christian Science Monitor* clearly identified its "Summer Food" (Fig. 7.9) feature as a pullout by using type and numbering the pages B1 to B8. However, unless the readers actually removed the section, they were unable to follow the double-truck layout that started on Page A12 and continued behind the B section on Page A13. The "Post-summit fallout . . . " head ties the two pages together only if the B section is removed.

Design is an important element in identifying sections. *Newsday* starts each section except sports with a magazine-type cover. The department is led with a large section identifier and a major illustration. The *Sun-Times* has one size of type to show the start of subsections, such as world news, and a larger size type to signal the start of a department, such as "Living." Because it is not easy to separate sections physically, it is important that tabloid sections have different typographical personalities. This can be achieved by using a different, though compatible, headline face; using different column widths on open pages; running unjustified type in one section and justified type in another; and altering the horizontal-vertical emphasis to fit the content.

For instance, in the softer feature or "Lifestyle" sections, ragged right type can be used to signify the less formal approach. In "Business," the layout can be a more conservative vertical structure in the image of the *Wall Street Journal*. In "Entertainment," it might be appropriate to use heavy rules freely, but in a "Fashion" section, thin rules (hairlines) would give a more dignified aura. Headline formats, if not the typeface, can also be changed according to section. The news can be presented in traditional style, while features rely on titles, labels, and readouts. The editorial section can emphasize summary decks to tell the reader the points made in the editorial column.

It is important to create different typographical personalities for each section, but the publication must be unified. This is done by providing standardized sectional identifiers (type and sometimes art) that convey the name of the section. Standardized identifiers can be designed by using the same headline face throughout, even if the format is different, using the same basic format for teasers on the section fronts throughout, or stipulating that all section fronts have summaries or standard indexes. The effort to unify the sections becomes more important as the differentiation between the sections increases. The points are not contradictory. Publications that do not choose to create separate personalities for sections have less need for standardized promotional approaches and indexes. On the other hand, publications that do create different personalities must show the reader that the sections are

Summer Food

Carrots in an antique tub decorate a Nantucket kitchen

Photo by Harriet Tell

Capitol Hill seeks limits on the use of consultants

Lawmakers want to cut abuses by US agencies, private consulting services

By John Yemma
Staff correspondent of The Christian Science Monitor

Post-summit fallout: Schmidt man

Margaret Thatcher sets the record straight

By Rushworth M. Kidder
Staff correspondent of The Christian Science Monitor

London

The fleeting flavors of unusual fruits, vegetables

By Phyllis Hanes
Food editor of
The Christian Science Monitor

Portuguese-US relations ease alliance strain

By Jimmy Burns
Special to The Christian Science Monitor

Lisbon

Ideas from a British picnic	Cool, refreshing chilled soups
Page B2	Page B4

THE CHRISTIAN SCIENCE MONITOR

12

Fig. 7.9.

part of the same family even though they are different in content and approach.

Publications such as the *Village Voice* and *Rolling Stone* have a different audience, different publication schedule, and different purpose than most tabloids. They are basically newsprint magazines. While sectionalizing is important to cater to reader preferences for the familiar, pullout sections are less important. Readers of these two publications spend considerable time with them and use them for entertainment during leisure time, not for information at the breakfast table or on the subway. Every design philosophy must consider the audience first. Inside pages from *Rolling Stone* (Fig. 7.10) and the *Rocky Mountain News* (Fig. 7.11) illustrate the differences between a newspaper and a magazine even though both are tabloids.

Fig. 7.10.   Fig. 7.11.

SPREADS. The manageable size of an open tabloid permits the design editor to treat facing pages as a single unit. Even when stories or pictures do not use the gutter between facing pages, the designer should treat the pages, or spread, as one unit for purposes of balance and flow (Fig. 7.12). In the tabloid, it is often possible to continue stories and pictures from the left-hand to the

Fig. 7.12.

right-hand page, and even the gutter can be used on the spread in the middle of a section. Using the gutter elsewhere is always risky because a continuous sheet of paper is not available, and headlines and photographs may not line up properly.

When a double truck is done properly (Fig. 7.13), it takes advantage of the extra inch or so in the gutter and brings two vertical pages together into a horizontal spread. Pictures in the hang-gliding feature take up two-thirds of the spread and copy occupies the rest. The layout makes the reader forget that two pages are being used.

RELATIVE SIZING. The most important design principle for tabloid editors to remember is that sizing is relative to the dimension of the publication. A 1-column picture in a broadsheet newspaper would look large in *Reader's Digest* or *TV Guide.* A 3-column picture in a broadsheet would look large in a tabloid. The fact that *National Geographic,* with its 33 by 52½ pica page size, has been able to establish itself as a quality photographic magazine is a testament to the principle of relativity.

Certainly a tabloid can never match the broadsheet newspaper's ability to run a picture 80 picas wide on Page 1. A photograph run as wide as the tabloid page will look large in relation to the size of the newspaper. Consequently, it is important for editors to use photographs properly in tandem to emphasize large and small shapes.

HEADLINES. Display type selection is also different for tabloids because there are fewer headlines and choices of size. Consequently, weight becomes the most effective way to show contrast. A headline schedule built around a bold or extrabold face would permit the editors to downsize heads, an appropriate measure for a tabloid. Smaller heads save space and preserve the proportions on a tab page. A lighter face should be available for decks and blurbs.

Tabloids are a more suitable format for mixing typefaces than a broadsheet. A broadsheet usually has several headlines on a page, but most tab pages have only two to four. As a result, a headline schedule that uses a serif for the main face and a sans serif for decks, or vice versa, does not have the potential for clutter that it would have on a broadsheet.

JUMPS. Jumps are a problem in any publication but, properly handled, are less of a problem for tabloids than broadsheets. In a tabloid, however, the writing must be tighter to avoid the necessity of jumping a large number of stories. A medium-sized story in a broadsheet might jump past several pages and, in the process, make it difficult for the reader to follow. The tabloid can capitalize on its magazine-like format and jump to the next page, which is less annoying to the reader and is a pattern familiar to magazine readers. Continuing a story to the next page poses problems for editors, however. If the story starts on one of the first three or four open pages, the jump might occupy valuable space normally used to attract readers with a variety of interests. If the story is important enough that it has to be jumped, it ought to be able to carry its own weight in competition with the other stories fighting for space. When tabs jump stories several pages away, they lose their advantage over the broadsheets. Readership surveys have indicated time and again that readers do not like jumped stories.

Tabloid philosophy

The Page 1 philosophy that tabloid editors adopt as well as the manner in which they handle sectionalizing and the special problems of dimension and proportion will determine whether the publication is treated as a mininewspaper or a genre with its own strengths and weaknesses. Too many editors of both broadsheet and tabloid newspapers never make the difficult decisions. The result is a publication that is unfocused in content and form. Although the basics of good design are the same for broadsheets, tabloids, and magazines, they each have their own special characteristics. Because the news tabloid serves the same audience as the more traditional broadsheet newspaper, editors often fail to distinguish it from the larger version.

With a clearly thought out philosophy, tabloid design editors can place their publications somewhere between the broadsheet newspaper and the weekly newsmagazine. The newsprint gives the tab a sense of immediacy. With only three or four columns to a page, the tabloid designer can use many magazine techniques.

Sunday magazines

Newspaper Sunday magazines often are similar in size to the tabloid format. Sometimes they are even printed on newsprint. Often, though, they are printed on better quality paper stock and have a personality distinct from the daily sections of the newspaper.

The principles of design are constant from format to format, but some general practices are common among Sunday magazines. Most of these practices are based on the belief that the magazine audience is more selective and will take time to read that section. The following principles should be kept in mind:

1. A good advertising arrangement and proper editorial space is essential to success. Ad sizes should be restricted to full, half, and quarter pages (except perhaps in a special section for small advertisers) to create modular spaces for editorial copy. There should be at least one open spread (two facing pages) for the cover story.

2. The beginning of the editorial content must be established clearly. Some Sunday magazines are so full of advertising that the reader must turn several pages before finding editorial copy. Some surefire reader interest material should be up front. *Time* magazine and the *Boston Globe* magazine run letters. The *Philadelphia Inquirer* runs a series of short items called "Inklings." The *Dallas Times Herald* publishes answers to questions about famous personalities in a feature called "People."

3. Begin each story with a strong focus. The reader should recognize

immediately where each story starts. Use large type and photographs or illustrations for openers. The *Boston Globe* magazine used both to open a story on the John Hancock Tower (Fig. 7.14).

Fig. 7.14.

4. Use plenty of white space in the magazine, especially around the type that starts the story. The magazine page should not be like the newspaper page, which is usually full from margin to margin. It is often more attractive to open a story abut 30 percent of the way down the opening page. White space in the margins is also important. The outer margin usually is larger than the interior, or interpage, margin. There should be more white space between the editorial copy and the advertising than there is between elements within the editorial spread.

5. Although the white space in the margins enhances the text that it surrounds, that margin area can also be used effectively for bleeds — running a picture to the edge of the page. Bleeds permit larger picture display and provide page contrast.

6. Design facing pages as one unit whenever possible. Create a strong horizontal left-to-right flow rather than a vertical flow. A spread on Bart Starr in "Insight," the *Milwaukee Journal*'s magazine, illustrates a good use of facing pages. Without using the gutter, the headline reads from one page to the next (Fig. 7.15).

Fig. 7.15.

7. Display typefaces appropriate to the content can be used without producing clutter because there will be only one typeface to a page. Newspapers with several different stories on each page cannot use different typefaces without producing a circus atmosphere. In a tabloid magazine, once a typeface has been selected, it should be used throughout that particular story to provide a unity of design and ensure reader recognition.

8. Use titles and labels rather than news heads. Within reason, the designer and staff should write the headlines and then determine the format rather than specifying a format into which the content must be squeezed. There is always room for compromise, but the magazine staff should take advantage of the use of fewer heads to tell and sell the way they want.

9. Avoid ending a story with a graphic explosion. In fact, it is usually better not to place art or photographs on the last page of a story because they may compete with the opening of the next spread.

10. Have a strong reader feature at the back of the magazine. A significant number of readers move from the back to the front. Do not let them sneak up on you. "Insight" uses a columnist on the inside of the back cover; the *Boston Globe* magazine runs a crossword puzzle.

11. Try to build a rhythm into your magazine. Do not bunch all the long or short stories together. Alternate. Work closely with the advertising department to be sure you get enough space to hook the reader before the story disappears into the columns of advertising.

12. Do not use jump lines when stories continue on consecutive pages. However, try to place a sales pitch on each page, even if it is nothing more than a blurb. One metropolitan newspaper ran a single story for nine consecutive magazine pages without so much as a standing title, let alone a blurb. Each page represents an opportunity to get readers interested in the story.

13. Anchor your standing elements. Readers need to know where things are located.

14. Use the cover to advertise the magazine. It is just one of several sections available to Sunday newspaper customers and something must attract their attention to make them pick it up. *Esquire* says "read me" from the newsstand; the magazine says it from the coffee table. All three of the covers in Figures 7.16 to 7.18 are posters that are used to sell an idea.

Fig. 7.16.

Fig. 7.17.

Fig. 7.18.

Newspaper

III

Design

CHAPTER EIGHT

Management by design

HERE a designer has a firm hand in the initial process of selecting material. He makes news judgments. Beginning on the front page, he helps shape the consensus of what to give the reader. He has real power! That's design.

Edward Miller
FORMER PUBLISHER
ALLENTOWN *Morning Call*

WHEN HENRY FORD INTRODUCED the assembly line to produce his automobiles quickly and cheaply, he started a revolution in mass production. Ford proved he could manufacture a car in 93 minutes; others who followed his lead adapted the technique to include everything from the manufacture of cans to toothpaste.

As Ford was tinkering in Detroit with his new concept, newsrooms were already operating on the assembly line principle; reporters reported, writers rewrote, copy editors edited and wrote headlines, and layout editors placed it all in the paper. As the copy moved mechanically down the belt from reporter to layout editor, additional interpretations were added to the meaning and importance of the story.

Even after photography became an integral part of the publication, the assembly line process remained unchanged. At some point, usually after a story was already written, an editor would order a photograph, often specifying what should be photographed and how. The photographer would comply, the picture would be placed on the belt, and the layout editor would add it to the text and headline. It did not seem to matter that the layout editor probably had no more knowledge of how to handle photographs than the average person.

Newspapers today carry more pictures and artwork and many have color, but their format is not unlike that in Ford's day. That is not surprising because newsroom organization has not changed substantially since that time.

Readers, however, and the ways they spend their working and leisure time have changed. Radio, television, and special interest magazines (and soon home information delivery systems) have captured some of the readers' time and interest. Although technological developments permit newspapers to publish a better, more legible product with increased speed, the organization of most newsrooms tends to fragment the work of highly trained, highly specialized journalists and put it in precast formats.

Traditional newsroom organization is a barrier to successful communication with the reader. Ever since photography became a part of the newspaper, the disadvantages of the assembly line process have outweighed the advantages, but few editors recognized the problem. The result is a product that is often disorganized, seldom thought out, and usually difficult to read. The system fails to take advantage of the combined skills of the reporters, editors, photographers, artists, and designers.

Traditional approach

The traditional newsroom is organized vertically to move the raw materials horizontally. As Figure 8.1 illustrates, the decision-making authority flows downward from the editor to the departments. Meanwhile, each department produces its own end product — stories from the city desk, photographs from the photography department, headlines from the copy desk, and layouts from the layout desk. All the elements come together at the layout desk where one, two, or three persons will make decisions about the proper mix. This structure creates unnecessary barriers. Reporters usually are not consulted about editing changes, and photographers are seldom asked about selection, cropping, or display. Artists, if there are any, are told to produce illustrations, graphs, and maps on short notice and with incomplete information. Furthermore, the editor who puts all these efforts together often does not know what is coming until it arrives.

Newsroom specialization is like the classic good-news, bad-news joke. It is good news when reporters know more about a particular field, such as medicine or the environment, or photographers know how to operate a camera, gather facts on film, crop for maximum impact, and display to attract attention. It is bad news when the division of labor inside the newsroom becomes so severe that journalists do not talk to each other any more than the employee who puts the engine onto the car frame talks to the employee who later screws in the headlights.

In the 1970s, some farsighted publishers, such as those in St. Petersburg, Fla., and Allentown, Pa., began to tinker with newsroom organization because of their growing awareness of the newspaper as a visual medium.

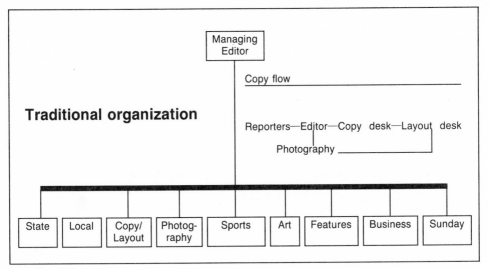

Fig. 8.1.

Oddly enough, at most newspapers it was not the management experts who started this newsroom evolution but first the photographers and then the designers.

Photographers argued loudly and often eloquently that the photo department needed to be more than a service agency that took orders but had no say about either the assignment or the display. These photographers saw themselves as photojournalists who were able to report with a camera, often more dramatically than reporters. They needed a chance to get into the newsroom flow and a voice in the planning and execution of the product as well.

It was only natural that journalists trained to deal with words were reluctant to invite photographers, much less designers, into the councils where news judgments were being made. There was, and still is, little appreciation for the total product in those councils. The efforts of professors Cliff Edom and Angus MacDougall, through the University of Missouri Pictures-of-the-Year competition, had a profound effect on the industry. Their students argued forcefully for the merits of photojournalism. Although many photojournalists went to magazines or free-lanced, many stayed in newspapers and fought the battle. Some won. Rich Shulman dramatically changed a small paper in Kansas before taking his talents to the *Everett* (Wash.) *Herald.* Brian Lanker, who worked with Rich Clarkson at the Topeka *Capital Journal,* helped transform the *Eugene* (Oreg.) *Register-Guard* into a visual medium. Bob Lynn brought the photographer's voice to the Charleston (W.Va.) *Gazette* and then the Norfolk (Va.) *Pilot and Ledger-Star* as graphics editor. For years, artist Frank Peters has reported for the *St. Petersburg Times* with maps, graphs, and charts. They and others like them convinced word-oriented editors of the importance of photographs and graphic presentation. Many editors resisted, and some still do, because they believed that a story, not a photograph, is the best use of space. Eugene Roberts, editor of the

Philadelphia Inquirer, disagrees. His newspaper won six Pulitzer Prizes between 1975 and 1980 and is considered one of the great newspapers in the country. Often overlooked is the fact that the editors at the *Inquirer* know they are working with a visual medium. In 1979, the National Press Photographers Association named Roberts Editor of the Year. Roberts responded, "If I have any virtue as an editor in dealing with photography, it's that I don't know much about it, and I am quite willing to admit it." At the *Inquirer,* the photo director has the title of assistant managing editor and answers only to the managing editor.

Photojournalism produced at papers such as the *Inquirer, Chicago Tribune,* and *Louisville Courier Journal,* combined with the growing body of readership research that showed that graphics does make a difference, began to change the face of U.S. journalism in the late 1970s. In 1980, Thomas Curley, director of research for Gannett, reminded his editors that "[the] causes of reduced readership and dissatisfaction with the newspaper are an unattractive appearance, poor packaging and the number of typos. Physical form often becomes an issue when something goes wrong . . . a small group, typically infrequent readers, finds reading a newspaper a chore. Good graphics attract them and help them understand a story" (Curley 1980).

It was not enough, however, to invite only the photojournalists into the mainstream of the newsroom. Artists, who were expected to work quietly in a corner of the room, and designers, who put the package together, started expressing their needs and showing editors how their involvement could attract attention and explain the content. As early as 1960, the *St. Petersburg Times* recognized that the presentation of information was as important as the content. At the Allentown *Morning Call,* art director Robert Lockwood and executive editor Edward Miller, revolutionized the newsroom process. The design director became an equal to the assistant managing editor in making news judgments and coordinating the paper's content. Miller and Lockwood also experimented with "villages," teams that worked together and included everyone from reporters and photographers to pasteup employees.

In each case, the newsroom organization was changed to make the newspaper more understandable and easier to read.

Reorganizing the newsrooms

Any reorganization of the newsroom must be based on the goal of the organization. If, as it should be, the goal of the publication is to communicate, it follows that whatever the publication can do to make sense of the message will increase reader satisfaction.

The most successful communicators are those who recognize they are selling, not newspapers or magazines, but information. Information consists of both content and form. Publishers and editors who use all the tools of their medium will be successful. Those who do not are like the fighter who goes into the ring with one hand tied behind his back; neither the publisher nor the fighter is using all available resources.

Newsrooms are not organized to produce stories, type, artwork, and photographs that work together. Many stories have no pictures or graphs, and the traditional system facilitates the need to meet daily deadlines. If stories do or should have pictures, maps, or graphs, the traditional system depends on the whim of the individuals doing the work.

At one newspaper, a five-member reporting and photography team worked for three weeks on a special fashion section. The two employees responsible for laying out the section found only the pictures and cutlines when they came to work. They put together the entire section without any of the stories. The layout editors were not involved in the planning, and the section was a disaster.

At another newspaper, a reporter worked for days on an exclusive story about a local judge who was a client of the prostitutes who were being brought before him in court. The story contained a vivid description of the judge meeting the pimp in a seedy bar, walking across the dark street to a three-story house, and going up the carpeted stairs to the third floor to visit a prostitute. Although nearly two pages were devoted to the story, it did not have a single picture or piece of art. Why not? The reporter and his city editor failed to tell other departments they were working on the story until it was too late to add photographs or artwork without delaying the publication date. The story was written, passed on for editing and a headline, and placed in the paper in classic assembly-line fashion.

The Gannett News Service won a Pulitzer Prize in 1980 for "The Story of the Pauline Fathers," an account of questionable financial dealings and fund raising and the church's reluctance to take disciplinary action against the order. Photo-graphics director Tim Manning and art director Pat Mitchell were key members of the team from the beginning. Gannett newspapers around the county had a complete package to present to their readers (Fig. 8.2), and the impact was greater because of it.

Fig. 8.2.

The news service took a team approach to the investigation. Such an approach will produce better newspapers too, but it is impractical to think that each story and picture that appears in a publication can or should be produced by a team. It is not unrealistic, however, to involve the appropriate departments in the planning, gathering, and preparation of all significant packages. That requires better management and a revised newsroom structure. In Figure 8.3, a new position has appeared on the newsroom chart, assistant managing editor – design (A.M.E. – Design).This position is at the hub of the newspaper. The design editor or a designate must be involved in both the daily production cycle and special projects and also have the authority to make news judgments.

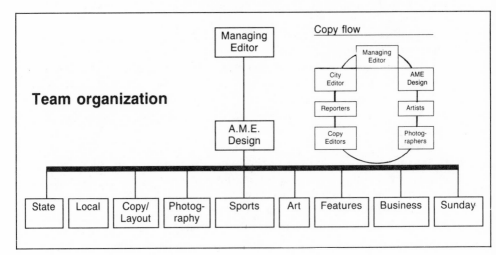

Fig. 8.3.

Design editors, whether they are called art directors, graphics editors, photo editors, or assistant managing editors, come from a variety of backgrounds. They may have been photographers, typographers, artists, or former copy editors who did layout. Because of the standards being established by these pioneers, those who follow will need to be even better qualified. For the design editors of the future, there are at least seven requisites:

   1. They must be journalists. Design editors must understand news values, know how news and features are gathered, and be aware of readers' expectations.
   2. They must be photo editors, though not necessarily photographers. They must be able to differentiate between potential picture situations and those that are not. In addition, they must know how to select, crop, group, and display pictures.

3. They must be artistic, though not necessarily artists, and must understand the principles of unity, contrast, balance, and proportion.

4. They must be typographers, know how to work with type and use it legibly.

5. They must have a working knowledge of publication reproduction processes. The editor needs to know everything from programming the computer for proper type spacing to color production methods.

6. They must be able to work with others. Design editors must be able to persuade others by earning their respect. In turn, they must respect others.

7. They must have the vision to think the unthinkable, the courage to experiment, and the wisdom to remember always that the reader must be served.

It is not necessary for the design editor to have firsthand knowledge of all the functions of the job. The designer needs to know the best spacing between letters in headlines and text, but a computer programmer can achieve the desired results. The designer needs to know how to use photographs, but a photo editor can make most of the day-to-day decisions. The designer needs to understand how color is reproduced, but the artist can make overlays.

Ironically, the smaller the publication, the more important it is for the design editor to have a broad base, because it is less likely there will be computer programmers, photo editors, artists, or lab technicians to do the actual work.

Because of the nature of the job specifications, photojournalists who have backgrounds in typography are likely candidates for design editor positions. Regardless of whether the design editor is a former photographer, the photography and art departments must be elevated from service agencies (as diagrammed in Fig. 8.1) to departments on equal footing with other newsroom divisions (as shown in Fig. 8.3). This will allow the photo editor to initiate assignments, make suggestions on photo orders from other departments, and even reject inappropriate requests. Such an action would be subject to an override only by the design editor or the managing editor.

It is essential that the authority of the design editor, photo editor, and chief artist be built into the newsroom structure.

If it is left to the preferences of the editor or managing editor, it can change overnight as editors move from one position to another. If authority rests on the shoulders of only one person, it also leaves with that one person. This is particularly true at small- and medium-sized newspapers that, like a campfire, glow brightly with the work of a single person but die as quickly as an ember when that editor leaves.

Once the structure exists, management must provide the means for the appropriate departments to work together. The assembly-line system requires cooperation but does not provide for the interchange of ideas or offer the benefits of collaborative efforts. The team system does.

The team system

Most newspapers still operate under a system in which reporters, working with the appropriate editor, gather the facts and write stories. When the stories are done, editors order photographs or artwork. As soon as those materials are available, they are given to a layout editor. Often, the preparation of the story takes days or even weeks, but the photography is expected to be completed in hours, and the layout must be finished by the deadline. The team approach, which involves more people earlier in the process, ensures adequate planning.

The composition of the teams is determined by the project. If it is a sports feature, the sports editor, reporter, and design editor (or designate) should be involved. At the initial conference, which may take only three minutes for some stories, the team determines the subject, focus, and deadline. The design editor might have suggestions about angles or tie-ins with other departments and may also assign a photographer to work with the reporter from the beginning. The reporter-photographer team might make decisions in the field that will change the focus. Even so, the words and visuals will still work together because of the team effort.

Planning sessions for other projects may need to include more people and be more formal. For instance, an investigative project should include the reporters and their project editor, the design editor, the copy editor, the photo editor, the chief artist, and the managing editor or assistant managing editor. The wide variety of perspectives strengthens the fact-gathering process. By involving all the persons who will be working on the package at some stage, management is making the most use of available talent, ego, and pride. Because everyone is involved and has a stake in the success of the project, they will work harder and understand what they are doing. Participating in idea and planning sessions is always stimulating to creative people. Ideas subjected to challenge and scrutiny become more clearly focused. The process is enriching for the participants and fruitful for the publication. The approach, however, requires more management ability than is needed to supervise the assembly line. It takes skill to select appropriate team members, conduct meetings, coordinate the efforts of various participants, and convince members to sacrifice some individual recognition or power to the group.

The advantages, however, far outweigh the disadvantages. The copy editor who is reading the daily memos along with the project editor is less likely to edit out essential information, edit in errors, or write a bad headline. Involving the design editor in the beginning of the project ensures that the photographers will have access, with the reporters, to people, places, and events as well as sufficient time to complete their work. Planning also permits artists to go in the field with the reporters, not two weeks later when conditions have changed. In addition, the design editor can have a series logo prepared ahead of time rather than one hour before deadline. Finally, the package can be designed for maximum impact in the appropriate space.

Scheduled events, such as elections, are naturals for the team approach because the date and participants are already known. It is the responsibility of the newsroom managers to assemble reporters, editors, designers, and photographers at the beginning of the election season to make plans for the entire campaign. Which reporters will be involved? Which photographers? How many out-of-town trips will be required? What kind of profiles should be done—issue-oriented, personality-oriented, or both? Should there be daily coverage or weekly wrap-ups? What will the campaign coverage be called? What would be an appropriate logo? What should the deadlines be for the major pieces? How much space will be available? What is the best method of reporting election results? Covering an election involves dozens of journalists. Those who work in newsrooms where all participants are involved from the beginning, goals are clearly defined, and ideas are sought from many persons instead of just a few will be more successful than those who work in an assembly-line plant.

Newsrooms where teams work together reflect the awareness that newsrooms can be managed and newspapers are a visual medium. Reporters are not the only fact gatherers in the newsroom; photographers and artists are too. Reporting for a visual medium includes gathering facts; writing the story; taking photographs; adding explanatory maps, charts, and graphs; writing headlines that tell and sell; and putting it all together so that it not only attracts and holds the reader's attention but is also legible and well written. Newsroom managers will be ready to compete in the twenty-first century if they recognize that photographers and designers are communicators, not decorators, and if they organize the newsroom to capitalize on their skills.

Principles of design

PAGE DESIGN should begin with the main illustration, and its size and shape should be regarded as a fixed element to which the other display elements have to adjust.

Harold Evans
EDITOR
LONDON *Sunday Times*

WE ARE ALL ENGULFED by the work of designers. We encounter it in the clothes we wear, the cars we drive, the buildings we live and work in, the art we buy, and the publications we read. The principles of that design spring from our natural environment. The geometric proportions of our universe are reproduced in great architecture and paintings. The forms of leaves and the rings of trees have influenced designers for centuries.

Though the principles of design are fixed, the results are fluid. Engineering, architecture, art, and fashion change as needs and desires change. In the 1920s, the Model T was the right car; in the 1980s, we look for sleeker lines, fuel economy, and brighter colors. The coliseums built in ancient Greece still influence architects, but today we build Astrodomes. Milton Glaser may owe something to Van Gogh, but even though we continue to appreciate Van Gogh's paintings, Glaser's colorful symbolic rendering of Bob Dylan appeared on the T-shirts of this nation's youth in the 1960s. Aldus Manutius published a book in 1499 that has influenced publication designers for centuries, but book publishers today use materials from the 1980s. The texture and the type are different even if the proportions are not.

Graphic design, the planning and arrangement of elements on a page, appeared in magazines in the 1920s, about the same time Henry Ford brought the Model T off the first assembly line. In 1930, *Fortune* became the first U.S. magazine to combine words and visual concepts (Hurlburt 1976). Six years later, *Life* was born. The developing concept of photojournalism was nurtured to adolescence before *Life* died in 1972. Newspapers, a much older medium of communication, have been slower to wed words and visuals in a carefully designed product. Beset by a cumbersome advertisement arrangement on inside pages, a printing surface that still smudges and allows the print to show through, and unyielding deadlines, newspapers have always been the kid on the block with a dirty face and tattered clothes. Perhaps editors have been unwilling or unable to clean him up because generations of readers have been charmed by this messy kid. The pressures of competition finally succeeded in achieving what many visually oriented persons had been urging for years.

Struggling to maintain its share of the marketplace, the *New York Herald Tribune* turned to Peter Palazzo in 1963 for a redesign. Until then, redesign meant primarily a new typeface and occasionally a new nameplate. Palazzo, however, demonstrated that it could be much more. A graphics designer, not a journalist, Palazzo lowered the story count per page and introduced wider columns, more white space, better proportion, better use of photographs, better packaging and organization, and a different typeface (Figs. 9.1, 9.2). For the first time, a U.S. newspaper had truly been redesigned.

Fig. 9.1.

Fig. 9.2.

The *Tribune* folded three years later, but the fallout from that redesign settled over the country. Suddenly, the design work at the *National Observer* and the *Christian Science Monitor,* both of which had been largely dismissed because they were not traditional newspapers, was emulated. Slowly, the momentum built. In the late 1960s, only a handful of newspapers had graphics directors or their equivalent. Ten years later, the pace had accelerated geometrically. Many newspapers began to look as contemporary and timely as their subject matter. Design had come to U.S. newspapers.

The look was changing because the process was changing. For nearly two centuries, layout editors served the unrelenting masters of deadline and story count in a repetitious process that was more concerned about production needs than readers (see Chapter 8). Layout editors react; designers plan. Layout is a manufacturing process; design is a creative process that traces its roots back thousands of years.

Design history

Most contemporary designers are products of one of two schools of thought: the Bauhaus/Swiss-Mondrian philosophy or the Push Pin Studio.

The Bauhaus school was established in Weimar, Germany, in 1919. The founders brought a Germanic precision and order to their teaching. When the Nazis closed the school in 1933, many of the faculty and students came to the United States. Some of them taught; others went to advertising agencies. Some, such as Paul Rand, worked for magazines. Their work was disciplined, functional, and imaginative because they had been influenced by the cubist revolution in painting. Piet Mondrian, a Dutch painter, developed many of the principles we still apply to the modular division of space and contrast in size and weight. They had also been influenced by the Swiss, whose application of functional Bauhaus thinking to typography produced the uncluttered approach to letter design. The popular sans serif typeface, Helvetica, (Fig. 9.3) is a product of this school of thought. Its austere, functional lines give it a quiet dignity.

	HELVETICA
Fig. 9.3.	The functional type

In physics there is a principle that every action has an equal and opposite reaction. The Push Pin Studio proved that this principle is as true in design as it is in physics. In 1957, a small group of illustrators, designers, and photographers formed a studio named a bit flippantly after a simple pin with a rounded head. That name was the only simple thing connected with this studio (Hays 1977). In the intervening years, the work of its designers has appeared in national advertisements as well as editorially in such magazines as *New York, Esquire,* and *Playboy.* Push Pin Studio is a genre of design that is as dissimilar to Bauhaus/Swiss-Mondrian as round is to square. While Bauhaus/Swiss is functional, formal, and rational, Push Pin is decorative, expressive, and intentionally irrational. For example, Bauhaus/Swiss eliminated curlicues because they were not essential to the reading process, but when Milton Glaser redesigned *New York* magazine, he reinstated them with gusto. His wild, colorful, abstract designs contrasted vividly with the austere look that was popular at the time. When Emilio Pucci, the fashion designer, was invited to a newspaper design seminar in Louisville, Ky., in 1974, he took decorative, hand-inked nameplates along and changed them each day (Fig. 9.4). The nameplates, he said, brought a "message of

Fig. 9.4. Emilio Pucci, best known for his fashion and interior designs, once proposed that the newspaper nameplate be changed each day for a new visual or esthetic message. (Louisville Times *photo*)

beauty, joy and serenity." They were impractical, fun, and straight from the Push Pin school of thought.

What had started as a backlash to functionalism became an established genre. By the late 1960s, art museum curators were cataloguing modern graphics in two groups: post Bauhaus/Swiss and Push Pin Studio.

Regardless of the philosophy to which designers subscribe, they all use the basic principles of design. Some follow them religiously; others know when to break them.

Principles of design

To know the principles of design is to know why you are doing what you are doing. No designer carries the list around consciously. Beginners, however, use the principles as guides until they are comfortable with the concepts. Although the names may be forgotten, the lessons never are.

There are five principles: balance, contrast, focus, proportion, and unity.

BALANCE. A square is perfectly balanced, but it is also monotonous. Similarly, formal balance in newspapers is dull and predictable, as were the people described as "square" in the 1960s. Formal balance is also the ultimate victory of form over content.

Formal balance had its heyday when the *New York Times* was its most visible proponent. It required balancing a 2-column picture at the top against a 2-column picture at the bottom and a 3-column headline at the top against a 3-column headline at the bottom. In short, balance was achieved by matching identical units. No matter what the news of the day, form took precedence over content.

While a formal balance format does not suit a newspaper's daily needs, any given design package can use formal balance successfully. The fashion spread on hats in Figure 9.5 is attractive, easy to read, and perfectly balanced. However, the photographic essay on Wyoming in Figure 9.6 is balanced, square, and dull.

Formal or symmetrical balance may be useful when building arches, but asymmetrical balance is more flexible and useful to newspaper designers. Balance is not achieved by merely using identical elements. Optical weights result from tones ranging from black to white. Tones, in turn, are provided by type in its various weights from light to bold, photographs and art, reverses and screens, rules, borders, and white space.

When two people are on a teeter-totter, they find the right balance by moving closer to or farther from the fulcrum. The weight is defined in measurable terms. Optical weight is not measured; it is observed. A small, dark shape balances a larger, lighter shape, and white space in the margin balances the grayness of text type. A longer, narrow horizontal rectangle is

Fig. 9.5.   Fig. 9.6.

balanced by a wider vertical one. The double-truck tabloid spread in Figure 9.7 uses contrasting sizes and shapes as well as white space to achieve balance. The dominant picture at the lower left and the small darker one above it are balanced on the right by the long vertical picture, the small nearly square photo, and the additional white space.

Fig. 9.7.

Designers balance the right against the left and the top against the bottom. To achieve this, the designer places the major display element close to the optical center, which is slightly above and to the left or right of the mathematical center.

Dividing the page into quadrants is useful only if the design does not divide itself into four equal parts. Each of the four divisions should have some graphic weight to balance the page, but the weight should not be confined to the quadrant. It should extend vertically, horizontally, or both into other quadrants (Fig. 9.8), just as the heavier of the two persons on the teeter-totter moves closer to the fulcrum.

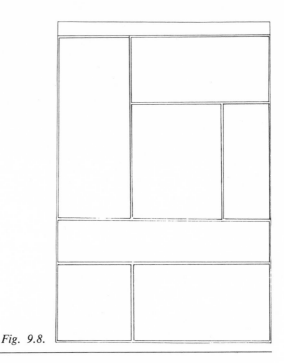

Fig. 9.8.

Designers working in modules have more control over weights on a page because their boundaries are defined. Meandering, irregular copy wraps make it more difficult to weight the elements visually.

CONTRAST. Writers contrast unlike things by using similes. For instance, My newspaper is like my slippers — comfortable to sit down with at night." Writers contrast form by varying sentence length. Some sentences are long, rambling structures that, when used correctly, slow the reader and complement the subject matter. Some are short.

Fig. 9.9.

Fig. 9.10.

Designers contrast weights to balance a page. A 3-column photograph at the upper right can be balanced with a 3-column photograph at the lower left. The photograph can also be balanced with a large multicolumn headline, white space, or a combination of all three. An 8-pt. rule can balance a block of text type.

Designers use type to provide contrast. For instance, bold type in the main head contrasts with light type in a deck or readout, sans serif type in the cutlines contrasts with roman type in the stories, all caps contrasts with lowercase, 90-pt. type contrasts with 24-pt. type, and sans serif type contrasts with serif type. The *Kansas City Star* uses Goudy as its basic display face (Fig. 9.9). By using Franklin Gothic as the accent head, designer Randy Miller was able to provide contrast. When a newspaper does not contrast serif with sans serif or vary weights within a face, the page will usually be monotonous (Fig. 9.10).

Designers also contrast forms. Strong verticals give the impression of taller space and longer stories; horizontals appear to make space wider and stories shorter. A page divided into quadrants has no contrast of form, but a page divided into modules of varying rectangular shapes is full of contrast.

Dimension is an aspect of contrast too. The closer the object, the darker it appears. A small photograph placed adjacent to a larger one provides a contrast in size and adds dimension. To teach this principle to children, Johannes Itten of the Bauhaus told them to draw an outline of their hand on a sheet of paper. Then they were told to draw, in their natural size, an apple, a plum, cherries, a gnat, and finally an elephant. The children said it could not be done because the sheet was too small. "Draw an old, big elephant — a young elephant next to it — the keeper . . . stretches his hand out to the elephant — in the hand lies an apple — on it sits a gnat" (Itten 1964). From that exercise, the children learned to contrast size by using light and dark colors and large and small shapes. Publication designers use the same devices.

FOCUS. Pages with focus clearly define the starting points and also show that an editor is not afraid to make decisions. To achieve focus, an editor has to decide what element or elements are most important or visually interesting and have the courage to let the design reflect that decision. Indecision confuses the reader and results in a meek or, worse, cluttered page. For instance, many editions on January 21, 1981, reflected their editor's indecision about dealing with both the release of the hostages from Iran and the inauguration of Ronald Reagan. Those editors who were unable to decide which of these two significant events should be the lead story often produced pages without focus. The *Minneapolis Tribune* (Fig. 9.11) solved the problem by clearly stating what had happened the previous day. In simplicity, the *Tribune* editors found focus.

Focus usually is provided by a dominant photograph. On a broadsheet page, this requires either a photograph wider than half the page or a vertical photograph of corresponding size. Three-column pictures on a 6-column page are just average and have little impact, but pictures wider than 3 columns provide both focus and impact (Fig. 9.12). Both the content of the picture and the importance of the event demand that the photograph showing the magnitude of Mount St. Helen's destructive force on the surrounding forestlands be played large, and the editors of the Baltimore *News American* did not miss the opportunity.

Type can also be used effectively to provide focus. Newspapers traditionally have used large type on big-news events. The editors of the *Des Moines Register* elected to use type rather than photographs to provide focus for their hostage-inauguration page (Fig. 9.13). More often, type is used to provide focus on feature pages or on packages within a page. Every design should have a focus, a major area of emphasis that identifies both the editorial decision and the reader's starting point.

From a broader perspective, the editor focuses on what is significant through the selection of elements for Page 1. Less important stories are found inside the paper. Similarly, department editors use their cover pages to pro-

Fig. 9.11.

Fig. 9.12.

Fig. 9.13.

vide focus for a section. There should be a progression from the focal point to the other elements on the page. It is not necessary for the designer to predict the readership path accurately. That is impossible. Readers will respond differently to printed stimuli. External stimuli, such as noise or lack of time, will also influence reading patterns. However, it is the duty of the designer to expose as many readers as possible to all the modules and remove anything that impairs legibility. Readers of poorly designed pages will skip some areas of the page altogether, not because they were not interested in the content, but because they did not notice the story. Readers move from large to small, (large photograph to small photograph), black to white, color to black and white, and top to bottom; but it all begins at the dominant element.

PROPORTION. Proportion, or ratio, has fascinated mathematicians, architects, and artists for centuries. Fibonacci, an Italian mathematician of the late twelfth and early thirteenth centuries, observed that starting with 1 and adding the last two numbers to arrive at the next created a ratio of 1:1.6 between any two adjacent numbers after three (1, 1, 2, 3, 5, 8, 13 . . .). Fifteenth-century architect Leon Battista Alberti believed that there was a relationship between mathematics and art because certain ratios recurred in the universe.

Leonardo da Vinci, who was not only an artist but also a mathematician, collaborated with a friend on a book titled *On Divine Proportion*. To Leonardo, proportions were of basic importance "not only . . . in numbers and measurement but also in sounds, weights, positions and whatsoever power there may be."

Finally, the classic definition of proportion was worked out by the architect-designer Le Corbusier in the early 1900s. He drew the human form with the left arm raised above the head. He then divided the anatomy into three uneven parts: from the toes to the solar plexus, then to the tip of the head, and finally to the tip of the raised hand. From this he developed what is known as the golden ratio. The ratio is 1:1.6, the same as Fibonacci's ratio. In nature, we see the same proportion in a daisy, a pinecone, and a pineapple, among others. The double-spiraling daisy, for instance, has 21 spirals in a clockwise direction and 34 in a counterclockwise position — a 3:5 ratio. The ratio of the printed to unprinted surface of a newspaper page with a 30-inch web is approximately 1:1.51; for a 28-inch web, it is 1:1.63. The 28-inch web, which the American Newspaper Publisher's Association began promoting in 1981 to standardize newspaper page sizes, is not only easier for the reader to handle but also closer to the proportions of the golden rectangle, which has the same proportions as the golden ratio.

Consciously or unconsciously, designers use that ratio when working with copy shapes on a page. The wider the story runs horizontally, the deeper it can go vertically and still maintain aesthetic proportions. On a 6-column page, a 4-column story 56 picas wide could be 30 to 35 picas deep from the top of the headline to the bottom of the story. As it goes deeper, it approaches the shape of the less pleasing square. Stories of 1 and 2 columns should be proportioned vertically in the same manner.

No designer actually measures the depth of the stories to determine if the ratio is correct. The eye recognizes what the calculator confirms. A sense of proportion is necessary for every designer.

In graphic design, proper use of proportion means avoiding squares unless they are required by the content. It also means being consistent about placing proportionally greater amounts of white space between unlike elements than between related elements. For instance, the designer might specify 24 points between the end of one story and the top of the next headline but only 14 points between the headline and the related story. The larger amount of space between the copy and the headline below disassociates the two when they are viewed against the lesser amount of white space between the headline and its related copy.

A good grasp of the concept of proportion is essential to anyone dealing with photographs. First, there is the proportion of the photo to the page. As we have already discussed, to dominate a page, a photograph must occupy more than half the width of the page or be sized proportionally vertically. The key is the size of the page. A broadsheet page requires one minimum size, a tabloid page another, and a magazine page such as *National Geographic* still another. Smaller pages require smaller visuals, a truism that many editors have not grasped. A 40-pica picture that runs margin to margin on a tabloid would not dominate a broadsheet page. In fact, 40 picas is a modest width on a broadsheet page, but impact is still possible with smaller sizes. A 40-pica picture in *National Geographic* bleeds the full width of a page.

Pictures should also be sized in proportion to each other. The 40-pica picture that looks so modest on a broadsheet page looks large when paired with one or more significantly smaller pictures. The smaller the subordinate picture, the larger the dominant picture appears.

Type also looks larger as the horizontal space it occupies grows smaller. A 48-pt. headline appears larger in a 2-column setting than in a 6-column format because it is larger in proportion to the space occupied. Type size is selected in part on the basis of the length of the story. Putting 3 lines of 24-pt. type over a 3-inch story would look odd, because the headline would be one-third the depth of the story. Proportionally, there would be too much headline type. Conversely, a 3-line, 24-pt. headline over a story 18 inches long would also look odd.

Designers who have cultivated a sense of proportion work, within the limits of the content, in rectangles having dimensions that approximate 2:3 or 3:5. The resulting pages are aesthetically more pleasing.

UNITY. The designer must unify the work on two levels: the content and form of the individual packages within the publication and the various parts of the publication itself.

On the broadest level, unity is the art of making all the departments and all the sections of the publication appear to come from the same family but still allowing individuality within the various parts. Typographical unity does not mean homogeneity but does require a familial resemblance among the sections. This requirement can be fulfilled by using one family of headline type and varying other elements such as text width or setting. An alternative might be the use of two basic compatible faces, one for the main head and the other as an accent head.

Unity of publication means that sectional identifiers and column logos are the same throughout the paper. If the paper is large enough, logos may change from department to department but not within the department. Publication unity flows from a set of rules that everyone follows with few exceptions. Spacing should be consistent between the lines of text type, headlines and bylines, and bylines and stories. In most newspaper plants, such control is possible because the specifications can be programmed into the computer. Most newspapers have design stylebooks for the same purpose as copy stylebooks — to provide consistency. The *St. Petersburg Times* book is 112 pages; the *Cincinnati Enquirer*'s is 94.

Publication unity is even more important as newspapers develop a series of special interest sections. It is important for these sections to have an identity of their own, but readers must recognize them as part of the parent organization. Before the *Los Angeles Times* was redesigned in 1980, John Foley, assistant managing editor for special projects, said the standard in-house gag was that the *Times* was six or seven papers under one banner. (A Newspaper Design Notebook critique of the redesign said, "If the true goal of the *Los Angeles Times* was to create one mediocre, outdated design instead of seven, it succeeded.") The *Dallas Morning News* runs a 24-pt. version of its nameplate underneath its sectional headings for such departments as "Today," "Metropolitan," "Sports," and "Business." The repetition of the flag also helps to unify the paper.

Unity of individual packages or pages is important, too. When the designer fails, the page becomes cluttered or confusing. For instance, the crayonlike border that was used around the story about children (Fig. 9.14) is appropriate to the content. Unfortunately, the same border was also used around the story of the woman professional. That immediately signals a relationship between the two stories, although there is none.

The capital dome that appears in the story on San Antonians (Fig. 9.15) is decoration and appears to have been added when the top line of the head fell short. When the same dome was built into the design of the story on the roots of power (Fig. 9.16) it helped to unify the package because it contributed to the message of power.

Fig. 9.14.

Fig. 9.15.

Fig. 9.16.

When form follows function, unity often results. Some stories, such as the Environmental Protection Agency's mileage ratings for new cars, are basically lists, and the design requires more chart than copy. Elections are stories of statistics and human emotions, and their design requires text, photographs, and charts. A fashion package has a different flow than one dealing with the eruption of Mount St. Helens. All of these stories can be told more effectively when the message and design are unified.

Following John Lennon's murder, the Newark *Ledger* published a page entitled "A look at Lennon" (Fig. 9.17). All three stories have simple titles, begin with an initial capital letter, and are boxed by 1-pt. rules. The page is unified, and the design is appropriate to the content.

Fig. 9.17.

On one level the principles of design are esoteric; they cannot be subjected to quantitative analysis. On another level, they all have specific applications to the day-to-day operations of a newspaper. The better you understand the principles, the more confidence you will develop in your own judgments about design.

Understanding type

LETTERS are to be read, not to be used as practice models for designers or to be moulded by caprice or ignorance into fantastic forms of uncertain meaning. They are not shapes made to display the skill of their designers; they are forms fashioned solely to help the reader.

Frederic Goudy
TYPE DESIGNER

TYPE IS TO THE GRAPHIC DESIGNER what the bat is to the baseball player. When a batter hits a home run, the fans appreciate the feat; they do not ask what kind of bat was used. When a graphic designer completes a successful spread, readers appreciate the pleasing presentation and the ease of reading; they do not ask the name of the typeface or the mechanics of reproducing it.

Because approximately 80 percent of the printing area in a newspaper consists of type, its selection and use is critical to successful communication. Yet, perhaps because it is so pervasive, type is often overlooked for the flashier tools of the designer—illustration, white space, and color. The headline face, the text type, and the design of the advertisements, which are primarily type, give each publication a personality. Many publications emit conflicting signals. The type says one thing, but the content says another. This Jekyll-and-Hyde effect is confusing and injurious to the communication process. Despite the importance of type, there are few typographers in newspapers or magazines. Consultants and designers may perform this function on a hit-and-miss basis, but often the day-to-day use of type is left to untrained personnel. Even so, given the proper type and instructions on how to use it, local staff members should be able to produce a daily or weekly product that is fundamentally sound typographically. Professionals who handle type every day should understand the basics of its use. This chapter discusses the design, language, grouping, and identification of type, Chaper 11 is concerned with legibility considerations, and Chapter 12 deals with the use of type.

Type design

Although the Chinese and Koreans first invented movable type, Johann Gutenberg was the first Western printer to use it. Furthermore, Gutenberg solved the problem created by the different widths of letters. Understandably, his first face was a modified reproduction of the handwriting used to produce sacred works, such as bibles. From that point, further modifications were made to reflect the tastes and nationalities of the type designers.

Although type was the first mass-produced item in history, nearly four centuries passed after Gutenberg produced his type before a typecasting machine was invented, and it was not until the end of the nineteenth century that the entire process became automated. By then, many of the great typefaces still commonly used today had already been designed.

William Caslon, for instance, was an English typographer who lived from 1692–1766. The rugged but dignified Caslon face has staying power. Over 100 years after it was cut, it became popular again following its use in the first issue of *Vogue* magazine. In 1978, designer Peter Palazzo brought it back once more in modified form when he redesigned the *Chicago Daily News*. In 1750, another Englishman, John Baskerville, designed a face that is known by his name and still commonly used today. Giambatista Bodoni, an Italian printer, developed a face in 1760 that was the standard headline in American newspapers from the post–World War II era through the 1970s. In 1896, another Englishman, William Morris, reacting to the conformity brought about by the Industrial Revolution, produced *The Works of Geoffrey Chaucer*. The Chaucer type he designed, combined with specialized initial letters and craftsmanship in design and printing, reawakened an interest in printing as an art form. Because his typefaces are highly stylized and personal, they are not used today for mass circulation publications, but his work influenced more than a generation of designers.

One of the people Morris influenced was Frederic Goudy, the first great

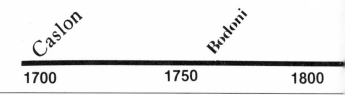

Fig. 10.1.

American type designer. Goudy, founder of the Village Press, cut 125 faces, many of which are still used today. Goudy lived until 1946. At one time, the types he had designed, including the one carrying his name, dominated the American press. They fell out of favor after World War II, but when the 1980s brought a revival of the classic faces, Goudy was dusted off. When the *Kansas City Star* was redesigned in 1980 and the *Dallas Morning News* was redesigned in 1981, Goudy was chosen for the basic headline face.

The 1900s brought a host of typefaces—some were new; some were modifications of classic faces. Century Expanded was cut in 1900, Cheltenham in 1902, Cloister Old Style in 1913, Baskerville Roman in 1915, and Garamond in 1918. The interval between the wars produced two startling new faces. Paul Renner designed Futura in 1927; in 1932, Stanley Morrison produced Times New Roman for the *Times* of London. Futura, a geometric sans serif that is monotone in cut, ushered in an era of sans serif faces that brought us the popular Univers and Helvetica in the mid-1950s. Univers is used at the *St. Petersburg Times;* Helvetica, the most popular sans serif face among American newspapers, is used, among others, by the *Minneapolis Tribune* and the *San Francisco Examiner.* Hermann Zapf is the most successful contemporary designer. In the 1950s, he designed both Optima and Palatino, the face used in the redesign of the *New York Herald Tribune.*

The majority of typefaces commonly used by newspapers and magazines today were designed before World War II (Fig. 10.1). Tastes in type run in cycles, and some faces that are more than 200 years old are brought back periodically and modified to take advantage of technological innovations and modern tastes. The "modern faces," such as Helvetica, Univers, and Optima, already are 30 years old, but they are mere infants in the life of a type. The newspapers that rushed to embrace the modern look of Helvetica in the 1970s found themselves slightly out of step with fashion in the 1980s when the country began to turn back to traditional values. If Helvetica is put on the back shelf, it will be dusted off again later—maybe in 20 years, maybe in 50—just as the Caslons, Goudys, and Bodonis keep reappearing.

The introduction of photocomposition essentially stopped the design of

| 1850 | 1900 | 1950 | 2000 |

new typefaces for use in general circulation publications. Foundries were busy converting their libraries to negatives for the new photocomposition machines. Most of the work involved modifying existing faces to take advantage of the new technology but still adhere to copyright laws. Bodoni, for instance, is now produced by six companies. Some of the alterations distorted the type and lowered the quality. By the late 1970s, great numbers of new faces were being designed for photocomposition.

Technological developments

The proportion of primary strokes and serifs in metal type changes as the type size increases. When the font is produced in one size on a negative and enlarged through a magnifying glass, these proportions are not preserved. Most people would not notice (the difference is something like that between a designer's dress and its look-alike sold at chain department stores), but up close there is a difference. The newest generation of digitized photocomposition machines have overcome this problem by eliminating the need to enlarge or reduce the type; each size is stored on a magnetic disk.

Because photocomposition permitted better control over letterspacing, kerning (letters set close together or even touching) and ligatures (two or more letters joined in a single unit) became common. When type was on individual metal slugs, the kern extended off the edge of the metal body and was vulnerable to breakage. That problem was eliminated in the phototypesetting process where the letters are on film rather than metal slugs. When Palazzo modified the Caslon face for the *Chicago Daily News,* he seized on the phototypesetter's ability to kern and create ligatures. He shortened the cross stroke on the capital *T* and lowered the dot on the *i* to align with the top of the capital letters. Many newspapers have been able to take advantage of photocomposition technology to make type more legible.

Now that designers are becoming comfortable with phototypesetting, a new generation of type designs will emerge to reflect contemporary tastes and demands. Type design has a history of fits and starts because it has been affected by such events as the Industrial Revolution, the world wars, and recent technological developments.

Language of type

The basic unit of all type designs is the individual letter. Just as we classify trees by the bark, leaves or needles, and shape, we classify type by its individual parts. Figure 10.2 provides a detailed examination of a piece of type. You need to acquire a working knowledge of most of these terms. The three main parts of the letter include:

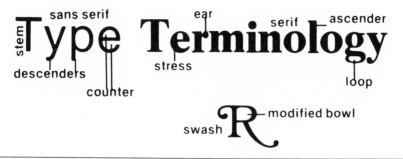

Fig. 10.2.

1. *X-line*—literally, the top of the lowercase *x*. The *x*-height is measured from the top of the lowercase *x*, or any other lowercase letter without extenders, to the bottom. Because type within the same size can have different *x*-heights, it is critical to know that measurement as well as the size; *x*-height is a more exact method of measuring type size than points.

2. *Ascender*—that portion of the lowercase letter extending above the *x*-line. Capital letters are all the same and do not have ascenders or descenders.

3. *Descender*—that portion of the lowercase letter extending below the base line, or bottom of the letter *x*. Together, the ascenders and descenders are called extenders.

The three basic parts are further divided as follows:

1. *Bar*—a horizontal or oblique (slanted) line connected at both ends. It is found in the letters *e* and *H*.

2. *Bowl*—the line enclosing a space. The letters *o*, *e*, *R*, and *B*, among others, have bowls. How the bowl is formed is one way of identifying a typeface.

3. *Ear*—on most faces, the *g* and *r* have a small distinctive stroke at the top right.

4. *Serif*—the unique cross-stroke at the ends of the basic letter form. A serif is ornamental, but properly done, it enhances legibility (see Chapter 11). Serifs are the principal means of giving a typeface a distinct personality.

5. *Stroke*—the primary part of the letter.

6. *Stress*—the thickness of a curved stroke, the shading of the letter.

7. *Loop*—a mark of distinction. The letters *o*, *c*, and *e*, particularly, may slant off center. Sometimes, the bottom of the *g* is left open.

8. *Terminal*—the distinctive finish to the stroke on sans serif (without serifs) type. It may be straight, concave, or convex.

With these terms in mind, let's look at Bodoni Bold (Fig. 10.3). Bodoni is most easily recognized by the distinctive tail of the *Q*, which drops from the center and slopes to the right. The serifs join on the diagonal stroke of the *W*, and the *T* has drooping serifs. The *O*, *Q*, and *C* are symmetrical; there is no distinctive loop. The strokes are composed of consistent thick and thin lines to give each letter a precise, balanced quality. The stress of such letters as *O, G,* and *P* is vertical rather than rounded.

Fig. 10.3.   **QWTOCGP**

Type grouping

To enable typographers to communicate about type and ensure harmonious use, type has been organized into races, families, fonts, and series.

RACES. The race is the broadest system of categorization. Unfortunately, typographers cannot agree precisely on the number of categories. Too many leave typographers splitting hairlines, but having too few forces them to lump dissimilar type into the same race. The discussion in this book follows the guidelines of the authoritative *Composition Manual,* published by the Printing Industry of America. The categories are roman, square serif, sans serif, text letter, cursive, and ornamental.

R O M A N.   The term roman has been used to refer to the straight up-and-down design of the type as opposed to the italic or slanted-right version. Originally, that was an incorrect use of the term, but it has became so common that it is now widely accepted. For the purpose of identifying races, roman is a classification of type that has serifs and thick and thin curved strokes. Some typographers believe roman is too general a designation and refer instead to three races: old style, modern, and transitional. These terms no longer have any relevance to the time when the faces were designed. Instead, the terms refer to the style of type. Each of the three will be considered under the broad umbrella of roman.

Old style looks more informal because the letters are asymmetrical. The horizontal and upward strokes are light, and the downward strokes are heavy, but the differences between the strokes are minimal. The serifs appear to be molded or bracketed onto the stems. Garamond, for instance, is an old style typeface that bespeaks tradition and dignity (Fig. 10.4).

Fig. 10.4.   Garamond is an Old Style face

Modern typefaces were introduced by Bodoni in 1760. His type was symmetrical and therefore had a more formal look. It also showed the influence of geometric forms. It is more precise than old style and has greater degrees of difference between the thick and thin strokes. The serifs were thin straight lines extending from the stems of the letters. As other faces were designed, the bowls became rounded, and the serif brackets were sharpened. Century Schoolbook, with its symmetrical, almost blocklike quality, is another example of a modern face (Fig. 10.5).

Fig. 10.5.   Century is a modern face

As a category, *transitional* was created when succeeding generations of designers produced type that took characteristics from both old style and modern. Baskerville and Caledonia, along with some members of the Century family, are generally classified as transitional (Fig. 10.6). They all have attributes of both old style and modern. Typographers do not all agree on which type merits the designation of old style, transitional, or modern, but a good reference book will help graphics editors avoid serious mistakes.

Fig. 10.6.   Baskerville is a transitional face

SQUARE SERIF.   In square serif type, the strokes are nearly monotone in weight, and as the name suggests, the serifs are squared off in rectangles. Clarendon and Karnak are from the square serif race (Fig. 10.7). The letters are not unlike the slab footings of the architecture common in ancient Egypt.

Fig. 10.7.   Clarendon Book is a square-serif face

SANS SERIF.   Befitting the mood of the day, the 1850s brought sans serif type. Sans is the French word for "without," and the type is without serifs. The type is easily identified not only by the lack of serifs but also by the uniformity in the strokes (Fig. 10.8). Sans serif type became popular in the 1920s as the Bauhuas school of thought (see Chapter 9) extended its influence. The purpose of the design was to eliminate all flourishes, including serifs, and produce a type that served the function of communicating without any of the aesthetic benefits that serifs offer. In the United States, the sans serif race was also referred to as gothic.

Fig. 10.8.   Helios is a sans serif face

T E X T   L E T T E R.   This race, also called black letter, has type that is medieval in appearance. It is the style that Gutenberg used to print the Bible. Its designers were influenced by Gothic architecture, which was popular at that time. Cloister Black Old English and Goudy Text are examples of this race (Fig. 10.9).

Fig. 10.9.   **𝕺𝖑𝖉 𝕰𝖓𝖌𝖑𝖎𝖘𝖍 𝖎𝖘 𝖆 𝖙𝖊𝖝𝖙 𝖑𝖊𝖙𝖙𝖊𝖗 𝖋𝖆𝖈𝖊**

C U R S I V E   O R   S C R I P T.   This race is also self-descriptive. The type is a stylized reproduction of formal handwriting (Fig. 10.10) and is most often found in formal announcements of events such as weddings and anniversaries.

Fig. 10.10.   *Murray is cursive*

O R N A M E N T A L   O R   N O V E L T Y.   This race is a catchall for those types that have been designed to portray a particular mood or emotion (Fig. 10.11) and is so unusual it cannot be used for other messages. The type is most frequently used in posters, movie advertising, cartoons, and display advertising. Newspapers occasionally use a novelty type on a feature page to reflect the content. For example, a computer type could be used over a story on the computer age.

Fig. 10.11.   **ROMANTIQUE IS NOVELTY**

FAMILIES. Like all families, type families are basically similar but have variations. The differences are based on width, weight, and form. Some families have several members (Fig. 10.12); Caslon has at least 15, Cheltenham at least 18, and Univers nearly 30. The average widths range from condensed to expanded; the weights from light to bold. Most types have two different forms, roman and italic. When the type is available in a special form, such as an outline or shadowed version, it is generally classified under the novelty race.

The width of a type is important when considering legibility and the amount of type that will fit on a line. It is figured on a character per pica (CPP) basis and is computed by counting the average number of letters that will fit in a given horizontal space and dividing by the number of picas. Thus, if the average number of characters that will fit on a 10-pica line is 32, the

Futura Light: abcdefghijklmnopqrstuvwxyz
Futura Medium Italic: *abcdefghijklmnopqrstuvwxyz*
Futura Medium: abcdefghijklmnopqrstuvwxyz
Futura Medium Condensed: abcdefghijklmnopqrstuvwxyz
Futura Bold: abcdefghijklmnopqrstuvwxyz
Futura Extrabold: abcdefghijklmnopqrstuvwxyz

Fig. 10.12.

character per pica count is 3.2. If the average is 32.45, retain the fraction. The length of an entire lowercase alphabet of a single type size is called the lowercase alphabet length.

Unfortunately, even though the method of computing the alphabet lengths and characters per pica is standard, the results are not because of the way type producers have altered the face and spacing between letters. The CPP for Baskerville with italic when manufactured by Linotype in 10 point is 2.68; manufactured by Intertype, 2.35; and manufactured by Monotype, 2.48. When comparing the CPP counts of typefaces, it is critical for the designer to know the type manufacturer.

FONTS. A font is a complete set of type. Nearly all families have fonts that include uppercase and lowercase type, punctuation, and symbols; some include an alphabet of small caps. Some also have ligatures, such as fi, fl, and ff. Others have special symbols. A font of Century follows:

ABCDEFGHIJKLMNOPQRSTUVWXYZ
abcdefghijklmnopqrstuvwxyz
1234567890 $ - % ¢
1234567890 $

1234567890
¡ ! □ ✔ ● ° © ° † * @ / £ & ( ) • / ¿ ? « »
+ = ÷
é ı ñ Ñ Ç ç
ß
a o
★ # [ ]
½ ¼ ¾ ⅓ ⅔

SERIES. The range of sizes available for each member of the family is called a series. When only metal type was available, size was an important consideration for the designer. Standard sizes of display type included 14, 18, 24, 30, 36, 42, 48, 54, 60, 72 and on up. Now that most newspapers have photocomposition systems, publications no longer buy a series; they buy a film font (Fig. 10.13). Most photocomposition machines can be programmed to set the type in any size desired, including sizes such as 25 or 47 points that were never available before. Newspapers that use cold type are also not limited by sizes because they can photoenlarge or reduce type to any size desired. As a result, the term "series" may soon be a thing of the past.

Identifying type

The Printing Industry of America has compiled the following list of ten ways to identify typefaces:

1. Serifs. All type immediately breaks down into serif or sans serif, but the differences between types with serifs can be startling.

2. Terminations on top of the strokes of *E*, *F*, or *T*.

3. Weight of strokes. Are they thick or thin, and how much contrast is there?

4. Shape of the rounded characters *BCGOPQbcgopq*. Are the bowls symmetrical or balanced diagonally? How is the weight distributed?

5. Length of descenders.

6. Formation of terminals on *J* and *F*. The curves or angles are good clues to the identity of the letter.

7. Formation of the ears of the letters. Look particularly at the *r*.

8. The shapes of key letters of the font. Look at *a*, *e*, *g*, *r*, *m*, and *H*.

9. General proportions of the letter. Is the bar of the *H* located above, below, or at center? Are the letters equally proportioned or do they tend to be condensed or extended?

10. Overall appearance on the page when the type is massed. What is its personality?

Fig. 10.13.

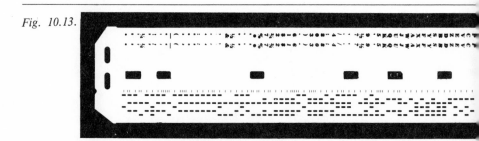

ABCDEFGHIJKLMNOPQRSTUVWXYZ
abcdefghijklmnopqrstuvwxyz — *Helios*

ABCDEFGHIJKLMNOPQRSTUVWXYZ

Fig. 10.14. abcdefghijklmnopqrstuvwxyz— *Univers*

Most graphics editors and designers have a working knowledge of 6 to 12 typefaces. For additional faces, they consult a type book. It is not necessary to memorize large numbers of typefaces, but you should become acquainted with those most commonly used in newspapers and, especially, the publications you read regularly. The popular sans serif Helios, for instance, is identifiable by its uniform but dignified cut. It has short extenders, a square dot on the lowercase *i* and *j*, a distinctive capital *G*, and a straight tail on the capital *Q*, which is slanted and starts on the inside of the bowl.

Compare Helios with another popular sans serif face, Univers (see Fig. 10.14.) Univers also has a uniform cut, square dots over the *i* and *j*, and short extenders. However, Univers has a sloped bracket at the cross-stroke of the *t*, does not have the finial or line extending downward from the *G*, and the tail of the *Q* does not start within the bowl and is lower on the letter.

Unfortunately, type identification is becoming increasingly difficult because of the barely distinguishable alterations performed for photocomposition fonts. The popular Helios, for instance, is produced with little or no variation under the names of Vega, Boston, Claro, Corvus, Galaxy, Geneva, Helvetica, American Gothic, Ag Book, Newton, and Megaron. Optima is marketed by different manufacturers under the name of Chelmsford, Oracle, Orleans, Musica, Orsa, and Zenith. Palatino also has several imitators including Palateno, Elegante, Patina, Andover, Palladium, Pontiac, Michelangelo, and Sistina. By whatever name they are known, however, they are still Helios, Optima, and Palatino.

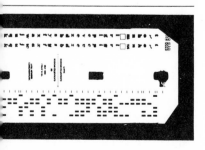

Legibility of type

TYPOGRAPHY is not merely design. It is the illustration of words. Whatever flourishes, fetishes, or serifs a designer may wish to use must always stand in humble relation to the words they articulate.

Art Direction
MAGAZINE, JUNE 1979

FOR MORE THAN 60 YEARS, researchers have been studying the variables that affect legibility. The findings have been enlarged significantly since Miles Tinker's pioneering studies in the 1920s. His work in later years, notably with D. G. Paterson, added significantly to the body of knowledge about legibility. The Merganthaler Linotype Company published *The Legibility of Type* in 1936 and a similar volume in 1947 in an attempt to distribute the research findings from the ivory tower to the grass-roots level. G. W. Ovink published *Legibility, Atmosphere-Value and Forms of Printing Types* in 1938. Sir Cyril Burt published the landmark *Psychological Study of Typography* in 1959. Tinker's 1963 *Legibility of Print* pulled together hundreds of studies that he and others had conducted. Bror Zachrisson and his colleagues at the Graphic Institute in Stockholm spent ten years researching legibility variables, and the results were published in *Studies in the Legibility of Printed Text* in 1965. The studies continue, but dissemination of the results to the people working with type daily in American newspapers still lags far behind the research. For example, in 1980 the assistant managing editor of design for the *New York Daily News* suggested in an industry newsletter that the American Society of Newspaper Editors should put together a presentation for editors on legibility of type.

For too long, knowledge of legibility has been buried in academic journals or limited to the province of professional consultants. It is necessary, however, for the men and women who work on newspapers every day to have the opportunity to learn and understand the factors that affect legibility. The daily examples of type that is overprinted; reversed; set too small, too narrow, or too wide indicate that many editors have still not awakened to the need to remove typographical barriers between the reporter and reader.

This chapter distills the results of hundreds of legibility research projects, but it is not a substitute for reading the original research. Several studies and books referred to in this chapter are listed in the References Cited section at the end of the book.

Perhaps the reason that many editors are just beginning to inquire about the proper use of type is that, for the first time, they have control over the typesetting and the flexibility to be creative. With video display terminals in the newsroom, the editor can program the type size, width, and leading for each story without slowing the production process. In addition, the letter and line spacing can be altered in both text and display type. A new era has begun, and editors are asking the right questions. The new graphics design editors will need to have the answers.

Legibility considerations

Legibility and readability are often confused. Legibility is the speed and accuracy with which type can be read and understood. Readability is a measure of the difficulty of the content. Legibility research has been conducted by typographers, educators, journalists, printers, and opthalmologists, all of whom have a stake in the printed word.

Some research methods are more useful for testing legibility factors than others. The visibility measurement, for example, tests reading speed by controlling the amount of light. This is useful for measuring the effect of contrast. Another method resembles the familiar eye test and measures what can be read at various distances. This test is most useful for work with large advertisements such as posters and billboards. Many other testing methods have been used through the years, but the most effective has been to measure reading speed while controlling all but one variable, such as line length. Researchers have also been able to track eye movement by using still cameras, television cameras, and various electrical devices. The results show that we read in saccadic jumps, the movements from fixation point to fixation point. For a split second the reader pauses, and reading occurs. The reader scans shapes, not individual letters, and fills in the context. The right half and upper portion of the letters are most helpful in character recognition. To illustrate how readers fill in the forms, one researcher gave this •xa•ple of • se•te•ce •it• mi•si•g l•tt•rs.

The results of all these tests are not uniform. Some of the discrepancies are attributable to incomplete control of the variables, others to the different measuring methods that are used. The measurement of legibility is an inexact science, but there are some general principles that can be extracted from the great body of research.

Legibility factors

Legibility is determined by at least nine factors:

1. The reader's interest in the text
2. Type design
3. Type size
4. Line width
5. Word and letter spacing
6. Leading, or line spacing
7. Form
8. Contrast
9. Reproduction quality

In the testing process, reader interest is controlled by comparing results against a control group. However, the editor who is publishing a daily or weekly product is interested in the level of reader interest because it is critical not only to legibility but also to sales and customer satisfaction. By the same token, the quality of reproduction, which depends on the paper and the printing process, is very important. In tests, researchers can control reproduction quality carefully. Editors, unfortunately, cannot. The newspaper is printed on an off-white, flimsy paper called newsprint. The texture is disagreeable, and the resulting contrast between the black type and the background is not as good as that found in magazines using coated paper. Other variables, however, can be manipulated with little or no expense to the newspaper. The most important factor to remember is that no one variable can be taken by itself. For instance, leading requirements change as the type and line width change; if the type size is changed, several other variables must be altered also.

TYPE DESIGN. For textual material, the basic choice is serif or sans serif type. A study conducted in 1974 for the American Newspaper Publishers Association by Hvistendahl and Kahl (1975) found that roman type was read seven to ten words a minute faster than sans serif type. The roman (serif) body type faces that were used included Imperial, Royal, and variations of Corona; the sans serif faces were Helvetica, Futura, Sans Heavy, and News Sans. The researchers found that the subjects in the study read the roman text faster and two-thirds of them said they preferred it. This study confirmed the earlier work by Tinker and Paterson, who found that a sans serif face was read 2.2 percent slower than a roman face (Dowding 1957). Robinson et al. (1971) found it took 7.5 percent more time to read sans serif than roman. Serifs are important in preserving the image of small letters.

This limited research does not mean that newspapers should never use sans serif in text. It does mean, however, that editors should seriously question the advisability of using it in quantity and perhaps might want to consider restricting its use to special sections or features. For instance, some newspapers that use a roman text type use sans serif in the personality, people, or newsmaker features. It is also often used successfully in cutlines.

Only a handful of the roman text faces are commonly used by mass circulation publications. Corona, Crown, Royal, Imperial, Times Roman, and Excelsior have proven themselves on newsprint. The *Los Angeles Times* chose an extended version of Paragon when it redesigned in 1980.

SIZE OF TYPE. The proper size of type is closely related to the line width and subject matter. Tinker (1963) found that moderate type sizes (9- to 12-pt. range) are the easiest to read. A discussion of type sizes in points, however, can be misleading. The *x*-height is a more accurate measurement of the actual size of the type (Fig. 11.1). When testing legibility, Poulton (1955) had to use 9.5-pt. Univers and 12-pt. Bembo to equalize the *x*-heights. Another researcher found that 60-pt. Univers Bold, 72-pt. Caslon Bold, and 85-pt. Bodoni Bold were needed to get an *x*-height of 12.6 mm. The *x*-height of Linotron's 9-pt. Helvetica is 4.8 points, but its Caledonia is 3.8. The difference is in the length of the extenders. If there are long extenders, the size of the bowl is smaller; if there are short extenders, the size of the bowl is larger and the type appears larger. *X*-height, then, is the critical determiner of type size.

X-heights

Fig. 11.1.   **9 pt.: Futura Univers   Helios   Clarendon Book**

A smaller type size can be used for reference material, such as sports scores, box summaries, or classifieds, because readers do not read large amounts of it. When the columns are wider, as for editorials, a larger type size is needed. Depending on the *x*-height, 11- or 12-pt. type is appropriate for material set wider than 18 picas.

Most editors acknowledge that newspapers should use a larger type size; the *Fresno Bee,* the San Diego *Evening Tribune,* and the *Arizona Republic* are among the few who use 10-pt. type. The *Charlotte* (N.C.) *Observer* uses 10.4-pt. type with 9.7-pt. leading, and the Providence (R.I.) *Journal* uses 10.5-pt. type with 9.8-pt. leading. Both use Bedford. The Bend (Oreg.) *Bulletin* uses 10.5-pt. Century type with 10.5 leading. Of the 314 American and Canadian newspapers that responded to a National Readership Council request for text type samples in 1980, 103 indicated their body type was less than 9 points. Most of those, however, were using Corona, which has a large x-height, or a modification manufactured under another name. Even though there have been improvements, more needs to be done. Editors reluctant to lose space to larger type are ignoring a significant portion of the potential audience. Poindexter (1978) found that 8.5 percent of the nonreaders did not read newspapers because of poor eyesight. A Gannett researcher found that 16 percent of the subscribers wanted larger type and that the percentage was even higher among people over 50, who are among the most loyal newspaper readers. Another newspaper found that one-third of its readers wanted larger type (Curley 1979).

WIDTH OF THE LINE. In newspapers, column widths range all the way from slightly less than 9 picas to 18 picas. Some newspapers do not have a standard setting for pages with no ads. The *St. Petersburg Times* permits settings between 11 and 22.6 picas for its 9-pt. Century Schoolbook. Other newspapers specify the widths for type. The *Minneapolis Tribune,* for example, permits only two widths.

Newspaper column widths have historically been shaped by advertising rather than legibility considerations. Advertising is sold by the column inch and 8 columns produce more column inches than 5 or 6 columns, even though the total space on the page does not change. Consequently, newspapers were loath to change to a 6-column format even when it became commonly known that it produced a more legible line length. Such a change also required a sizable increase in advertising rates on a column-inch basis to maintain the same income per page. As a result, some newspapers converted to a 9-column advertising format and a 6-column news format. The result is some extremely narrow news columns when 8 columns are filled with advertising.

The 6-column format was an improvement over the 8-column format because the line widths are between 12 and 14 picas for most newspapers. Tinker and Paterson (1929) found that a line width of 18 to 24 points provides the easiest reading when 10-pt type is used. This width provides 10 to 12 words per line, which they found to be the optimum number. Because most newspapers use type at about 9 points, the 12- to 14-pica range produces nearly the same number of words per line. Hvistendahl and Kahl (1975) found that the highest reading speed was obtained when they set roman type in 14-pica columns.

WORD SPACING. We read by perceiving shapes and groups of words. If words are   widely   spaced   like   this, it slows reading speed considerably. More stops are necessary, and words must be read as individual units rather than as parts of phrases. For newspaper purposes, type is read most comfortably when word spacing is between 3 to the em and 4 to the em. (An em, you will recall, is the square of the letter *m* in the type size being used.) The term 3 to the em means one-third of an em spacing. Word spacing should not be greater than the leading.

The spacing between letters also affects the speed of reading. By tightening letterspacing, more words can be printed in the same amount of space. With proper handling, this can increase reading speed. Condensed type in particular, whether text or display, should not have a large amount of letterspacing.

LEADING. The correct amount of leading depends on the width of the line and the size and design of the type. Unleaded material generally slows reading speed (Becker et al. 1970), but too much leading can have the same effect. For newspapers that have columns in the 12- to 15-pica range and use 9-pt. type, Tinker (1963) found that 1-pt. leading is desirable. He also found that 10-pt. type set solid (no leading) was read faster and was more pleasing to the readers than 8-pt. type with 2-pt. leading (Figs. 11.2 to 11.4).

9 pt. with no leading
The amount of leading required depends upon the width of the line, x-height and design of the type. For newspaper purposes, 9 pt. type set at 12 to 14 picas should have about 1 pt. of leading.

Fig. 11.2.

9 pt. with 1 pt. leading
The amount of leading required depends upon the width of the line, x-height and design of the type. For newspaper purposes, 9 pt. type set at 12 to 14 picas should have about 1 pt. of leading.

Fig. 11.3.

9 pt. with 3 pts. leading
The amount of leading required depends upon the width of the line, x-height and design of the type. For newspaper purposes, 9 pt. type set at 12 to 14 picas should have about 1 pt. of leading.

Fig. 11.4.

There are some situations where the designer will have to apply common sense because research does not answer all the questions; for instance:

1. Type with a large x-height generally needs more leading than type with a small x-height because the large x-height has shorter descenders and gives the impression of less space between lines.

2. Sans serif type generally needs more leading than roman type because sans serif has a strong vertical flow and leading will counteract this. Roman type with a strong vertical flow, such as Bodoni, also needs more leading.

3. Less leading is needed on special copy such as editorials because the reader does not spend much time on it.

4. Leading for headlines can be much tighter than for body copy because the reader does not spend much time reading them. In fact, some newspapers have gone to minus leading in headlines. The *St. Petersburg Times* sets 24- and 30-pt. headlines at minus 2-pt. leading; type above 36 points is set at minus 4-pt. leading.

FORM. The design of the type and how it is used affects legibility. For newspapers and magazine purposes, editors are primarily concerned with the legibility of text type between 8 and 12 points. Readers prefer moderate designs, neither too condensed nor too extended, for textual material. The shape of the bowls and, for roman type, the design of the serifs are also factors. The space within the bowls determines legibility (Roethlein 1912), which is why boldface is less pleasant to read in large quantities. Boldface type has heavier lines and less white space within the letters. As a test, compare a typewritten page from a typewriter that has not been cleaned against one that has. It is far more difficult to read the page when the letters are filled in. If the serifs are too fine, they may not reproduce well on newsprint in small sizes. That is why some modern roman types such as Bodoni, with its hairline serifs, are not used as text type. Among the sans serif types, the differentiation among letters is even more important than it is for roman faces. News Gothic has been successful in this regard (Poultan 1955).

Once the typeface is selected, the editor must decide how emphasis will be added. Boldface in small amounts is a good method. Italic type, on the other hand, takes longer to read and readers do not like it. "In general," Tinker (1963) concluded, "the use of italics should be restricted to those rare occasions *when added emphasis is needed*" (italics added).

Text or headlines in all capital letters should be avoided, except as special treatment because it slows reading speed and displeases readers. Because readers perceive shapes, IT IS MORE DIFFICULT TO READ ALL-CAP MATERIAL. THE SHAPES BECOME UNIFORM, AND THE READER IS FORCED TO LOOK AT INDIVIDUAL LETTERS RATHER THAN WORDS AND PHRASES. A headline style that requires capitalization of the first letter of the first word and proper nouns only is more legible than one that requires capitalization of all words. In addition, the more capitals used, the more space required. All-cap style in text or headlines is not economical. An occasional headline or title in all caps, however, has a negligible effect on legibility.

Another aspect of form that is increasingly coming into question is whether to justify the copy to produce an even right margin or run it unjustified (ragged right). The research to date suggests that there is no significant difference in reading speed between justified and ragged right copy (Fabrizio 1967). Hartley and Barnhill (1971) found no significant differences in reading speed when the line length was determined by grammatical constraints and hyphenation was avoided whenever possible, when about 33 percent of the lines were hyphenated, or when type was set ragged right over double column formats of varying widths.

While there may not be a difference in reading speed between justified and unjustified lines, there certainly is a difference in appearance (Figs. 11.5, 11.6). Justified type in narrow newspaper columns requires a great deal of hyphenation and causes variation in the space between words. Unjustified type permits the editor to standardize the word spacing and avoid illogical breaks in words. When type was hand set, unjustified type was much faster to produce, but now that a computer justifies the lines, that advantage has been nullified.

Type set justified

Type set justified looks more formal. It is appropriate to news content. Type set ragged right is more relaxed. It is appropriate for soft news and features. There is no significant difference between the two in reading speed.

Fig. 11.5.

Type set ragged right

Type set justified looks more formal. It is appropriate to news contents. Type set ragged right is more relaxed. It is appropriate for soft news and features. There is no significant difference between the two in reading speed.

Fig. 11.6.

The choice of justified or ragged right type is reduced to a question of personality. The *Hartford* (Conn.) *Courant* claims it was the first American newspaper to use ragged right throughout the newspaper. When the Allentown *Morning Call,* which had used ragged right frequently, appeared set entirely in ragged right, the publisher did not notice for two weeks. Neither, apparently, did the readers. There were no objections.

Justified type is formal, and the orderliness of the margins gives a feeling of precision and control, factors that may enhance a news product. Ragged right type is informal, more relaxed, less precise. Consequently, it may be more appropriate for feature sections. If ragged right is chosen, it is preferable to use a modified ragged right type, which permits hyphenation whenever a line is less than an established minimum length, such as 50 percent of the potential line. This eliminates unusually short lines, which are noticed for their contrast rather than their message.

Ragged left type should be avoided except in small amounts, such as a short cutline set to the left of a photograph. If the reader does not have a fixed left-hand margin, reading speed is seriously impaired. Ragged left should never be used in textual material of any significant length.

CONTRAST. The contrast in color between the type and its background is another important factor in legibility. Black and white offers the most contrast and therefore is the most legible. The reverse, however, is not true. White print on a black background slows reading speed significantly (*J. Appl. Psych.* 1931). The dramatic effect that can be achieved by reversing type must be balanced against the loss of legibility. Reversed type should only be used in small quantities, such as a paragraph or two, and in larger-than-normal type, such as 14 or 18 points.

When color is laid over type, it should be treated the same as reversed type — larger-than-normal and in small quantities. Only pastel colors should be considered, and they should be screened. Black print on yellow paper, and red print on white paper have scored well in legibility tests (Tinker 1963).

Newspapers are fighting an increasingly difficult battle to produce a legible product. As newsprint prices have increased, the quality of the paper has decreased. In the mid-1970s, in an attempt to restrain increasing costs, newsprint mills dropped the basis weight of newsprint from 32 to 30. The lighter paper is easier and cheaper to make but, according to an analysis by the Knight-Ridder group, has caused expensive web breaks and reduced printing quality. Now the newsprint industry is proposing to lower the basis weight to 29 or 28.5. The result for newspapers will be more show-through of ink from one side of the page to the other. This in turn will decrease legibility.

QUALITY OF REPRODUCTION. If the quality of the newsprint continues to decrease, it will become even more difficult to control the other variables, such as camera and press work, that affect the quality of reproduction. Offset presses need a good quality paper. As the basis weight for newsprint decreases, the pressroom operators have to work even harder to control the amount of ink. Unfortunately, there is a limit to how much the operators can do to prevent show-through with lighter paper.

While the texture of the paper does not directly affect legibility, it does affect the reader's attitude toward the product. It is almost impossible to read a newspaper these days without getting ink all over your hands and perhaps even on your clothes. NBC television correspondent Irving R. Levine always wears gloves when he reads a newspaper, a practice that invites curious glances, not to mention comments.

Summary

Editors must avoid the temptation to change the size of type without considering the line width, leading, and type design. Editors must eschew the dramatic at times to produce the legible. Nevertheless, every factor discussed here can be violated to a minimal extent. Type can be reversed if it is done in small quantities and with large type. Newspapers·that publish editorials in 10-pt. type but run only one editorial a day can probably get by with little or no leading even though 10-pt. type is usually not set solid. Screening type decreases the contrast and thus the legibility, but as a labeling device it can be effective. There is no doubt that all-caps type is more difficult to read than lowercase, but a two- or three-word headline in all caps is not going to make an appreciable amount of difference in reading speed. All these factors should be considered in relationship to one another, but any can be violated within reason.

CHAPTER TWELVE

Using type

A MESSAGE that we hear is soon forgotten, but the one that we see and read is more permanent because it penetrates memory on more than one level and can be referred to over and over again. This explains the growing significance of typography as a world-wide communication tool — a tool that we must improve steadily by studying it as we use it.

Will Burton
TYPOGRAPHER

JUST AS THE CLOTHES WE WEAR reveal our personality, the type that is used to dress our newspaper says a great deal about the publication. Type is an essential part of a newspaper's personality. Imagine reader reaction if the *New York Times* was set in Cartoon typeface, the *Wall Street Journal* in Egyptian, or the *Philadelphia Inquirer* in Futura Light. Those type choices would be as inappropriate as wearing a T-shirt to a formal dinner party. Researchers have shown that lay people are able to attribute characteristics to type similar to those used by professionals (Tannenbaum et al. 1964) and that the selection of a correct typeface appears to make more difference with some types of content than others (Haskins 1958). Benton (1979) found that the sans serif face Helvetica was not perceived as differing significantly from serif faces Garamond, Bodoni, Palatino, and Times Roman, except that it was considered more modern. For years, many newspapers used a more feminine face in the women's section than elsewhere. Haskins and Flynne (1974) found that even though readers ascribed feminine characteristics to certain typefaces, the use of those faces in the section did not affect readership. Not enough research has been done to determine whether readership is enhanced by appropriate typefaces, but it is generally conceded that selection of type does have connotative impact. That is, type imparts an emotion, a feeling. The successful designer uses type with the understanding that the form is part of the message and not a decoration.

For instance, former *Washington Star* designer Eric Seidman selected Egyptian Bold Condensed as his sectional headface because he found he could vary the size to provide different messages and still maintain unity (Fig. 12.1).

Fig. 12.1.

The selection of a proper headline face rests on legibility considerations, the image the editors wish to project, the tradition that needs to be preserved, and the mood and life-style of the community. After World War II, Americans were hungry to improve their lives. A home, two cars, and vacations became possible for millions. Americans trashed the old and devoured the new. During a period like that, a modern typeface such as Helvetica has a strong appeal. Moods change, however.

When the oil embargo overturned the world economy in the late 1970s, Americans elected a president who preached self-denial. Throughout the country, there was a strong yearning for the "good old days," and political conservatism enjoyed a revival. For the first time in years, functionalism became more important than looks. Nowhere was this shift in moods more evident than in the auto industry. The smaller, fuel-efficient imports outsold the heavier, bigger, and fancier U.S.-made cars. While the nation was buffeted by recession and inflation, caused in large part by the problems in the automobile industry, engineers frantically sought to design small, competitive U.S. cars.

The theme of the administration that took office in 1981 was "A New Beginning," but it was based on a return to classic American values. At that time, many American newspapers going through redesigns selected classic typefaces instead of the more modern ones. The *Dallas Times Herald* and the *Los Angeles Times* adopted Times New Roman. The *Kansas City Star* chose Goudy Bold. The *Milwaukee Journal* adopted Baker Argentine. Other newspapers sensed the mood of their readers and followed suit. Times change; tastes change. There is no "right" display face. Type should be chosen on the basis of its legibility, its connotative image, its credibility, and the mood of the community in which the paper is published.

Type is a large part of the newspaper's personality. A sudden change is shocking. For example, if nameplates were exchanged between the *New York Times* and the *Idaho Statesman* (Fig. 12.2) or the *Milwaukee Sentinel* and the *Philadelphia Inquirer* (Fig. 12.3), the resulting combinations of type would immediately indicate that something was wrong. The personalities would have been changed.

To check the personality of your paper, draw up a list of opposite characteristics (traditional, modern; credible, not credible; old, young; aggressive, passive; cold, warm) and put them on a 1 to 10 scale. Compare the staff's perception with that of an audience sample. This kind of measurement is also a good way to field test a proposed type change.

Assuring contrast

Once editors have decided upon the image desired, they have four basic methods to provide contrast with the display face.

Fig. 12.2.

Fig. 12.3.

1. Choose one weight of one typeface and use size differentiation only.
2. Choose one typeface with two or more weights.
3. Choose one typeface and use italic or oblique of the same face.
4. Choose different but complimentary typefaces.

A fifth option, which is not desirable, is the use of any typeface from condensed to extraextended. These styles should be avoided for the main display face because their legibility is not good; the readers do not like them; and with the extended faces, editors cannot get as many letters into a headline. Although a condensed version can be built into the basic headline chart, it should be used judiciously. It is better to use these special faces for standing features such as departmental identifiers and column logos.

SIZE DIFFERENTIATION. Traditionally, newspapers have relied upon more than one size of type to relieve the dullness that is inherent in the use of a single weight of type. When the size differentiation is not present, the page lacks interest (Fig. 12.4). It is possible to produce successful pages that rely only on size to provide contrast with type, but the task is formidable. In fact, it is impossible if the basic face is a bold weight. As type increases in weight, type size should decrease. Newspapers such as the *St. Petersburg Times,* which uses Univers Bold for its basic face, do not need as much size to carry a page. As a result, the range of type sizes used is much smaller. A typical *St. Petersburg Times* front page, for example, ranges between 30- and 60-pt. type. Most headlines are 36 and 42 points. However, newspapers that use a medium weight often range above 80 points, and 48-, 60-, and 72-pt. type is seen frequently.

Fig. 12.4.

Fig. 12.5.

WEIGHT DIFFERENTIATION. If designers select a single display typeface for editorial content, contrast can be achieved from weight differentiation. One face helps to ensure the designer of concord, the blending of typographical elements to give a uniform impression. When all the type is the same weight, however, the uniformity produces dullness; bolder and lighter weights provide pleasing contrast. A designer should work with at least two or three weights. The basic headline face is usually in the medium-to-bold range. Different weights are used most effectively in readins, readouts, blurbs, and decks. Some newspapers, *Newsday* among them, obtain contrast by alternating heavier and lighter weight type in main heads throughout the page. However, the interplay between the bold and the light in the same story shows off the contrast to better advantage (Fig. 12.5). Even with weight contrast, size differential is important. Editors need to downsize heads when using a bold or extrabold weight for hammers or labels. For instance, if the hammer is usually twice the size of the deck, the size differential may be only one step (from 36 to 30 points), particularly if the hammer is set in bold or extrabold type and the deck is medium or light. In each of the examples in Figure 12.6, two weights of type are used. In the first, there is one size difference; in the second there are two.

Fig. 12.6.

Bold weight
It can be used in smaller sizes

Medium weight
It requires more size to set it off

CONTRAST BY FORM. Some designers prefer to achieve contrast by using the italic or oblique of the basic face. *Time* magazine, for instance, uses a serif italic as a contrasting deck head to the sans serif main head. Because of the small page size and subordinate position in the headline, italic type usually is only 12 to 14 points. Some italic faces lose their graceful lines in larger sizes and are not as suited for newspaper use where larger sizes are needed. The *Milwaukee Journal*'s Baker Argentine has an attractive italic, and the *Dallas Times Herald* uses the italic of its Times Roman successfully. The oblique, or slanted right, versions of the sans serif and square serif faces have none of the elegance of italic and are best used in small sizes, such as in blurbs. Some newspapers, however, do use oblique as a contrasting face.

CONTRAST BY FACE. A few newspapers are starting to use contrasting typefaces in their basic formats. It is a noble but risky experiment. If the proper types are not matched, the effect will be the same kind of clash that results from mixing a striped shirt with plaid slacks. In addition, because of the high story count on most newspaper pages, clutter is always a danger when two typefaces are used.

A knowledge of the type continuum can help avoid mismatched types, and lower story counts can mitigate the clutter. The type continuum arranges type much the way a color wheel arranges colors. The continuum (Fig. 12.7) ranges from text lettering to square serifs. To be effective, the contrast must be sharp. Timidity in type choice produces conflict. That is why a designer would not mix two types from the same race, such as Helvetica and Futura. The *Kansas City Star* selected Goudy Bold (modern) for its basic face but uses Franklin Gothic (sans serif) for decks. The mix works. The types are from adjacent races, a basic rule when mixing type. The weight contrast, however, is not as successful because both typefaces are bold. A sans serif in a lighter face would have been more effective, but the bold was chosen so smaller sizes could be used to save space. *USA Today* uses Times Bold

Fig. 12.7.

𝕿𝖊𝖝𝖙

Old Style

Transitional

Modern

Sans serif

Square serif

and Times for weight contrast in decks. But it also uses Helvetica Extra Bold Condensed for its teaser lines and over its special cover story. Richard Curtis, assistant managing editor, said their goal was to produce a high-energy paper without being circusy.

The Long Beach *Independent Press-Telegram* successfully uses Helvetica Bold in some sections with a Century Light Italic as a contrasting deck head. Century and Helvetica are from adjacent races, and the eye finds the relationship pleasing. The *Los Angeles Herald Examiner* uses Helvetica Bold and a lightweight Garamond Italic as a deck head (Fig. 12.8). Garamond is an old style type too far removed from Helvetica, and the combination is less pleasing. Whatever the combination, one of the faces should be designated as the main display head and the other should be used in subordinate positions.

Fig. 12.8.

In the days when most newspapers had as many as 20 stories on the front page, it would have been impossible to have two basic faces. Now that most newspapers have lowered their story count to 10 or less, it is possible to work with two typefaces without cluttering the page.

SPECIAL OCCASIONS. It is often difficult to decide when to deviate from the newspaper's basic face to choose a type that reflects the content of a specific story. A newspaper page has several elements on it; the use of a special typeface for one or more of them invites discord. Even the newsweeklies (*Times, Newsweek,* and *U.S. News and World Report*) stick to their basic face or faces. Like newspapers, their element count is high. Other magazines, though, have fewer stories, and their openings are often separated by several pages. Consequently, the use of type appropriate to the content of each story does not cause disharmony because each spread is a separate unit of the magazine, and the type from one story is not adjacent to the type of another. In certain circumstances, however, newspaper designers can use type other than the basic display face with great success. For instance, type appropriate to the content might be used without risk to the unity of the publication on section fronts, particulary those with one subject; on picture pages, which often give designers an opportunity to meld mood and type; and in special sections, such as investigatory projects or evaluations of new car models. Care must be taken, however, to tie the section to the main paper with identifying symbols such as a reduced version of the newspaper's nameplate or repetition of the department identifiers.

It is not advisable to change faces, even on one-subject pages, because it might disrupt the reader. If readers fail to recognize the page as part of their paper, the designer has failed. It is more appropriate to change faces on pages that do not appear regularly, such as picture pages or one- or two-page special reports.

Judicious use of a special type, often a novelty face, for a story heading (Fig. 12.9) can be exciting. This technique is best relegated to feature sections.

When a typeface is selected to reflect the content of the only story on a page, it can attract attention without producing clutter. When the *Daily News* at Longview, Wash., published a feature on oriental fashions, the type set the tone for a strikingly successful page (Fig. 12.10).

Working with display type

Headlines inform and entertain. They make history, incite emotion, and cause people to laugh and cry. In most cases, however, they are dull.

Newspaper headline writers have been straitjacketed into some unusual formats. Once it was fashionable to write headlines that exactly filled each

Fig. 12.9.   Fig. 12.10.

line. At another time, headlines had one or two counts less in each succeeding line — the stepped-down format. Narrow columns and capitalization requirements further restricted the ability of headline writers to tell and sell stories. Developments in newspaper design that accompanied the introduction of cold type eased some of the restrictions but also took away an essential element of the headline — the deck. Functionalism was incorrectly interpreted to mean that decks were superfluous. The fact that decks allow headline writers to tell the story more accurately and fully was overlooked. The elimination of decks for design purposes was a case of form over content. Both form and content are served by the increased use of well-designed display type.

For the most part, the decks that are reappearing are decks only in the sense that they are subordinate to the main head. Traditionally, decks were 1-column wide and 3 or more lines deep. Now, type that is subordinate to the main head appears in a variety of forms — readins, readouts, one-line, multicolumn, summary boxes, and blurbs. Main heads bring with them the tyranny of headline counts, but some of the subordinate head styles avoid the restrictions of count. Readins and readouts, for example, are not counted. The readin leads into the title or label of the story (see Fig. 12.11).

Writing headlines can be a
frustrating experience. But the
readin format is one way to avoid

HEADLINE TYRANNY

Fig. 12.11.

A readout is not tied to the main head in the same sentence (see Fig. 12.12).

The aftermath of a VOLCANO

When the grief subsides,
the residents discover that
they have to get back to business.
But what do you do when your
business is buried under mud?

Fig. 12.12.

Designers should take advantage of every opportunity to use display type to attract the reader's attention. For example, to sell a story on a freshman football recruit, the editors of the *Columbia Daily Tribune* used a takeoff on a well-known advertising line (Fig. 12.13). It is not a traditional headline, but combined with the deck set in a lighter face, it tells and sells the story. Special stories should have special treatment, but run-of-the-mill stories such as city council and school board meetings need display treatment too. Summary boxes are especially useful when reporting on meetings where several votes are recorded. The lead of the story will probably be the issue judged by the reporter to affect the most readers. Even if the reporter is right, "the

COLUMBIA DAILY TRIBUNE

Sports

When Mack speaks, his teammates listen

MU's versatile recruit from Webster Groves proves he's not afraid to speak his mind

By DAN KELLY
of the Tribune's staff

Tracey Mack will bring a full supply of self-confidence to Missouri this fall.

Soviet man scores 10, wins gold

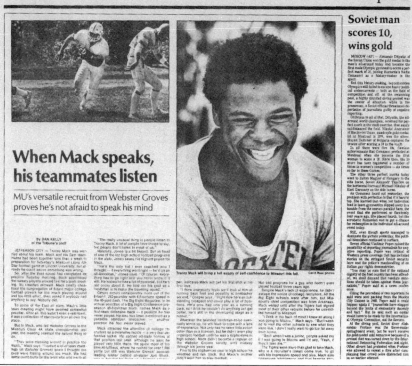

Fig. 12.13.

most readers" will probably be a minority. Because the headline reflects the lead, readers who are not affected by that particular issue will probably ignore the entire story. Readers are self-centered; they look for information that helps them. A summary box is one way to reach readers, many of whom are essentially newspaper scanners (see Fig. 12.14).

Council approves $20 million sewage project

xxxxxxxxxxxxxxxxxxxxxxxxxxxxxxxxxxxxxxxx
xxxxxxxxxxxxxxxxxxxxxxxxxxxxxxxxxxxxxxxx
xxxxxxxxxxxxxxxxxxxxxxxxxxxxxxxxxxxxxxxx
xxxxxxxxxxxxxxxxxxxxxxxxxxxxxxxxxxxxxxxx
xxxxxxxxxxxxxxxxxxxxxxxxxxxxxxxxxxxxxxxx
xxxxxxxxxxxxxxxxxxxxxxxxxxxxxxxxxxxxxxxx
xxxxxxxxxxxxxxxxxxxxxxxxxxxxxxxxxxxxxxxx

In other action, the council:
- **voted to widen Broadway;**
- **cut the West and Tenth street buses;**
- **put the north side fire station on hold**

Fig. 12.14.

Without the summary box, scanners who travel or live on or near Broadway, ride the buses, or live on the north side would never have known the council took action that might affect their lives.

The scanner can also be stopped by type used as blurbs, readouts or quoteouts. These terms refer to the use of type (usually in the 14- to 18-pt. range) to highlight a quote or anecdote or set the stage for a confrontation. The Allentown *Morning Call* used type in this way when it quoted some of the people involved in the school closing issue (Fig. 12.15). Readers who had a connection to the school probably read the story regardless of the headline; those who were only peripherally connected or not interested at all were teased by the way the story was sold as a confrontation between a small individual and a large institution: "We're not wealthy businessmen. We can't say, 'If you're going to close our school, we'll pull our factories out of Allentown.'" This story involved human drama, and the editors used display type to sell it to the scanners. The average reader spends about 15 minutes with the daily newspaper. Even if scanners are not enticed to read the whole story—and some will be—they should be given as much usable information as possible. Readers who find their newspapers useful are likely to continue subscribing.

Fig. 12.15.

CONTENT CHANGES. Designers are using a greater variety of headline formats. Some newspapers are also reevaluating rules about content. The standard rules are sound: use the active voice; use a subject and verb. For years, the headline has done yeoman's work and permitted journalists to process hundreds of stories against a deadline. However, such admonitions as "never use titles or labels" need a rehearing. Combined with subordinate type, titles can help editors avoid the extreme statements that traditional headline rules often force. Flexible headline formats and content rules alleviate the problems of attribution in headlines over controversial stories, highlighting only one of many charges and one of the denials, and using large bold type for only one of several findings of an investigation. Do not hesitate to deviate from the tried and proven headline approach if the message can be told better by using alternative formats or content.

Type can talk

Now that designers have the flexibility to use type more creatively, it can do more than just carry the letters; it can talk. When we speak, we add inflection to emphasize a point. We speak softly sometimes; other times, loudly. Similarly, inflection can be added to type by capitalization, changing the size or weight of type, or varying the form from regular to italics. Most of the time, type only carries words. For instance,

Let my people go

Printed in that manner, it directs the reader to give each word equal emphasis. If the story's theme has a different focus, inflection can be added to the last word as follows:

Let my people GO

Without changing the words, the meaning can be changed again:

Let MY people go
or
LET MY PEOPLE GO

In the last line, the speaker is shouting. Additional variations include changing the shape of the headline and using size differentiation

Let my people GO

or changing the shape and form:

Let
my people GO
or
Let my **GO**
people

   Type can speak in other ways too. In Figure 12.16, internationally known designer Herb Lubalin makes type speak with great simplicity and strength. The "Families" nameplate is the work of a genius. By overlapping the *O* and the *U*, the designer of the "Our Town" page (Fig. 12.17) created a visual pun. What could be more appropriate than joining two letters in the word "our" — yours and mine?

   It does not take a genius to improve the use of type in newspapers, but it does take a knowledge of the alternatives and the willingness to try. It is time to unleash the power of type to reach our readers.

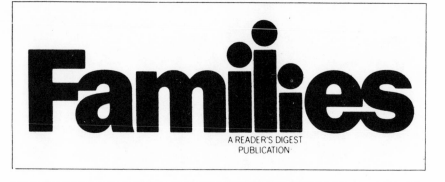

Fig. 12.16.

Fig. 12.17.

OUR TOWN

You can talk about the
mountains and you can
dream of the ocean.
You can sing your songs
of a home far away.
But when all is said
and done, William
Shakespeare was right:

**What is the city
but its people?**

Written by Jim Herweg
Photographed by David Rees

Ask a man where he's from and as often as not he'll tell you a lie.

These days, anyone who ever changed places in Portland says they're from the Northwest. Years ago, it was always San-something-or-other, and, "Oh, what's become of my cars?"

For some folks, a town is simply something to embrace if it enhances your walk.

Columbia usually doesn't appeal to such folks. Fans here owe $35, and when you've finished one of your 20 running installments you're back on Walnut Street with a nose full of twin chopped cow. Somehow it's just not like a trip to the beach.

But you're here because you've chosen to be here, or at least chosen not to leave. Retired Stephens College English instructor C.S. Miller puts it this way: "Despite the winter, this is where we base social life. This is where we know lots of people."

And there's the gist of it. It always comes down to people. Cities are built by people, exist for people. And when everyone sings their line on key, the city is like the barbershop quartet that magically turns four voices into a chorus, far transcending the sum of its parts.

And it is those sounds that seem to come from nowhere that is the voice of the city. Here, then, are a few of the singers.

WILLIAM AND MAIMIE STEPHENSON:
two turtle doves

On Christmas Day 1929, William and Maimie Stephenson were married in a little cottage in northern England.

At 4 a.m., she climbed out of bed to prepare everything, just as always for the whole celebration, as always has been her way. At 4:30 a.m., she lit the oil lamp and went to dress for the day.

Fifteen minutes later, she returned to find everything in the room covered with soot from the lamp. Everything.

We started spring cleaning at quarter to five when I was to be married at nine," she says. "I always said that was the inviting beginning of a very exciting life.

In 1948, William Stephenson left his post at Oxford University, and the two moved to Chicago where he became a visiting professor of psychology at the University of Chicago.

In 1958, they moved to Columbia after he accepted a position at the University of Missouri's School of Journalism. Two years later, she joined the Columbia Art League. It's been 30 years now, she says.

For many people in town, she represents the art league; at one site has worked six jobs, you'll never forget her or the English accent, her exacting punctuation, her ebullient energy—she is one of a kind.

This year at Christmas, she and her husband celebrated their 50th anniversary. Sitting, unaware of anyone asking, mincemeat pie and ice cream, they suddenly found voices on the radio singing. Two Turtle Doves at Christmas.

And every time the tears welled in her eyes, the two were determined with precision pages pages, she caught them on her fingers until her tears were full.

It would be another Christmas in remembrance.

ROBERTA AND PHIL JACKSON:
hamburger, for now

Eleven years ago, after a short but sweet courtship, Phil and Roberta—Bert "too sloppy"—Jackson sort of ran off and got married. She's 30, she's 29, and with a little bit of help they'd like to change that soon.

They mean it, but today. Probably not tomorrow. When the time is right.

The reason for their end is clear. The two own the car at the White Rock Prairie Ranch, opened after the sale of Rock Prairie area of northwest Missouri, where the two lived for three years, barely making ends.

There are, who Phil Jackson said, so many ways to run the White Rock House, build starters and work on the chicken house. Together each diameter firm distinct, "It's his real name—they came to cultivate to their horse and cow, Lisa.

I learned from us to be able to understand the business, for," says Roberta Jackson, who considers a harmony nice balance between the big, city and nature and tries to find harmony.

The far-kooney life with all town, one sees a cafe with a bedroom, a kitchen and a bath bath. The music of Dave's steak house, the world's. They've own making a song by the name. But it's sent its part of home and the Club and the it might rather do that the making sense.

The name of this game is making money, he says. "You can do performance in after performance, but it's not rounded, it's not there on the next day.

The band has recorded a few songs and hopes to put out a 45 record shortly. But they don't sell those pricing serial measures. Part of it came color comes.

The band members are part of the fun folks that have built a group formed last year to organize and promote local musicians. White Rock Prairie has ten songs on the fair bid who attention and fast performers at Columbia's Blind Apple Party Palace.

They hope it's a suite of good things to come. "If you can keep your heart together, you can arrange things," she says. "So, do you know comedy with some money?"

NARCY TRASS:
all in the family

If you like your salad served with the meat instead of before, simply tell her once. That will do just fine every time you go to "the view," as she's known to us.

If I do something wrong, they tell me and I'm sure not to do it again," she says. "If I was perfect, I'd be bored."

Tran is banquet manager at the Columbia Country Club where she has worked for 34 years. Her style is elegance, one manager specific offering the next, arriving throughout and always in perfect style with the manager.

When a member blows the cork on the seventh green, she knocks on the dining room glass and tells him knows she's watching. And when his daughter gets married she throws a reception perfect to the last detail, she wouldn't have it any other way.

"I'm self-conscious about my job," she says. "I want everything to go just so it gives you a good feeling. I love to see a person's name in smiling and love to see them going out smiling."

Membership at the club is about 460, which includes some out-of-town members, mostly folks from St. Louis and Kansas City, who use the club during football season. Tran serves as host guide across club transfers travel in many games. It's all, 4 1/2 or 85 to 90 here a week, on the hour.

But it's nothing you wouldn't do for someone in the family. And that's how she sees the members—one's not great. Once a year the club hosts Nancy Day in her honor; the only day each year she swings golf clubs.

The club is private, and members are basically rich and older. But with Tran, the barriers are lowered.

"I don't know. I'm back, and I don't know they're all around active," she says. "People always say they think of them as really. They're all human beings with a heart. They're all down-to-earth people. They have feelings too.

"It's just nice to be here, nice to be here. Anyone you love to come to work, that's nice."

Continued on following pages

CHAPTER THIRTEEN

Design challenges

THE design of a daily newspaper is a difficult undertaking. Compromise on the niceties of typography is inevitable, control of layout minimal, and perfection unobtainable.

Alan Fletcher
GRAPHICS DESIGNER

"SOMETIMES I FEEL THAT THEY [the local paper] are out to hassle me," a participant in a readership study said. "You can't find things, you're always turning pages, and the whole paper begins to fall apart."

Enter the designer with the tools to keep the paper from falling apart. The tools include organizational talents, labels, and unifying devices. Like a carpenter, the designer constructs the newspaper from the solid footings of sections. When the designer is finished and the occupants move in, they soon become familiar with every nook and cranny. It is hoped they will also feel comfortable with it.

The designer should approach the job with an understanding of how people go through a newspaper, why they read it, and what competes for the reader's time and attention. Most of all, the designer should have an appreciation for the function of a newspaper. As long as that function is primarily to inform, there can be only one guiding principle: Keep it simple.

Keeping it simple does not mean talking down to readers in writing or graphics. It does mean that designers should use writing and typographical devices to explain rather than decorate, to organize the paper, to favor the familiar over the dramatic, to be more concerned about reader reaction than peer reaction, and to create an environment suitable to the content.

With these goals in mind, the discussion now turns to the specific parts of the newspaper. We will work from the nameplate through the various sections, deal with some of the specific challenges within the sections, and then study how newspapers handled one of the biggest news days in modern times.

Nameplate

The nameplate, or flag, sets the tone for the newspaper. Its design is important because it is usually the first thing the reader sees. Seven factors should be considered:

1. Personality
2. Flexibility
3. Importance of each word in the name
4. Insignia
5. Letter and line spacing
6. Customizing
7. Subordinate elements

PERSONALITY. The nameplate can say to the reader, "This is an old-fashioned newspaper," or "This newspaper is up-to-date." The difference between traditional and old-fashioned is a thin line that often involves the elements included in the flag. When it is unnecessarily cluttered, it can communicate an amateurish quality. The type in the nameplate of the *Plainsman Herald* has a weak personality and is surrounded by clutter that detracts from the credibility of the newspaper (Fig. 13.1). One solution would be a visual pun that makes the nameplate as simple and "plain" as the name (Fig. 13.2).

OFFICIAL CITY AND COUNTY PAPER
IN BACA COUNTY IT'S THE
Plainsman Herald
ESTABLISHED IN 1887
Exclusively Serving the People of Baca County, Colorado
VOLUME 91
SPRINGFIELD, COLORADO 81073
THURSDAY, JANUARY 4, 1979
NUMBER 25

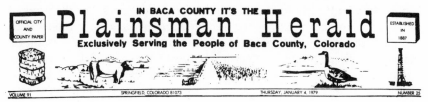

Fig. 13.1.

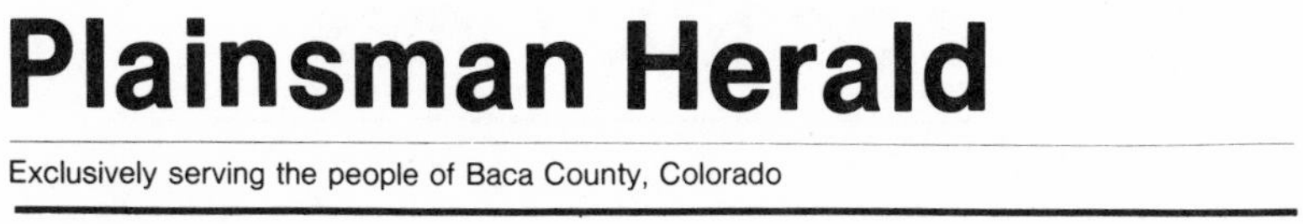

Plainsman Herald
Exclusively serving the people of Baca County, Colorado

Fig. 13.2.

The type chosen to convey the name can be old without being old-fashioned. The *New York Times* and the *St. Petersburg Times* both use a variation of Old English type. The nameplate of the *New York Times* speaks of tradition and credibility, and the news section, at least, is in tune with

Fig. 13.3.

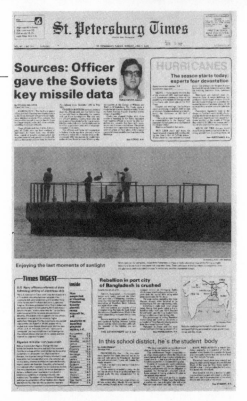

the tone set by the nameplate. The *St. Petersburg Times* is a modern paper with a traditional flag (Fig. 13.3), which is the newspaper's way of saying that it has a long and proud tradition but also recognizes that the product and its form are continually changing. The *Seattle Times* uses a modernized version of the Old English face (Fig. 13.4) to preserve the image of tradition while updating the product. Other newspapers have completely severed ties with the past. Some, like the *Sun* near Biloxi, Miss. (Fig. 13.5) have no past. The *Sun* was started in 1973 and its flag says as much. The nameplate conveys the message that this newspaper is a young, bright product.

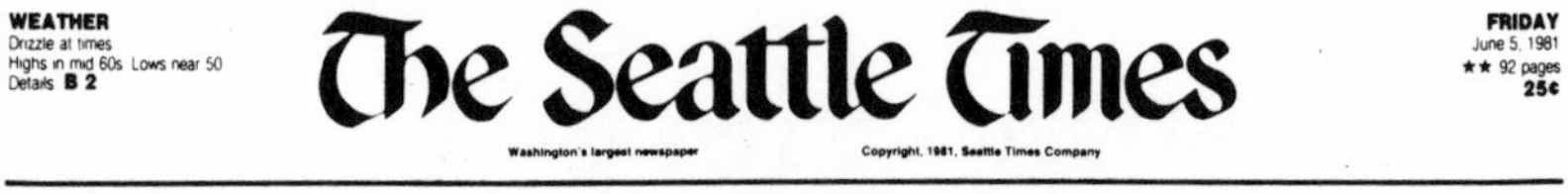

Fig. 13.4.

Fig. 13.5.

Personalities do not change overnight, and neither should nameplates. Proposed replacements should be allowed to simmer in the newsroom. Determining the connotation of a type is an inexact science at best, and editors should get as many reactions to the proposed replacement as possible before making a decision.

FLEXIBILITY. Some editors like nameplates that can run the entire width of the paper or can be used in a narrower format. Newspapers with short names may be able to run either a 5- or 6-column flag by adjusting the amount of white space at both ends. Editors should be reluctant to vary the flag width more than one column because it is the major identifier each day. Flexibility is less important than familiarity.

IMPORTANCE OF WORDS. Because all the words in a newspaper's name are not of equal importance, the designer can subordinate some words to others by changing size and boldness of type. This gives the designer a chance to use larger type for the main part of the name. For example, if Stillwater were of equal importance with *News Press* (Fig. 13.6), the type would have to be much smaller to accommodate all the letters. Instead, the designer subordinated Stillwater, and as a result, *News Press* is big, bold, and brash. In Baltimore, when *Sunday* is added to the name of the *News American* (Fig. 13.7), it is run in bolder, larger type to announce its special status. Some newspapers have dropped "The" from the name; others have subordinated it by running it in smaller type. In Figure 13.8, *Columbia* is subordinated to emphasize *Missourian*.

Stillwater, Oklahoma

NewsPress

Partly Cloudy, Warmer
Considerable cloudiness with chance of showers and becoming partly cloudy through Friday. Warmer. Winds becoming southwesterly 10 to 20 mph Friday. High Friday low 80s.

Thursday
April 16, 1981

15 Cents
Vol. 72 No. 60
26 Pages

Fig. 13.6.

60¢

The **Sunday** News American

FINAL
**

Baltimore, Maryland

Sunday, May 25, 1980

Fig. 13.7.

𝕮olumbia
𝕸issourian

75th Year — No. 167   Good Morning! It's Tuesday, March 29, 1983   2 Sections — 14 Pages — 25 Cents

Fig. 13.8.

INSIGNIA. It is easy to clutter a nameplate, but a simple insignia can help establish the identity of the paper. The insignia can reflect the area (as it does at the *Sun* in Biloxi) or a major landmark, or it can be a trademark for the newspaper. Whatever the insignia, it should be simple and fit neatly into the nameplate. The eagle in the *Albion News* flag (Fig. 13.9) overpowers the type, but the cotton boll in the nameplate of the *Greenwood* (Miss.) *Commonwealth* (Fig. 13.10) is integrated into the design.

Fig. 13.9.

Fig. 13.10.

SPACING. As a rule, the spacing between letters should be tight. Kerning and even ligatures should be investigated. Horizontal spacing should also be minimal. In Figure 13.6, "Stillwater, Oklahoma" lines up with the top of the *N* to produce a compact nameplate. In contrast, "The Stuttgart" floats uncomfortably above the rest of the name in Figure 13.11. Anchoring it to the *Daily Leader* would eliminate the float and save space.

The Stuttgart

Daily Leader

| Vol 97 172 | Thursday, April 16, 1981 | Stuttgart Ark Rice and Mallard Capital of the South | 16 pages | 25c |

Fig. 13.11.

CUSTOMIZING. Some nameplates can easily be duplicated by anyone with access to typesetting equipment, others are hand drawn, and some use standard type in an individualized manner. It is impossible and unnecessary to design a nameplate that cannot be duplicated, but it is desirable to customize it. The *Detroit News* has a simple nameplate, but notice how it was customized (Fig. 13.12). The *Th* is run together as a ligature; the ear of the *r* overlaps the *o*; the *e* and *s* sit under the serifs of the *w*. As already mentioned, an insignia, especially when neatly integrated as in the *Sun* (Fig. 13.5), individualizes the nameplate.

Fig. 13.12.

SUBORDINATE ELEMENTS. The design of the nameplate includes the name of the paper and all those elements that surround it—insignia, folio lines, cutoff rules, weather blurbs. Too many elements cause clutter; the fewer there are, the better. For example, in Figure 13.13 the *Daily Sentry-News* almost gets lost between the folio information to its left and the index at the right. The insignia even extends into the promotion boxes above. The *Gleaner,* which uses the same Helvetica type, is much cleaner (Fig. 13.14).

Fig. 13.13.

Fig. 13.14.

The weight of cutoff rules should be selected carefully so there is a clear delineation to show where the nameplate ends and the news begins. When this is not clear, the lead headline often sits uncomfortably close to the type in the nameplate. If the flag is ever dropped to permit promotion boxes or a story to run above it, at least a 1-pt. rule should be placed between the flag and the material above. Generally, the weight of type in the flag dictates the weight of the cutoff rule—bold type, bold rule.

Information that goes with the nameplate should be handled as simply as possible. Folio information usually runs below the name in small type. Occasionally, when the name of the paper is short, it may be run vertically at the left or right of the nameplate.

Section identifiers

Sectional logos, or identifiers, are labels to tell readers where they are in the paper. They are read differently than headlines and text. They receive only a glance, like the sign on a restroom door. Large sectional logos, such as the ones used by the *Seattle Times* (Fig. 13.15), make a bold statement at the beginning of each section. The *Dallas Morning News* uses 72-pt. type

Fig. 13.15.

for its logos, a 4-pt. cutoff rule, a 24-pt. reproduction of its nameplate, and a 2-pt. cutoff rule (Fig. 13.16). The *Columbia Daily Tribune* runs a 24-pt. all-cap version of its name. (Fig. 13.17).

Metropolitan

Tuesday, June 9, 1981   ©The Dallas Morning News, 1981   𝕿𝖍𝖊 𝕭𝖆𝖑𝖑𝖆𝖘 𝕸𝖔𝖗𝖓𝖎𝖓𝖌 𝕹𝖊𝖜𝖘   15 A

Fig. 13.16.

COLUMBIA DAILY TRIBUNE   Show
Page 31, Sunday, April 17, 1983   me **M**issouri

Fig. 13.17.

With space at a premium, some newspapers have looked at sectional logos as oné place to conserve. This can be done by using variations of a typeface. For instance, bold type can be run smaller without losing impact and condensed or extended variations might be appropriate, although extended would save more space than the more vertical condensed type. If the type in the nameplate is not customized, using a variation of it in the sectional logos provides unity and contrast at the same time. Screening the type produces the same effect.

Refers or teasers to inside stories can be built into the sectional logos, but if it is done in one, it should be done in all. The teasers should be handled carefully to avoid clutter.

Whatever typeface is selected, it should be compatible with the type used on the rest of the page and in harmony with the personality being created throughout the publication.

Section pages

As the reader moves from section to section, there should be a sense of continuity (recognition that the section is a part of that newspaper's family) and a sense of individuality (recognition that each member of a family can develop in its own way). Section identifiers provide a sense of continuity, and so do the same text and display type and column logo design. However, designers still have an opportunity to match the form to the content of each special-interest section. Even newspapers that do not have sections need to achieve the twin goals of unity and individuality.

A discussion of the special characteristics of five sections common to most newspapers ("Lifestyle," "Sports," "Editorial," "Business," and "Entertainment") follows.

LIFESTYLE. When it was known as the women's or the society page, this section lagged far behind societal changes. Now that most newspapers have converted to a lifestyle approach, the sections have become leaders in developing both alternative writing and graphic styles. Lifestyle editors have an opportunity to develop a personality different from the other sections of the paper because, unlike news, sports, and business, they are not tied to day-to-day news developments. This basic difference shows up in the graphic presentation. The story or element count is usually lower than in other sections of the paper, and there is generally more time to do stories and designs than in any other department besides the Sunday magazine. These opportunities also present special challenges, however. Editors of this section must involve writers, photographers, and designers in planning conferences to ensure a variety of ideas. When the system works, interesting and entertaining pages such as the takeoff on a popular movie (Fig. 13.18) are produced. This page has a dominant picture and story but maintains a high element count with its attractively packaged "amenities" feature that contains five short stories. Combined with the promotional items on the top of the page, this cover contains a high element count without creating clutter. The *Miami News*

Fig. 13.18.   *Fig. 13.19.*

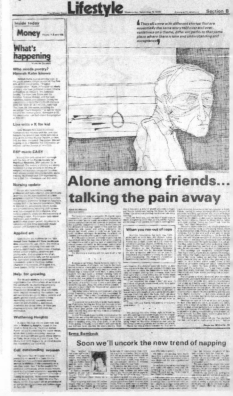

achieves the same high element count (Fig. 13.19) by combining a dominant illustration with a major story, anchoring Erma Bombeck's popular column at the bottom of the page, and using a long vertical element down the right for a series of short items. The "What's happening" feature illustrates how designers can deal with a problem common to many lifestyle sections — handling short items. Lifestyle sections often contain club news, short advances, and calendar items. Because running each of them as separate stories would clutter the pages, they should be grouped according to topic. This permits the designer to treat a series of short items as one large graphic element and helps readers find what they are looking for.

In Figure 13.20, the dramatic interplay of black and white (the reversed type and the lighting on the photograph) produces an appealing "People" page. Despite the size of the picture and story, the standing features are anchored, as they always are, at the bottom of the page.

Lifestyle sections that are not built around a dominant story can use a busier approach, as the *Washington Star* did (Fig. 13.21). The challenge is to organize the page well. The weakness of this approach is that too many stories jump. In this example, the *Washington Star* jumps four stories.

Because of the special nature of the content, designers can consider several options in lifestyle sections:

Fig. 13.20.

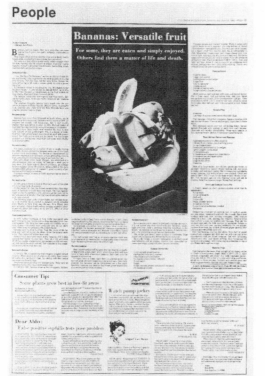

Fig. 13.21.

1. Ragged right type. It is less formal and more appropriate to the content of this section.

2. Wider settings, at least on open covers.

3. More use of alternative headline formats. Titles, labels, readouts and blurbs should be used regularly. Traditional news heads should be reserved for stories that have a strong news peg.

4. Large photographs and art work for impact. Good photo editing is essential because many lifestyle sections waste space by using too many photographs that are too large. Good editing permits more stories.

5. Beware of one-subject pages. They miss too many readers.

SPECIAL PROBLEMS. We have already mentioned that the number of short stories is one problem common to lifestyle sections. Grouping them under common subject headings creates a larger graphic element. The "Milestones" page (Fig. 13.22) brings many small items together on a well-organized, easy-to-read page.

Weddings and engagements present another common problem. As discussed earlier, one of the principles for handling related photographs is to group them, but this must be done carefully. If they are scattered about (Fig. 13.23), the page looks as though it has measles. Designers must try to keep the stories with the pictures so the readers can see the relationship and relatives can clip the articles. The solution is to create photographic clusters (Fig. 13.24). This technique could also be used in the previous example.

While it is important to cluster weddings and engagements, it is also important to anchor standing columnists. Most life-style sections publish "Dear Abby," Ann Landers, Erma Bombeck, and sometimes a local writer. These recurring columns should be located in the same place every day, but that creates a problem when the size of the section varies from one page to several pages. Daily columnists should be located on the front of the section, which is always available. Weekly or twice weekly columnists can be scheduled on days when the section is larger.

SPORTS. The key to the design of the sports section is whether it is a morning or afternoon paper. The morning sports section focuses on sports news; the afternoon usually has more features. As in any section, columnists should be anchored. Papers that have a horizontal format often find it useful to anchor a columnist in a vertical format down the left side, which is how the *Dallas Morning News* runs its popular columnist Skip Bayless (Fig. 13.25). This gives the page a built-in vertical element, especially when the column is set 1½ columns wide.

Sports is both news and entertainment. Big headlines and big pictures reflect the excitement and activity of the content. The "Sports Monday" section of the *New York Times* speaks louder than any other section of the paper

Fig. 13.22.

Fig. 13.23.

Fig. 13.24.

Fig. 13.25.

Fig. 13.26.   Fig. 13.27.

(Fig. 13.26). The bold, square serif "Sports" logo appears daily; the screened "Monday" signals the special nature of the section.

By contrast, the *Columbia Daily Tribune* is an afternoon paper, and its sports section concentrates on features and background stories (Fig. 13.27). The cover story count is low, headlines are moderately sized, and the personality is more leisurely than newsy.

SPECIAL PROBLEMS. Sports editors have been inundated by the expansion of organized sports and overlapping seasons. Many editors have elected to publish columns of agate type approximately 5½ to 7 points, in order to have some room left for stories. Organizing the agate into a neat, readable package is a challenge.

To improve sports agate pages:

1. Use narrow columns. Regardless of the newspaper's normal format, agate should be set on the equivalent of a 7- or 8-column format. Depending on the width of the page, that produces column widths of about 10 picas, an efficient size for box scores. Thirteen picas is too wide for agate type because it wastes too much space.

2. Build in a variety of light and bold type. Readers need the visual relief.

3. Use sans serif type. It is more legible in agate than serifs. In agate size, serifs often disappear.

Fig. 13.28.

4. Use bold headings to signal different sports. Some newspapers use drawings or symbols of the sports, but be careful; it is easy to get junky. A bold cutoff rule is also effective.

5. Use column rules. Narrow columns with small gutters need column rules to separate the type.

The *Cincinnati Enquirer* uses 10½-pica columns, ruled gutters, bold condensed type for subheads, cutoff rules, and also a sports comic strip to add interest to a well-designed package (Fig. 13.28).

EDITORIAL. The editorial or opinion pages traditionally are the most static of any page in the newspaper. The news, sports, features, and entertainment change daily, and the pages reflect that change. The editorial page content generally consists of opinions from the newspaper editors, columnists, cartoonists, and readers. A few newspapers use photographs to drive home an editorial point; some use photos or artist's drawings to illustrate the concerns in readers' letters. These are admirable improvements. Photographs, especially, are strong editorial devices that increase readership and add impact.

Nonetheless, the editorial page is properly static in format. Most newspapers prefer to create an environment in which issues are discussed rationally. Credibility could be damaged by flashy display, but that does not mean the pages have to be dull. The appropriate use of photographs aids and does not hinder the editorial viewpoint. Deviation from the traditional format should be saved for special occurrences.

The designer's first goal is creation of the proper editorial personality, which should be noticeably different than the news pages. Once the personality has been identified, there are two other major concerns: providing contrast to differentiate between the newspaper's opinion and the opinion of others on the page and anchoring the recurring elements.

Because form is part of the message, contrast must be built into the page to separate the newspaper's opinion from the rest of the page. This can be achieved by setting the editorial column significantly wider than the rest of the copy, using larger type, or using a different text face. When the contrast is missing, the readers have to guess whose opinion they are reading. Labeling is important, too.

The *San Francisco Examiner* (Fig. 13.29) sets its editorials 10/18½ and uses an inset capital letter to start each one. The rest of the copy is set 9/12. The difference in type size and width clearly differentiates the editorials. Editorials that are set wider usually need to be set in larger type with more leading.

On an editorial page, anchoring means finding a standard place for everything on the page because all items are standing features. Editorials are usually run vertically down the left, but this is not a necessity. Some newspapers, such as the *Lewiston Morning Tribune* (Fig. 13.30), run them

Opinion

Carter's approach to the refugees

Marianne Means / A look at Anderson's record

Hotel-union talks

The construction-conservation link

Editor's mail box

Carl Rowan / Hungering for a humane budget

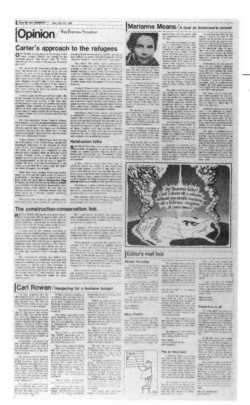

Fig. 13.29.

horizontally across the top of the page. The *Providence Journal* often takes the top half of the page for its editorials, which are set wider and larger than the columnist's copy (Fig. 13.31).

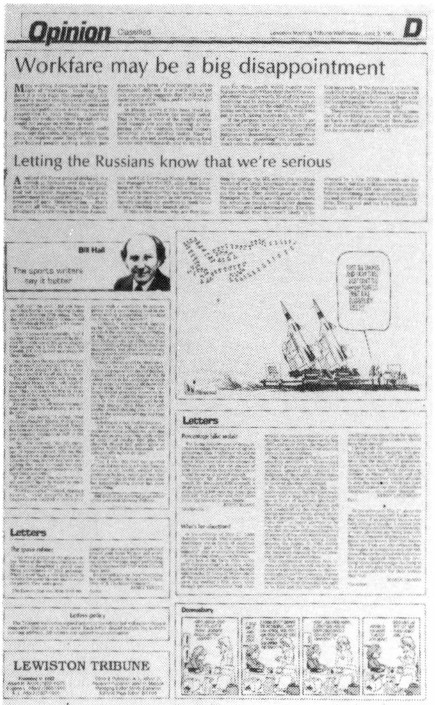
Opinion

D

Workfare may be a big disappointment

Letting the Russians know that we're serious

Bill Hall

The sports writers say it better

Letters

Doonesbury

LEWISTON TRIBUNE

Fig. 13.30.

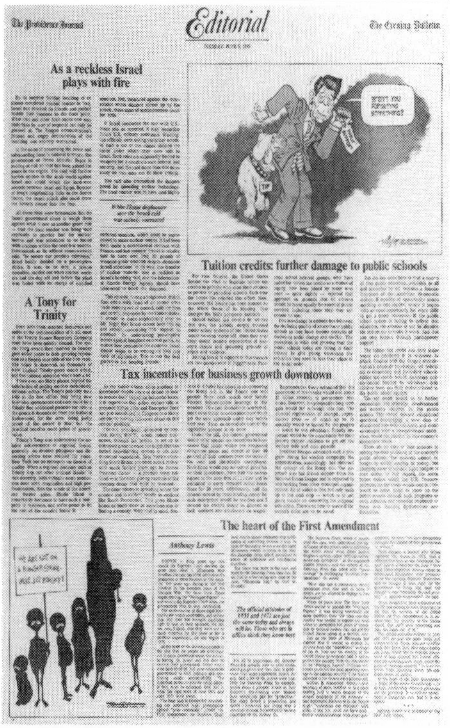
Editorial

As a reckless Israel plays with fire

A Tony for Trinity

Tuition credits: further damage to public schools

Tax incentives for business growth downtown

The heart of the First Amendment

Anthony Lewis

Fig. 13.31.

THE SPOKESMAN REVIEW
monday, feb. 2, 1981
page 4

opinion

'Well, all wasn't lost . . . I got him to sign my gun control petition!'

TOPIC A: Good for FAFB!

Fairchild Air Force Base, our military neighbor, makes front pages as **one of four** *Strategic Air Command bases chosen to host cruise missiles. They come to roost after Oct. 1, 1982. About 200 new personnel and $23.5 million in construction. Fairchild's a hefty next-door* **friend.** *"Economic impact" was $206,196,456 in '80. Fairchild folks are part of* **us** *; they live here. Now come missiles to live here, too. That's* **nothing to fear.** *Strong* **defenses serve peace.** *We've lived in peace with the B-52s. We'll live with the missiles, too.*

our views

Why we look different today

Today's Spokesman-Review has been printed on new presses, in a new plant and features a new typographical design.

As a result we hope you find today's paper easier and more attractive to read.

The new presses, plant and design are the latest of numerous changes we've undertaken during the last two years in order to provide a more modern and comprehensive newspaper.

The new design of the paper is characterized by a change of typeface in headlines, a change in the style for picture captions and bylines, a greater emphasis on presenting the news in a logical order and an increased use of summaries.

Part of the design, the Almanac package on Page 2, was instituted last month as a means of briefing readers on the morning's news, weather and sports. It also provides a quick look at what's happening to people on the move and gives readers tips on personal planning.

By consolidating the briefing on Page 2, the front page of the paper has been opened up so it can feature more stories and better display them.

The graphic device in the upper left corner of today's front page enables us to convey the most important news of the day in a telegraphic manner. A similar device on the Editorial Page, called Topic A, conveys a brief opinion on a current event demanding comment.

The editorial page has also been changed to enable us to better separate our editorial positions from the views of readers and syndicated columnists.

There are other changes: comic strips ("Dallas" premiered Sunday), an expanded sports staff, and new columnists to supplement the ones that have appeared regularly. Also, a new Sunday Spokesman-Review will debut February 8. It will feature the best—and, we think, biggest—Sunday comics section in the Northwest, a new home and garden section, a special TV viewing guide, the Ann Landers column and a separate section for local and regional news.

In making the changes, attention was given to keeping many things the same — our nameplate on Page One, for example.

Redesigning The Spokesman-Review was more than a matter of fashion or change for change's sake. In essence, it was another step toward continuing to achieve what Publisher William H. Cowles, 3rd has called the "fundamental purpose of the First Amendment", that of guaranteeing "an effective system of free expression."

Summary: Because there is always some resistance to change, we suspect that some readers may find the new design uncomfortable at first. We believe, however, they'll come to like it as much as those who will find it refreshing from the start.

THE SPOKESMAN-REVIEW

Founded 1883

William H. Cowles, 3rd, *Publisher*
Donald W. Gormley, *Managing Editor*
Dorothy R. Powers, *Editorial Page Editor*
John F. Phillips, *Asst. Managing Editor* — Shaun Higgins, *Asst. Managing Editor*
John E. Smithmeyer, *General Manager*
John P. Troyer, *Advertising Manager* — Norman Gervais, *Circulation Manager*

your views

Peck column 'petty'

This is a response to the petty, cynical and politically immature article that Chris Peck wrote on Jan. 27 concerning Ronald Reagan and what his presidency means to America. I, like Mr. Peck, have reservations about Mr. Reagan. However, I also have an understanding of why he was elected and why so many Americans are turning away from the politics of liberals and leftists.

People are tiring of the absurd changes liberals have wrought or appear to have wrought upon our society: a lower standard of living, increased taxation, strains upon the family, six million fetal deaths and forced busing are just a few of the reasons why. I believe, liberals and leftists are responsible for their own political demise.

The social consequences of their domestic politics and ideas are so repulsive and ridiculous that most Americans are driven into the waiting arms of conservative opportunists.

To conclude, if Mr. Peck wants liberal politics to be taken seriously by the populace, the traditional liberal social politics of the last decade must be abandoned. This is not a reversal to the 1950s but an admission that much of the politics of the left has been a mistake. We as a nation must preserve the positive aspects of our society and, simultaneously, seek change when change is in order.

Unfortunately, many of the changes this society has been forced to accept in the last decade have not been positive steps for the people as a whole — hence, the election of Ronald Reagan.

J.B. DELACOUR
Spokane

Commends S-R

I'm writing to you today in order to commend you for your news coverage of the Human Life organization's pro-life billboards and other activities a week or so ago. Additional publicity was added to our own effort by this action of yours.

MARY R. WIEMAN
Human Life board member
Spokane

Save colleges

I would like to respond to a recent letter from a man who thinks the solution for a balanced state budget lies in closing the community colleges.

Many of the people who attend these colleges do so because they cannot afford the high cost of a four-year college or university. The community colleges provide excellent training for trades and occupations including mechanics, carpentry and law enforcement, courses not always offered at other schools. Also, the community colleges' proximity makes them convenient for people who have transportation problems.

The main reason, however, is that they offer people careers, education and a chance for self-improvement. The closing of the colleges would only serve to slow the supply of qualified people entering the job market, while at the same time stifling the education of many people, people who pay to learn.

DEAN SPRAGUE
Student
Spokane Community College
Spokane

Asks Iranians why

I read Bart Preecs' story, "A glimpse of theirs . . .", about four Eastern Washington University Iranian students. Their perceptions of the hostage crisis are interesting. They are wondering why America intervened in Iran; they support "Khomeini cancer." One of them didn't seem to mind being beaten in Seattle.

I understand there are some 53,000 Iranians attending colleges and universities in this country — there must be many, many more Iranians who are U.S. citizens. Would I be a "redneck" if I asked why these Iranians are here going to school? Or why they became U.S. citizens?

GEORGE C. KREUTZER
Spokane

Angry at dent

Today I had the experience of finding a good-sized dent on my car which I didn't put there. I am mad at whoever did, since he or she didn't have the decency to leave a name and number. I am also mad because the three times I have bumped someone else's car I have left my name and number.

Sure, I have insurance, but my insurance company doesn't love getting claims. I feel like a chump because I'm so super honest I wouldn't think of doing what was done to me. I was brought up to believe that honesty is the best policy.

BELLE RITA ROBBINS
Spokane

Society has rights

I would like to make a comment on one of the last escapades of Dixy Lee Ray.

She found it necessary to commute the life sentences of eight convicted criminals. I am so sick and tired of hearing about the rights of criminals!

If someone commits a cold-blooded murder or other serious crime, he or she deserves the punishment set down by the laws of the land.

The only rights deserved in these cases are the rights of society to protect itself from these people.

RANDY WADE
Coeur d'Alene, Idaho

their views

Cranston criticizes presidential primary

Tom Wicker
New York Times

NEW YORK — Sen. Alan Cranston of California has proposed that no more than a third of the delegates to the next Democratic National Convention be elected in primaries and pledged to a particular candidate. That would move perhaps too far in the right direction.

Cranston has not been active in party reform movements. But a senator from the largest state, particularly one who was re-elected by 1.8 million votes in the teeth of the Reagan landslide, is likely to be listened to. It also appears probable that Charles Manatt of California will be elected the new Democratic national chairman, with Cranston's enthusiastic support — another reason why the senator's proposals carry weight.

Cranston insists that he was only throwing out one of many ideas that should be discussed by a party whose last two nominees were George McGovern and Jimmy Carter, and which suffered an election disaster in 1980. Nevertheless, in his speech to a California Democratic luncheon, he also delivered a severe indictment of "over-reliance" on primaries.

Primaries 'seldom test courage and never test wisdom.'

He conceded that primaries disclose something about a candidate's fund-raising and organizational abilities, his or her effectiveness on television and "electability" in specific situations. But primaries do not, he insisted, necessarily disclose whether a candidate can appeal to "the larger constituency" necessary for victory in a general election.

Nor, Cranston said, do primary victories necessarily demand of candidates the qualities needed by a president — for example, those required for dealing with Congress and "moving the national power structure." Primaries, he added, "seldom test courage and never test wisdom," and say little about "how good an educator of the American public a candidate would be as president."

Cranston's remedy would be to rescue the national convention from its present "empty symbolism" and make it a body capable of reaching "value judgments" and forming a consensus as to which candidate can best win election and lead the nation. He termed it "irresponsible" to abandon that process to the primaries.

Many Democrats, however, opted for primaries precisely because they came to see the national convention not as a representative body but as boss-dominated. Party reforms followed the 1968 convention, at which Hubert Humphrey was nominated without having entered a single primary; but in fact, the last multi-ballot convention in EITHER party was held by the Democrats in 1952 — 20 years before primaries began to dominate the nominating contests.

State primaries — 36 of them in 1980 — or caucus systems operating under the same rules of proportional representation and pledged delegates, were seen as means of achieving a more powerful popular voice in presidential nominations. To that end, they have worked well and it is unlikely that the Democratic Party would agree today to such a major rollback of the 1970s reforms as Cranston proposes.

He would divide the states and the District of Columbia into three groups of 17. One group would conduct binding primaries as at present; a second would select delegates through "various grass roots precinct or neighborhood meeting systems", and the third would leave delegate selection to the state parties. Only those delegates chosen in the primaries would be legally pledged to a particular candidate. The three groups of states would rotate delegate selection methods from one election to the next.

The senator's sensible aim is a national convention not bound by primary decisions, many taken months earlier in far different circumstances, and one able to reach a broad consensus on a party platform and nominee. But aside from the procedural difficulties of his three-group plan — who is going to force New Hampshire to give up its primary in two of every three election years? — many Democrats will balk at returning two-thirds of the delegates, as they are likely to see it, to organization control.

Do national party conventions need 'rescuing'?

Something like the convention Cranston envisions might more realistically be sought by leaving the states to choose their own delegate selection method under a national party rule providing that at least a third, and perhaps 40 percent, must not be pledged to any candidate. That would permit 60 to 67 percent of the delegates to be chosen by binding primary or caucus, if the states so chose; it would nevertheless demand of any winning candidate that he or she pull together a broad party consensus at the convention.

That might not always produce a winner. But it might more nearly to assure that a party nominee knows more about being president than just how to win primaries.

Tax reductions, spending cuts needed to tame inflation

New York Times

In his first news conference President Reagan could hardly have been more emphatic about his determination to control the inflation monster. "I do not intend to make wildly skyrocketing deficits and runaway government simple facts of life in this administration," he said. Instead, he will cut taxes and cut back government spending; no caretaker presidency for him. So much, then, for the back-room battling within his Cabinet over which to cut first, taxes or spending. The truth is that Reagan must do both. And the question is whether, even together, the cutbacks will do the job.

Lowering business taxes, as Reagan has proposed, WILL encourage investment and growth while dampening inflation. Cutting the budget — humanely — can calm fears of continuing inflation, and help hold down interest rates, which will also stimulate investment and growth. But Reagan still tenaciously advocates cutting billions out of personal income taxes for three years running.

Guest editorial

It is not his tenacity that is in question here, but his wisdom. For at a time when inflation is still untamed, such a tax cut risks making it worse. Any tax cut that is not aimed at encouraging anti-inflationary behavior is a wasted opportunity and a needless danger.

A wiser approach would be for the administration to conquer its ideological fear of using governmental power to influence wages and prices by cutting taxes more imaginatively. It may prefer to rely on the market; but in some sectors, the market needs help. Consider the auto industry, or steel. Large companies and big labor have managed to insulate themselves from competition for years, imposing inflationary prices and wages on the economy.

In general, though, the administration's first noises about budget cuts deserve encouragement. Feeling politically strong in their early days, the Reaganites appear willing to challenge sacred spending cows. The target list includes dairy price supports, future Social Security raises, federal pensions and Medicaid, trade adjustment assistance and extended unemployment benefits.

There will, and ought to be, argument about details and priorities, especially about protecting the weakest and poorest segments of society. But only a willingness to cut from every major constituency can overcome special pleading. If the wealthy are to give up subsidies, so must the middle classes.

Fig. 13.32.

The designer usually approaches the page by first anchoring the editorials and then the lead columnist, if there is one. The editorial cartoon often is the only art on the page. Most cartoons are horizontal; some, such as the popular Berry's World, are vertical. Letters to the editor should also be given good display.

Traditional news headlines are used on many editorial pages, but titles and labels are more appropriate to the content. Although blurbs and summaries are not often seen, their use should be considered. When the *Spokesman Review* in Spokane, Wash., was redesigned, the editors introduced a "Topic A" feature, a minieditorial in 18-pt. type (Fig. 13.32).

The masthead, which usually contains a listing of the top editors, the name of the paper, date and volume of publication, and sometimes the newspaper's creed, should be neat and space efficient. It can be placed at the top of the editorial columns or anchored at the bottom of the page (see Figs. 13.30, 13.32). Some newspapers have eliminated the masthead altogether.

BUSINESS. Business sections have become good business for newspapers. As a consequence, many newspapers have added pages or sections on the subject. Many have emulated the *Wall Street Journal*'s vertical format, but others have remained horizontal (Fig. 13.33). All have one problem in common—how to tell the stories visually.

Fig. 13.33.

Many editors think that stories dealing with numbers cannot use photographs or illustrations. However, it is precisely these stories that need the most help. The example set by *Fortune, Forbes,* and *Time* magazines, with their array of art, charts, and graphs, is proof enough that illustrations are helpful. The NEA illustration (Fig. 13.34) and the illustration from the *New York Times* Corn Belt story (Fig. 13.35) show what can be done to help readers understand a complicated story. In addition, a photo editor can point out many photographic opportunities for business stories.

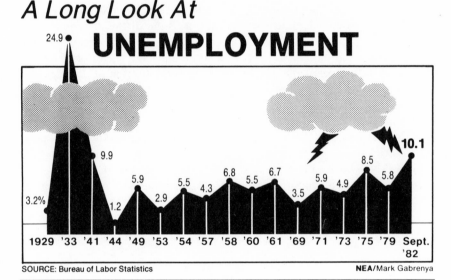

Fig. 13.34.

SPECIAL PROBLEMS. Formatting the agate stock listings is an important job for the designer. By its nature, this material presents problems of grayness. Like the sports and classified agate, it is not going to be "read" in the sense of story text; it is a reference. Columns should be narrower, but their width depends upon the amount of information on each line. Some newspapers run only the name of the stock, its price, and the change from the previous day. Others also include the number of shares traded and the high and low for the day. The designer's primary concern is breaking up the long columns of gray. The natural break is at each change of letter in the alphabet. The *Louisville Times* runs a white letter against a black strip. Other newspapers run a 2-pt. rule above and a 1-pt. rule below the letter. The *San Francisco Examiner* boldfaces the names of the stocks and lightfaces the numbers.

Business Day

The New York Times

BUSINESS Digest

The Economy

The I.C.C. denied railroads the authority to set freight rates collectively. It said the long-standing practice, which Congress sanctioned in 1948, stifled competition. Under the Reed Reform Act of 1976, railways must meet new competitive standards. The agency said shipping analysts predicted that some shippers would be disappointed, because they realized the order most likely would bring that the practice assured. [Page A1.]

Sales by the Big Three car makers dropped 31.1 percent in the first 10 days of August. Analysts said the slide was expected, and that customers were awaiting much-publicized 1981 models. Chrysler reported an 11.9 percent decline, G.M. 30.5 percent and Ford 40 percent, despite a quality incentive program. [D1.]

New York's seven biggest stores said sales climbed 9.6 percent in July, despite the month's heat and humidity. An influx of tourists helped retail sales. In the metropolitan area, the same retailers posted a 7.9 percent gain over comparable 1979 period. [D1.]

Savings bonds will no longer be touted as a good investment, the Treasury said. Responding to a complaint filed with the F.T.C. by a senior citizens' group, the Treasury said it would instead advertise the bonds as a means of regular saving. The complaint said that returns from inflation exceeded the bonds' yield of 7 percent. [D6.]

Companies

Proceedings against Paine Webber are being considered by both the S.E.C. and the New York Stock Exchange, the brokerage house disclosed, because of operational difficulties it experienced early this year. Paine Webber also reported a 14.7 percent earnings drop in the quarter ended June 30; revenues surged 68 percent. [D1.]

Merrill Lynch voiced interest in buying the Chicago White Sox, a major-league baseball team. R.S. Oleman, a vice president of Merrill, the nation's largest brokerage house, said the firm had not yet submitted a formal bid, but he had discussed buying the club for syndication with Bill Veeck, the White Sox president. The club would enjoy its six-year partnership in Chicago. [D13.]

Texaco and Mesa Petroleum agreed to form a partnership to explore for oil and gas on 1.9 million acres of undeveloped American leases held by Mesa. Texaco would put up $150 million in cash, while Mesa, a leading independent producer, would hold a 75 percent interest, put up the fund and operate the venture. The companies valued the six-year partnership at $600 million. [D1.]

G.E.'s voluntary price guidelines were raised by the Council on Wage and Price Stability to take the company's increased labor costs into account. In the first such move it has taken, the council raised G.E.'s home price ceiling, rather than losing the increase on profit margins, but it would not disclose the amount. [D6.]

The S.E.C. accepted a settlement offer from Playboy Enterprises, which it had accused of illegally failing to report more than $2 million in bribing and other benefits given to Hugh Hefner, its founder, and other officers. Without admitting guilt, Playboy agreed to undergo an internal shakeup and change its accounting procedures, and Mr. Hefner, his daughter and three executives have transferred the company more than $900,000 for the benefits. [D6.]

Burton Oil and Gas rejected an offer by Scopros Resources to "undercount and substantially harass" recent modification of its assets. Scopros, a Canadian company, however, reaffirmed its offer of $24 a share, or $196 million overall. [D6.]

Markets

The stock market's consolidation continued, with the Dow Jones industrial average slipping 3.16 to 903.23. Big Board volume contracted to 44.3 million shares. Computer issues were among the biggest losers. [D6.] Bond buyers shrugged off $400 million in corporate offerings, following Tuesday's successful sale of $500 million in Illinois Bell Telephone debentures. [D6.] The dollar strengthened against other major currencies, and gold rose $3 an ounce in New York to $645. [D6.] Cocoa and soybean futures prices slipped in Chicago, but livestock futures advanced. [D6.]

Today's Columns

The most promising solar-energy technology — photovoltaics — has been too expensive for general use. Now, Westinghouse and two California utilities are working toward the low-cost, high-efficiency production of such cells. Technology [D2.]

Is a speculative climate heating up in the current bull market? The appearance of new certain new issues suggests it is. For example, materials filed with the S.E.C. for the Digital Switch Corporation, written by John Muir & Company, list nine "special" and 17 "high" risks. Market Place. [D1.]

Index

Telecommunications Bill At Congress Crossroads

By ERNEST HOLSENDOLPH
Special to The New York Times

WASHINGTON, Aug. 13 — A watershed communications bill that would greatly expand the Bell System's area of business goes before the House next week when the conference report on the bill, has moved to the floor. [...]

(continued — text largely illegible)

Continued on Page D8

The Corn Belt's Costly Drought

Damage Likely To Force Rise In Food Prices

By H.J. MAIDENBERG
Special to The New York Times

HUDSON, Ill. — "Walking corn" has never been a pleasant task. While the lush green fields attract the eye, the choking heat generated by the closely planted crop, roughly 26,000 stalks an acre, can reach 120 degrees in August. This season, however, "walking corn" — going through the fields to check the progress of the crop — is a particularly distasteful duty for most corn growers, as they assess the damage inflicted by the drought.

The farm income squeeze of 1980:

The Farm Income Squeeze of 1980

<table>
<tr><th>COSTS</th><th>1980</th><th>1979</th></tr>
<tr><td>Seed</td><td>$ 17.10</td><td>$ 17.40</td></tr>
<tr><td>Fertilizers</td><td>61.69</td><td>68.64</td></tr>
<tr><td>Herbicides</td><td>12.77</td><td>11.85</td></tr>
<tr><td>Insecticides</td><td>8.82</td><td>7.93</td></tr>
<tr><td>Hail Insurance</td><td>5.50</td><td>5.50</td></tr>
<tr><td>Combining</td><td>8.00</td><td>8.20</td></tr>
<tr><td>Drying Corn</td><td>24.00</td><td>26.24</td></tr>
<tr><td>OPERATING COSTS</td><td>$137.88</td><td>$145.76</td></tr>
<tr><td>Real Estate Taxes</td><td>34.00</td><td>29.84</td></tr>
<tr><td>TOTAL COSTS</td><td>$171.88</td><td>$175.60</td></tr>
<tr><th>INCOME</th><th></th><th></th></tr>
<tr><td>Gross Income*</td><td>$270.00</td><td>$487.20</td></tr>
<tr><td>Less Costs</td><td>171.88</td><td>175.60</td></tr>
<tr><td>Income per acre</td><td>$ 98.12</td><td>$311.60</td></tr>
<tr><td>Times 250 acres</td><td>$24,530</td><td>$77,900</td></tr>
</table>

*These figures are based on a yield of 174 bushels an acre times $2.50 a bushel.

(article continues, largely illegible)

Continued on Page D4

Paine Webber Is Facing S.E.C., Exchange Action

By ROBERT J. COLE

Paine Webber Inc., parent company of Paine Webber Jackson & Curtis, the nation's fourth-largest stockbroker, disclosed in a statement yesterday that both the Securities and Exchange Commission and the New York Stock Exchange were "considering possible proceedings" against the company in an outgrowth of its highly publicized operational difficulties early this year.

(article continues, largely illegible)

Continued on Page D4

10-Day Auto Sales Drop 31.1%

Announcements On 1981 Models Called a Factor

Special to The New York Times

DETROIT, Aug. 13 — Sales of new American-made cars fell 31.1 percent below last year's pace in the first 10 days of August, according to the nation's Big Three auto manufacturers.

(article continues, largely illegible)

Continued on Page D4

Texaco in Oil Accord With Mesa

By ANTHONY J. PARISI

Texaco Inc., the nation's third-largest oil company, and the Mesa Petroleum Company, a leading independent producer, announced yesterday that they had agreed to form a six-year partnership to explore for oil and gas on some 1.9 million acres of undeveloped leases held by Mesa in the United States.

(article continues, largely illegible)

Continued on Page D4

New Respect for Remainders

By N. R. KLEINFIELD

To authors, they appear to be indisputable evidence that the work is against them. To publishers, they are a painless way of unloading books that have run out of steam. And to the public, they are unexpected bargains.

Remainders — those books with reduced prices that remove un-worthy titles in the lives of bookstores — are coming into their own. Long snubbed by booksellers as unwanted items, remainders have won new respectability in recent years. Now that the torpid economy and rising book prices have kept many new titles glued to retail shelves, more and more bookstores are greeting remainders as if they were Care packages.

(article continues, largely illegible)

Alan Mirken, left, president, and Robert McGee, Outlet Books sales chief

Continued on Page D8

Fig. 13.35.

ENTERTAINMENT. When form follows content, entertainment sections are more informal and more relaxed than news pages but still are part of the newspaper family. More informal sometimes means a lower story count and larger pictures, but is also can mean a series of short, bright items, often illustrated with humorous cartoons. News-style headline formats are not used, and the copy and graphics are more personal.

A *San Francisco Examiner* page illustrates this informality (Fig. 13.36). The main story has a title, not a headline. There are only two stories, and one of them is a "Pie in the Sky" gag story that is set ragged right. Although the section has a different personality, the top-of-the-page logo is consistent with the style in the rest of the paper.

Fig. 13.36.   *Fig. 13.37.*

"Weekend" (Fig. 13.37), a cover for an entertainment and recreation section, is a poster front, and the design is not as busy as that found in the news pages. The "Weekend" logo is larger than other sectional logos, but is in the same typeface.

The Allentown *Call-Chronicle*'s "TV/Entertainment" page (Fig. 13.38) combines the slower-paced story count with the high-element count in the neatly packaged TV preview. The page makes excellent use of rules, reverses, and screens for page contrast.

Newsday's cover for its entertainment section is a startling change of pace (Fig. 13.39). Unity is achieved by picking up the hairline boxes from the rest of the publication, but the cover is used for a series of short, snappy reader items on things to do, and the page is anchored with teasers to inside material.

Fig. 13.38.

Fig. 13.39.

SPECIAL PROBLEMS. Both the *Call-Chronicle* and *Newsday* examples illustrate solutions to a problem common to many weekend sections—how to handle the many briefs. The *Call-Chronicle* divided the highlights column of its TV preview into categories. The boxed schedule is clean and easy to read. The reverse label and screen over the print, permissible here because it is a reference feature rather than a reader item, give the page needed weight at the bottom. *Newsday* packaged four upcoming events with pictures and short descriptions in a series of four boxes. This is a device that also works well for broadsheet papers. The pictured items can be used to lead a larger package that includes line items.

Calendars, often found in entertainment sections, present designers with the challenge of presenting columns of information in a graphically pleasing manner. The *Call-Chronicle* solves this problem by relying on oversized dates and headings to break up the gray (Fig. 13.40). Oversizing the dates also forces a bank of white space into the columns. Other devices to break up gray columns are discussed later in this chapter.

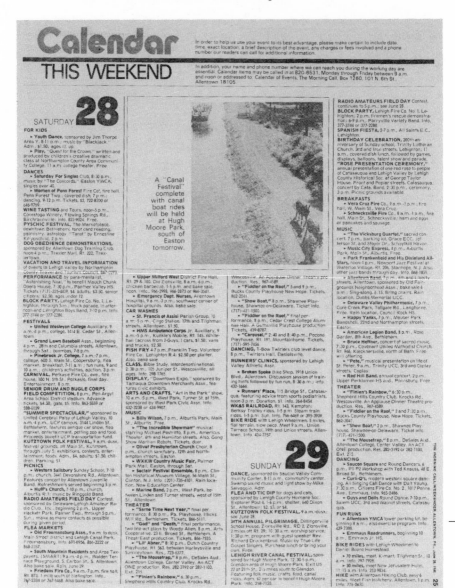

Promoting the paper

Selling the content of the paper is becoming an increasingly popular as well as necessary function of the editorial department. Page 1 teasers are usually placed across the top of the page or anchored at the bottom. The location depends on how the newspaper is trying to market itself. Papers that have significant newsstand sales often run the teasers over the top; those located in smaller communities with insignificant newsstand sales can move the teasers to the bottom of the page. In either location, it is generally better to lay out the teasers in a horizontal format to make them less intrusive on the body of the news page. For papers that have limited access to news pictures, the bottom-of-the page teaser box serves as a needed visual anchor.

The following guidelines should be observed:

1. Be careful not to let the teaser feature get too deep. Two inches, from top rule to bottom rule, is about maximum. If the teaser feature is at the top of the page, a depth of more than two inches will push the flag and the lead story too deep into the page and counteract whatever advantage the teaser might provide on the newsstand.

2. Teasers appearing above the flag should be boxed to provide a visual border at the top and set them off from the flag.

3. Do not try to jam too many items into the space available. Keep it simple. This is essentially a billboard.

4. Do not overuse special effects. Photography and artwork should be used, but silhouettes and special screens for photographs can be overdone. This is a quick-check reader feature, not a freak show.

5. Bold, extrabold, and bold condensed type are effective for titles because they can be downsized and still retain impact. Use lighter faces for the details.

6. Do not get too predictable. The format should not be so static that the teasers look the same every day, or the readers will soon regard them as a reference point instead of a reader feature.

The *Seattle Times* runs a typical over-the-top promotion box (Fig. 13.41). It is uniquely theirs because of the AM logo and fold at the left. Bold and light type provide contrast. The AM logo and 14-pt. rule at the bottom, which gives a shadow box effect because it does not extend to either end of the box, is run in color.

The *Columbia Missourian*'s teasers provide a strong visual tug to the bottom of the page (Fig. 13.42). Because the teasers are designed for readers who already have the paper, text instead of display type is used to sell the stories.

Fig. 13.40.

AM
SATURDAY

HOTEL STRIKE
Tearful employees
were outside;
paychecks inside
D 12

SPORTS
Barker holds
M's to 5 hits
in 8-1 win
D 1

WEATHER
Some rain, a little sun.
High, mid-60s; low, lower 50s.
Details, A 11

The Seattle Times

Washington's largest newspaper

Copyright, 1981, Seattle Times Company

SATURDAY
June 6, 1981
★★ 58 pages
25¢

Reagan human-rights nominee withdraws

3 Queen Anne generations

Enid Lair takes a picture of her husband's relatives — three generations of Queen Anne graduates.

Staff photo by Alan Berner

Decades of grads to bid school good-bye

By Don Duncan
Times staff reporter

From city, town and suburb the alumni will come at 2 p.m. today — thousands strong — to pay their last respects to the sandstone columns at Third Avenue North and Galer Street, for 72 years the home of the ancient and gold and just of the ferocious Grizzlies.

They'll talk — these old Queen Anne High School grads — of Otto Luther, who opened the school in English and reigned as principal 16 years, and of George Farmer, who was born for the next 16.

They'll speak of the athletic exploits of Edo Vanni, Bob Hastings and Steve Anderson, the cartooning skill of Hank Owens the Monaco Ketchum, the musical skills of Jackie Souders, who wrote the lyrics of the school song, and of strength & students who did OK, and of it, students who became captains of industry.

They'll be joined by the Class of '81, fresh from commencement exercises at the Seattle Center, who will add their own memories of what it's like to finish one's senior year in a school to be closed forever.

Many vintage Quays will walk around until the doors finally are closed at midnight. They will look across the street, at the muddy athletic field, and wonder where the Grizzly fire has gone, and look up the street and recall spending their lunch money at Ping's.

Three generations of Queen Anne High graduates from one family gathered on the sidewalk yesterday to talk about the school, symbolic of the continuity that is about to be broken by dwindling enrollments and demographics. They included:

Catherine Lair Van Brunt, the Class of '19, who was on the campus from and played basketball in bloomers and a middy blouse and met her late husband, Edward, in the halls. And, yes, she remembers. The lovely trees across the street and how beautiful and white the building was and how clean they kept it — there.

Jack Lair, Catherine's younger brother, Class of '24, who lived a block from the school and "got a good education" and then wound up marrying Enid, a girl from Broadway High, which had its own chance some years ago.

Gaene Van Stone Findlay, Catherine's daughter,

Class of '41, trim and smart-looking with beautifully coiffed grey hair, who was an honor student and active in the Girls' Club and remembers "the lasting friendship and how everybody was going to Queen Anne."

Andrea Angus Findlay, Gaene's husband and classmate of her Uncle Jack, Class of '52, who recalled it as "a comfortable school — I hate to see it go."

Sally Lair McCrilis, daughter of Jack, Class of '51, who gets "goosebumps just thinking about the school being closed; it's a part of our lives; we've always lived on Queen Anne."

Shelly McCrilis Nelson, daughter of Sally and Frank McCrilis, class of '79, who was "into journalism and drama," and who will never forget her roles in "The Boy Friend" and "Hello Keller."

Shelly brought her two daughters, Jennifer, 4, and Heidi, 2.

"We thought they'd go here, too, as part of the tradition," said their mother. "Now they won't."

The girls didn't seem to mind.

But they were the only ones who didn't.

Lefever acts after rejection by committee

Compiled from news services

WASHINGTON — Ernest Lefever, stinging at his critics even in defeat, withdrew as President Reagan's nominee for the assistant secretary of state for human rights yesterday after his rejection by the Senate Foreign Relations Committee.

"I do not wish any longer to put up with the kind of suspicion and character assassination that some of my adversaries have used to besmirch my name," he said in a letter to Mr. Reagan, who remained a staunch supporter and who was surprised by the withdrawal.

"I am so weary of the charges and innuendos against my integrity and my compassion," Lefever wrote.

The committee voted, 13 to 4, against Lefever's nomination. Five of the committee's nine Republicans, including the chairman, Senator Charles Percy of Illinois, sided with the committee's eight Democrats.

At issue were Lefever's statements that he would be more tolerant of human-rights abuses in countries friendly to the United States, his ties with Nestle Corp., a leading exporter of infant formula to Third World countries, and his reported statements to two brothers that blacks were genetically inferior to whites.

It was the first time in 41 years that a Senate committee had rejected a presidential nominee and the action stunned Lefever's chances for Senate approval.

After the committee vote, Senators Howard Baker of Tennessee, S.I. Hayakawa of California and Jesse Helms of North Carolina met for an hour and decided it would be best not to try a full Senate fight, where the nomination faced almost certain defeat. All were Republican supporters of the nomination.

Reaction to Lefever's withdrawal was immediate.

The White House said that Mr. Reagan "reaffirmed his confidence in the integrity and competence of Dr. Lefever."

The State Department said "We regret that this matter has occurred, but we respect Dr. Lefever's wishes. We were unaware of his plans and we were not asked about them in advance of his decision."

Eric Bochstette, coordinator of the Washington-based Ad Hoc Committee of the Human Rights Community, called the withdrawal "a resounding victory for human rights across the world."

Senator Edward M. Kennedy, Massachusetts Democrat, said Lefever "acted wisely (because in reality) he did not demonstrate the sensitivity and commitment required to carry out the duties of this office."

"He is a great patriot," Hayakawa said of Lefever. "He has been a deep commitment to human rights. I am sorry that he will not be serving in the position to which the President has appointed him. Our government has lost a potentially great public servant."

Senator Nancy Kassebaum, a Kansas Republican who voted against Lefever, said she hoped him until he was questioned at a hearing Thursday. She said she became convinced then that he was not the right man for the job. "The job requires a great deal of sensitivity and skillful diplomatic ability," she said.

Oversupply: Pharmacy study may be cut at W.S.U.

by Julie Emery
Times education reporter

A state study has recommended that the college of pharmacy at Washington State University be eliminated as part of a dollar-saving move in an era of pharmacist oversupply in the state.

The University of Washington would have the state's only pharmacy college under the controversial proposal made by the staff of the state Council for Postsecondary Education.

The study grew out of a report on pharmacies the two universities gave the

enacted about 18 months ago. The plan would reduce the present annual total of 140 graduates to 100.

Gail Norris, the education council's executive coordinator, said the recommendations give strong support for development of a new doctoral pharmacology-toxicology program, focusing on the effects of pesticides on plant and animal life, at Pullman.

W.S.U. regents and Dr. Glenn Terrell, university president, reacted immediately, saying they strongly oppose the plan as dismantling the Pullman college and incorporating it in the U.W. program.

Terrell said he will present W.S.U.'s

case to citizen members of the council's academic-affairs committee Wednesday at The Evergreen State College. The full council will consider the matter Thursday.

"We are not going to give in on this issue," Terrell said. "It has been documented in every turn that our program is one of the finest and most cost-effective in the nation."

He said the council's cost study shows that at W.S.U. it costs $3,686 a year to educate a student, compared to $4,391 at the U.W.

He noted that W.S.U. as just completing the total remodeling of teaching and re-

search facilities in Wegner Hall to accommodate the full pharmacy program, which graduates nearly 80 students each year.

W.S.U. pharmacy graduates are providing an important service for the citizens of this Washington which would be seriously threatened by the proposal, Terrell said.

Norris said a switch to one college eventually would serve the state about $700,000 a year. He said the change should be done with extreme care over a phase-out of several years.

After the council makes its decision the plan it recommends will be presented to regents of the two schools.

Talks to resume today in hotel-restaurant strike

Compromise offered by union

by Svein Gilje
Times staff reporter

Striking hotel and restaurant workers and their employers will return to the bargaining table today, five days after the walkout began.

Doug Hammond, federal mediator, called a session for 10 a.m., hoping for a conciliation based on development yesterday, when the union put forth a compromise proposal.

Hammond called the meeting as 2,000 to 3,000 workers were striking more than two dozen hotels and restaurants in Seattle and along the Seattle-Tacoma Airport strip.

The call came after Marco Vaticano, union business manager, warned that the strike could go on "indefinitely" if talks are not restarted. No one was backed up

by James K. Bender, executive secretary of the King County Labor Council, who said organized labor in the area will become "tougher and tougher as we go down the line" of the dispute.

The union's compromise proposal called for wage increases generally between 10 and 12 per cent in the next year. The union leaders also agreed to submit to binding arbitration on wages in the second and third years of the unexpired new contract.

There was no immediate comment from the employers.

The employees, whose contract expired at midnight Sunday, started walking out at 2 a.m. Tuesday, gradually closing establishments. Eventually 2,000 to 3,000 could be on strike if there is no settlement.

Struck as of yesterday were the Benson, Camlin Hotel, Dog House,

HOTEL STRIKE
The fifth day

Edgewater Inn, Executive Inn, Four Seasons Olympic, Hyatt House and Four's Acres of Oasis and Salmon, Drive-Ins, Salmon House and Captain's Table.

Others being struck were Jet Inn, Sea-Tac Red Lion Inn, King's Inn's 400 and The Other Place, Sherwood Inn, Sixth Avenue Motel, Space Needle, Towne

Manor Hotel, University Tower, Vance Hotels (Sheraton and airport), Washington Athletic Club, Washington Plaza and Wharf.

One of the sticky issues, the control over gratuities, should be left unchanged from the old contract, which expired at midnight Sunday, said Rhonda Alguire, secretary-treasurer of Local 8.

The union's proposal calls for wages increases over the next 12 months amounting to:

Dining room and food service — 10 per cent increase in all classifications (for hotel waiters and waitresses on regular shift it would boost them to $3.47 an hour).

Beverage service — 10 per cent, for all classifications (for bartenders serving hard liquor it would go to $6.87).

Kitchen — 12 per cent, all classifications ($6.85 for dinner cook).

Hotel service — 72.5 per cent

for all employees (room attendants, housekeepers, laundry) with one or more years of service ($5.50 steady on regular shift); 10.7 per cent for those with less than a year.

Hotel maintenance workers and operating engineers — 12 per cent ($8.66 for maintenance worker).

In all other classifications, the union calls for a 10 per cent increase.

The union pledged not to strike (in return for no lockouts) in the wage negotiations for the second and third year should there would be total reliance on binding arbitration if negotiations failed to produce agreements by June 8 of each year.

The union also asked two additional, floating holidays, but dropped a demand that sick leave, if asked additional vacation time, going to three weeks after eight years of service and four after 15.

Fig. 13.41.

Headline strip teasers (Fig. 13.43) are brasher. They are effective on Page 1 to attract newsstand sales, but here they are used to promote an inside section. These teasers use white type against a gray background; white against black is also effective if it does not unbalance the page.

Fig. 13.42.   Fig. 13.43.

Relieving grayness

Some stories are like the Great Wall of China; they go on forever. The Great Gray Mass is a forbidding sight even to a willing reader. Several devices can be used to break up the gray. Some provide visual relief; others also tease the reader. Among the possibilities are:

1. Blurbs. Used primarily to tease the reader, blurbs also provide visual relief. Usually set in 14- or 18-pt. type, they should be set off by rules. The

weight depends on the overall design of the paper. The Allentown *Call-Chronicle*'s design is bold and uses 4-pt. rules over and under its blurbs (Fig. 13.44). Figures 13.45 and 13.46 show less traditional ways of handling blurbs.

CDC links tampon use to toxic shock syndrome

ATLANTA (AP) — The use of tampons has been linked to a rare disease called toxic shock syndrome that primarily affects young women, but preliminary studies show no reason for most women to discontinue tampon use, national health officials said yesterday.

The Center for Disease Control reported the results of three studies of the syndrome, a sometimes fatal disease characterized by high fever, vomiting, diarrhea, a sunburn-like rash and a rapid drop in blood pressure, which frequently results in shock.

Ninety-three women who had the disease were included in the three studies, which were conducted by federal and state health officials in Wisconsin and Utah. Of the women surveyed, 92 regularly used tampons, CDC officials said in their Morbidity and Mortality Weekly Report.

Since 1978, 128 cases of toxic shock syndrome have been reported, with 10 resulting in death, the officials said.

The federal agency said most cases of toxic shock syndrome occur in women under 25, and more than 90 percent begin during the menstrual period. But the report said a small number of cases have been identified in men.

Dr. Kathryn Shands, an epidemiologist with the center, said researchers have not determined exactly how tampon use is related to the disease, although tampons may "provide a good culture medium" for bacteria.

Earlier studies have indicated the syndrome may be caused by a toxin associated with Staphylococcus aureus, the common bacterium which causes pus to form in boils and abcesses, the federal report said.

"Because we expect only a small number of women to get the disease, we are suggesting that women not discontinue tampon use unless they have had toxic shock syndrome already," she said.

The center's report added, however, that women "who wish to decrease their small risk of TSS may choose to use tampons during only part of their menstrual period or to use napkins or minipads instead."

. . . The use of tampons might favor growth of the (toxic) bacterium in the vagina or absorption of the toxin from the vagina or uterus — but these possibilities have not been investigated.

Dr. Kathryn Shands
CDC epidemiologist

Women who have had the disease should refrain from using tampons for at least several menstrual cycles after their illness, Dr. Shands said. Antibiotics can be used to reduce the risk of recurrence.

No particular brand of tampon has been associated with the disease, the CDC said.

Dr. Shands said 2-15 percent of American women may carry the Staphylococcus aureus bacterium in their bodies, but "we don't know why some of them get sick and some don't."

Health officials do not recommend testing for the bacterium unless a woman has shown symptoms of toxic shock syndrome, she said. Women who believe they

Fig. 13.44.

Study finds women tending to stay in 'traditional fields'

By FRANCES CERRA
© New York Times

NEW YORK — Although the number of women enrolled in law, medical and business schools has been increasing dramatically in recent years, most college women are still studying for traditionally female occupations where jobs are scarce and relatively low-paid, according to a recently published study.

The study, conducted by Pearl M. Kamer, the chief economist for the Long Island Regional Planning Board, and published in a recent edition of *The New York Statistician*, concludes that if women "continue to cling to traditional, female-intensive professions," the gap between their earnings and those of male college graduates will remain wide.

According to 1978 figures compiled by the U.S. Census Bureau, the average female college graduate working full-time earned 60 percent of the salary of a man with the same education.

Miss Kamer reported that this gap was likely to continue well into the 1980s. A.J. Jaffe, special senior research associate at the Columbia University Graduate School of Business, developed projections indicating that in 1987, 71 percent of all doctoral degrees earned by women would still be in such fields as education, library science, fine and applied arts, English and foreign languages.

The author of the study says there is a need for a 'major push to guide women into faster-growing "nontraditional" professions such as mathematics, economics, business and the physical sciences.'

Miss Kamer said in an interview that she had been surprised by her findings. "We tend to focus on the exceptional women as role models, but this obscures the fact that most women are not moving into traditionally male fields rapidly," she said.

As a result, Miss Kamer asserted in her article, there was a need for a "major push to guide women into faster-growing 'nontraditional' professions such as mathematics, economics, business and the physical sciences."

Miss Kamer's study documents the presence of more and more women on college campuses, both as undergraduates and graduates.

Between 1950 and 1976, the number of female college graduates increased by almost 400 percent, while the

Fig. 13.45.

Senile conditions often misdiagnosed in elderly

By Brenda Stewart
Missourian staff writer

Edith Jansen is 75 years old. When her husband died several years ago, she moved in with her daughter.

Lately she has been having a difficult time recalling events and facts. She often wakes up in the middle of the night confused about the time, date and place. She no longer enjoys shopping or visiting with her friends.

Mrs. Jansen's children are concerned about her depression and poor memory. They watch her closely, reading more into her behavior than is really there. She realizes she is ill and is afraid that her family will not want to take care of her.

Mrs. Jansen is one of the 15 percent of people over 65 in this country who are affected by senile dementia, a condition affecting the elderly which impairs thinking and causes personality changes.

Fifteen percent of the people over 65 in this country are affected by senile dementia, a condition which impairs thinking and causes personality changes. Amnesia is a common symptom of dementia along with a general disorientation concerning place and time. Other warning signs are lack of initiative and lack of interest in activities outside the home.

Bartling. "There is less concern for the underlying cause of the depression. It is assumed they are depressed just because they are old."

The misdiagnosis of symptoms brought about by the multiple use of drugs by some elderly persons also is a serious problem. "They may be taking drugs their doctor gives them along with drugs their friends give them," Bartling says. "This use of multiple drugs may very well produce symptoms that are diagnosed as senile dementia. It is a very real problem with the elderly."

Bartling says families of the elderly should understand that "the longer the person can remain active, the less likely problems will develop." He also recommends regular physical checkups with a doctor who is aware of emotional problems in the elderly.

But when problems occur, Bartling advises consulting several doctors and considering differences in diagnoses.

Fig. 13.46.

Blurbs should never extend over more than one column of the story's setting. When they do, some readers will incorrectly decide to return to the next column of type rather than jumping over the blurb. The same problem occurs when you drop a photograph wider than one column into the body of the story.

2. White space. When you have a long story, it may be possible to put additional white space at the right or left margins. (Blurbs can be placed in this additional space.) Additional space can also be built in between paragraphs every few inches.

3. Inset cap letters. Columns of gray can be broken up effectively by starting out a paragraph with a capital letter, normally in 30- or 36-pt. type of the same face as the headline. With inset cap letters, the first line of copy reads out of the top of the letter. The *Kansas City Star* starts all its stories in this manner (Fig. 13.47).

Fig. 13.47.

4. Rising cap letters. The first line of copy reads out of the bottom of the letter and creates an additional band of white space at the point of the letter. The rising cap is especially useful on long stories.

5. Rules. A simple cutoff rule, shortened so that it does not cross the entire column (jim dash), can provide visual relief in a subtle way. If the design for the story is elegant, a simple hairline with white space built around it may suffice. If the design is bolder, a 4- or 8-pt. rule may work better.

6. Photo takeouts. A headshot of someone in the story, with a quote, can be effective both as visual relief and as a teaser. The example in Figure 13.48 emphasizes black and white, and that technique is picked up in the rising cap. If less contrast is desired, a screen can be used.

Fig. 13.48.

registered nurses in south central Missouri, an area facing a tremendous growth in population. The 14 students who have been accepted into the Mizzou nursing program are spending their first two years of baccalaureate education at Rolla. Their last two years of study will be done at Mizzou, but the students will return to their home areas to get learning experiences in community nursing, senior nursing and mental health nursing with the hope that the nurses will live there after graduation.

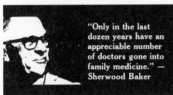

"Only in the last dozen years have an appreciable number of doctors gone into family medicine." — Sherwood Baker

Providing a health care "bargain" for 150 families in five counties (Audrain, Boone, Callaway, Cole and Cooper) is a community nursing outreach program, sponsored jointly by the School of Nursing and the Missouri Division of Health. In this program, about 50 community nursing students and faculty members make an estimated 2,000 home visits per semester, as well as work with school or community groups and participate in activities of existing community health care and social agencies.

NOTHER WAY nursing is lending a helping hand to rural health is through graduate education programs. Courtney hopes Mizzou graduates will "strengthen faculty in other nursing schools in Missouri."

die, I would list the manufacturer and the expected price.
4) Using the above, establish a five-year projection on sales and potential profits, which would include the most important item of all, a cash flow budget.
5) Finally, having dealt with money people before, I knew they would want a complete list of my personal assets and liabilities.

Organizing the business plan

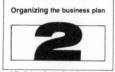

All of the above data became the outline of my business plan—a road map with which I could approach both the manufacturers and the money lenders in my attempt to go into business.
The first step was to broaden the objectives into a market plan. This sub-plan to the master business plan would detail the approach we would take to reach and sell the market we had decided to capture.

Fig. 13.49.

publisher, especially in areas of accounting and engineering.
b) The industrial trade magazine in the higher scientific disciplines. Here earlier experience as a production manager on industrial trade magazines would allow me to relate to the problems of schedule and content that the publisher faced.
c) Journals dealing specifically with the medical and professional field, including accounting and engineering.
The next step, in conjunction with the market plan, was to forecast the current size of the market and project its growth for the next five to 10 years. This was necessary to encourage the money lenders to advance the needed capital for equipment and machinery. For basic industry statistics we used those of the U.S. Dept. of Commerce and the annual industry review of INLAND PRINTER.
We were now ready to project share-of-market and growth for the next five years, and more importantly, could relate these numbers to the total market. This approach provided the necessary credibility for the business plan as well as the

7. Subheads. Traditionally run in the same size as text type but boldfaced, subheads are more effective on long stories if they are boldfaced in 10- or 12-pt. type.

8. Invent your own. The possibilities are endless. One enterprising graphics editor who was working with a story that had five steps designed

a series of copy breakers that not only broke up the grayness but also delineated each step (Fig. 13.49).

Bylines

Bylines help readers make the transition from the headline type to the text. There are several possibilities, some of which are shown here. The byline style that is selected should be harmonious with the overall style of the paper. Do not, for example, use a thick and thin line over and under a byline unless the overall design is black and white. Unity is the controlling principle.

There are two general guidelines for all bylines:

1. Flush left is best because we read from left to right. A style that runs bylines flush right is an affectation done without regard for readership patterns. However, if headlines are centered, it would make sense to center bylines.

2. Bylines normally are larger than text type. The size differentiation provides contrast and eases the transition from headline to text. Contrast can also be achieved by using a different form such as sans serif if the text is serif. In that instance, size differentiation is not necessary. The examples in Figure 13.50 illustrate several possibilities.

		By Gary Roets Staff Writer
By GARY ROETS Staff writer	**By Gary Roets** **Staff Writer**	*By Gary Roets* *Staff writer*
BY GARY ROETS Staff Writer	**by Gary Roets** staff writer	**By Gary Roets** *Staff Writer*

Fig. 13.50.

Column logos

If you opened your local paper every day and saw a variety of column logos like that in Figure 13.51, you would probably wonder if anybody at the newspaper was reading it. Designers rely on column logos (also known as sigs and standing sigs) to achieve unity, create a personality for writers,

Fig. 13.51.

and help readers locate standing features. Because these three functions are critical to the success of a newspaper, designers spend a lot of time working on logos.

Good logos reflect the marketing philosophy of the newspaper. If the newspaper is trying to develop and sell personalities, the logos should contain a picture of the writer. If the newspaper is not trying to establish a personal relationship between reader and writer, a logo of type only is sufficient.

Good logos that are used correctly help guide the reader through the newspaper. They should be used as locators, not headlines. Headlines attract the casual and infrequent reader to the content of a specific column; logos identify the feature for the faithful readers. The phenomenon is not unlike highway travelers who look for the billboard of a specific hotel chain. For some, the billboard is sufficient; others take a look at the motel itself before they decide whether to stay.

Logos also unify the newspaper. A consistent logo style identifies the paper to subscribers no matter which section they pick up. This consistency is one more indication that the editors are in control of the product. Inconsistency, whether in writing, editing, or graphics style, damages credibility. Some newspapers, particularly large ones, have different logo styles in different sections. Variation on a logo theme is a better approach than completely changing the style.

When designing column logos, five considerations should be kept in mind.

1. Size. Logos should be compact. They have more in common with the Izod alligator than a neon sign.

2. Flexibility. Are they proportioned so they can be set in 1, 1½, and 2 columns? Normally, 1-column logos are slightly wider than they are deep, and larger ones should be horizontal rectangles.

3. Marketing. If you are trying to sell the name of the column, emphasize it. If you are trying to sell the author, use a photograph. Column logos without pictures are not as warm or personal as those with them. Even artists' realistic renderings of authors are less personal than pictures. Caricatures convey humor and informality.

4. Reproduction. Because most newspapers are offset now, reproduction is less of a problem, but even offset newspapers must produce fresh logos on a regular schedule. Most pictures in column logos are Veloxes, a screened photograph that is pasted on the page. Eventually, they get muddy and must be replaced. Some newspapers use special-effect screens, often to produce high-contrast pictures. At most large newspapers, column logos are produced through the VDT system, which provides new copies easily.

5. Personality. Design of the column logos should be consistent with the design of other standing elements (such as the nameplate and sectional logos) and the tone of the publication. A bold publication, one that emphasizes blacks and whites, would use bold type and bold rules in the logos. A grayer publication would use lighter type and rules.

The column logos shown in Figures 13.52 through 13.60 illustrate the variety of marketing approaches and personalities that can be created.

Bold type and rules are consistent with the *Los Angeles Herald Examiner*'s design (Fig. 13.52). The logo does not permit the reader to make contact with the author.

CAROLE HEMINGWAY

Fig. 13.52.

Bold type and rules are combined with a photograph in a space-efficient logo from the *St. Petersburg Times* (Fig. 13.53).

FOREIGN NEWS EDITOR

WILBUR G. LANDREY

Fig. 13.53.

The *Minneapolis Tribune* uses a three-sided box throughout the paper in all its graphic elements (Fig. 13.54). This technique gives editors unlimited flexibility in changing column widths. The photo is a line shot, a picture without halftone dots.

Fig. 13.54.

The *Charleston* (W.Va.) *Gazette* emphasizes the columnist's name over the column title (Fig. 13.55). The picture is a posterization, a technique in which white and black is combined with only one middle tone. The result is a picture that looks grainy. The *Gazette*'s format is flexible.

Fig. 13.55.

The *Arizona Daily Star* combines a line shot with a name in a simple and space-efficient logo (Fig. 13.56). Reproduction of line shots, even in offset newspapers, is not particularly good, however.

Fig. 13.56.

The *San Antonio Express* personalizes its columns with a halftone and name in a light logo (Fig. 13.57).

Fig. 13.57.

The Baltimore *News-American*'s tight cropping on the columnist makes him look threatening (Fig. 13.58). The thick and thin lines are consistent with the paper's design.

Fig. 13.58.

A drawing signals informality if not humor. The *Birmingham* (Ala.) *News* logo also makes use of heavy rules (Fig. 13.59).

The *Seattle Times* sells a personality by running a large photograph of the author (Fig. 13.60). The thick and thin lines are repeated throughout the newspaper's design.

Fig. 13.59.

Fig. 13.60.

If logos for columnists are run vertically, they should appear above the headline and be the same width as the type underneath. If run horizontally, columnist logos should be tucked under the headline in the second leg of type.

Story logos

Any story that runs more than one day should have a graphic identifying element that reminds readers that it is a continuing story. Graphic logos help editors get around the problem of series, which readers generally avoid unless the content is gripping. Do not scare off readers who do not want to make a long-term commitment or may have missed one or more parts by labeling related stories as a series. Each story should stand alone, while the graphic logo provides the continuity. Space for a teaser line for the next day's story can be built into the logo.

Logos for continuing stories are common, but logos that pick up an element of the coverage itself are relatively uncommon. When the *Columbia Missourian* opened its coverage of the race for the board of education, it began with a portrait of the three candidates running for two available positions (Fig. 13.61). That portrait was reduced and used as a logo for campaign coverage (Fig. 13.62). The logo appeared for a final time with the results of the election (Fig. 13.63).

Fig. 13.61

The School Board Race

The economy
Council shifts guide, but opposes controls

WASHINGTON (UPI) — The government Thursday tightened its voluntary price guidelines to discourage businesses from moving forward with price increases during the next three months in anticipation of wage-price controls.

The Council on Wage and Price Stability said the change is designed to assure that price increases are imposed gradually and not taken all at once between April and June.

Carter's anti-inflation plan called inadequate by Burns

From our wire services

WASHINGTON — Arthur Burns, former chairman of the Federal Reserve Board, sharply criticized the president's new anti-inflation policy Thursday.

Inflation is changing lifestyles

United Press International

People throughout the country say inflation is changing their lifestyles, forcing them to drive, shop and eat out less.

Joel Harris: Teachers key

By Valerie Battle
Missourian staff

Revised Carter budget proposes millions for cities

From our wire services

WASHINGTON — President Carter, siding with liberals on one marked budget issue, will call for $440 million in aid to cities likely to be hurt by elimination of their revenue-sharing, it was learned Thursday.

Administration opposes tax cut

From Page 1A

Ignacio murder trial jury to retire

By Michael Otel
Missourian staff writer

Columbia Missourian

72nd Year — No. 170   Good Morning! It's Wednesday, April 2, 1980   3 Sections — 26 Pages — 15 Cents

Voters reject Flat Branch plan 2-1

Sole ballot jams gears in election

Election Returns at a Glance

FLAT BRANCH
(Approve Redevelopment?)

Yes	3058
No	5323

CITY OF COLUMBIA BOARD OF EDUCATION
(Top Two Elected)

Middleton	5489
Harris	6495
Krysiak	5320

NEW HAVEN SCHOOLS
(Join Columbia District?)

Yes	281
No	138

NEW HAVEN SCHOOL BOARD
(Top Two Elected)

Gamble	188
Moore	184
Hafey	159
Pauley	175

MIDWAY SCHOOL BOARD
(Top Two Elected)

David	65
Partner	95
Duncan	138
McConnell	163

CALLAWAY COUNTY HOSPITAL BOND ISSUE
(Failed — Two-Thirds Required)

Yes	4019
No	2037

ASHLAND GYM BONDS

Yes	542
No	145

CENTRALIA PARK LEVY

Yes	564
No	280

HALLSVILLE SCHOOLS BOND ISSUE

Yes	336
No	100

Janet Harrison and daughter at the polls

Harris captures education spot; Middleton wins

CITY OF COLUMBIA BOARD OF EDUCATION
(Top Two Elected)

Middleton	5489
Harris	6495
Krysiak	5320

New Haven seeks annexation

The dilemma: Fulton or prison?

Insight

Strike halts construction

Inside today

Carter, Reagan win

In town today

The Rochester (N.Y.) *Times-Union* used a similar device when it sought reader participation in a fun feature to pick the best bar food in town (Fig. 13.64). The photograph combined with reversed type served as the identifier for the ballot and the follow-up story.

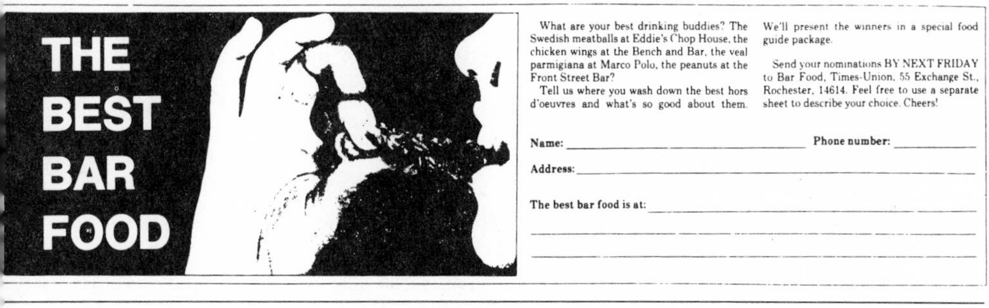

THE BEST BAR FOOD

What are your best drinking buddies? The Swedish meatballs at Eddie's Chop House, the chicken wings at the Bench and Bar, the veal parmigiana at Marco Polo, the peanuts at the Front Street Bar? Tell us where you wash down the best hors d'oeuvres and what's so good about them.

We'll present the winners in a special food guide package.

Send your nominations BY NEXT FRIDAY to Bar Food, Times-Union, 55 Exchange St., Rochester, 14614. Feel free to use a separate sheet to describe your choice. Cheers!

Name: _____ Phone number: _____

Address: _____

The best bar food is at: _____

_____

_____

Fig. 13.64.

The Big Event: A case history

The designer should make every effort to provide good news displays, but no newspaper will have a well-designed news package unless its editors are willing to make tough decisions. Such decisions may include lowering the story count, making choices between good stories, and selecting fewer pictures and running them larger. Occasionally, however, editors are confronted with a combination of events, such as the inauguration of a president and the release of the hostages from Iran, and must make decisions that permit the designer to extract focus from confusion. The following review, based on a study of 75 newspapers published coast-to-coast, shows how editors coped with the news of January 20, 1981.

When the *Minneapolis Tribune*'s 4 P.M. news huddle began in managing editor Frank Wright's office, editors went over the local list first, as always, and then the state and business reports. The order of discussion was all that was normal. At the *Tribune,* as at newspapers across the country on January 20, editors were trying to determine how to report a momentous news day. Just minutes after Ronald Reagan took the oath of office, 52 American hostages left Tehran on a flight to freedom. When the time came for the wire report, Steve Ronald, the *Tribune*'s assistant managing editor, suggested they tell the story with two pictures, two headlines, and two copy blocks. Recalls Wright: "We all said, 'Okay, let's do it.' Then we sat and sweated for a while."

It was five hours to first-edition photo deadline. In that, at least, the *Tribune* was fortunate. Papers in the eastern time zone were squeezed. It was after 8 P.M. in New York when the planes landed in Algeria; 12:45 A.M. January 21 when they arrived at Rhein-Main.

In Minneapolis, the editors already had selected a picture for Page 1 that showed the Reagans waving toward the camera. A few hours later, they would have a picture of two hostages walking toward another camera (see Fig. 9.11).

The *Tribune* editors' goal was to display the day's two major stories with impact even though most readers already had seen many of the events on television. By focusing clearly on the events with two strong photographs, the *Tribune* editors brought order to a chaotic news day.

Editors of other papers had varying degrees of success. The events of January 20 presented the temptation to do too much. The hostages were coming home, Reagan was going to the White House, and in some cases, there were local sidebars to go with both stories. If there is a single universal principle of successful communication, it is that less is more. Too many newspapers tried to convey the impact of the day by shouting rather than explaining.

The occasion called for more than large type, although there was plenty of that. Freed from the limits of hot metal, newspapers photoenlarged type until it roared. The *Shreveport* (La.) *Journal* used a quarter of its front page to proclaim "FREE AT LAST." The *Miami Herald* said the same thing in type only a couple of points smaller. The *Des Moines Register* used a condensed type for both size and count (see Fig. 9.13). In a 2-line banner that was 4 inches deep, the *Register* proclaimed in all-caps: "HOSTAGES FREE AT LAST AS REAGAN TAKES OFFICE."

That headline represents the compromise many editors made; they combined or equated the two events. It is questionable, however, whether the inauguration of Ronald Reagan, a scheduled event of more symbolism than substance, rated equal play with the freeing of the hostages, an event that burst a coast-to-coast bubble of emotion. Writing, design, and marketing are all improved by sharp focus. Most editors provided that focus by subordinating the inauguration to the hostages in the lead headline. Emotionally, however, many editors could not make the break cleanly; while the banner went to the hostages, the play went to the inauguration. The result was often babble when a single strong voice was needed.

Only a few papers chose the inauguration as the top story. One, the *New York Times,* had a special historical tradition to maintain; another, the *Dixon* (Ill.) *Evening Telegraph,* reported on its most famous native son.

Because the hostage story was developing throughout the evening, western editors had a substantial advantage, particularly in picture availability. The outstanding photographs of the freedom flight came from Rhein-Main. In what looks like a combination of defiance and ecstacy, David Roeder has both arms in the air as he emerges from the plane. In the AP picture, the "Welcome Back to Freedom" sign on the open door to his right says it all. UPI captured the same dramatic moment. Although the sign is missing, UPI's vertical cropping captured not only the exuberant Roeder but also the painful emotion of another hostage's face.

Both pictures came too late for next day (Wednesday) morning papers except those in the western states. The *Los Angeles Herald Examiner* ran AP's Roeder picture 5 columns wide (Fig. 13.65). The *Atlanta Journal* played it the same way Wednesday afternoon.

Fig. 13.65.   Fig. 13.66.

The second-best picture from the freedom flight was the most widely used because it was sent early enough for papers in the eastern and central time zones to publish it in Wednesday morning editions. From AP, the picture shows Elizabeth Swift and Kathryn Koob holding hands as they walk across the runway in Algiers. It led the *Minneapolis Tribune* (see Fig. 9.11). The *Chicago Tribune* played it four columns. The *Boston Globe* ran it two columns but paired it with an oath-taking picture of the same size (Fig. 13.66). In a perfectly balanced page, the *Globe* equated the two news events. Even if the news events could have been considered equal, the pictures were not.

Fig. 13.67.

The most bizarre photo usage popped up at the *Boston Herald American* where an AP photo of a group of hostages, apparently shot from a television screen, consumed the entire front page (Fig. 13.67). A good idea was wasted because the photograph was poor.

The *Boston Herald American,* however, at least had focus. At many newspapers, the record-keeping urge overpowered the drama of the hostages' return. Some of these papers had planned color coverage of the inauguration and were unable or unwilling to change gears. *Newsday* had the bad luck to choose the inauguration for its first color cover; the hostages only rated a mention at the bottom of Page 1. The *Virginian-Pilot* of Norfolk, the *Houston Post,* and *St. Louis Globe-Democrat,* among others, played color inaugural pictures at the top. By contrast, the *St. Petersburg Times* moved its color inaugural picture to the bottom of the front page to focus on the hostages above.

Even some papers that were not wedded to color failed to capitalize on the available hostage pictures. The *Washington Post* led Wednesday's issue with a forgettable black and white inaugural parade shot but regrouped and published an extra on the hostages' release. The *Courier-Journal* of Louisville, Ky., hedged its play by running a picture of the Reagans and two small hostage pictures at the top of Page 1 (Fig. 13.68). In Portland, the *Oregonian,* with both the Roeder and Swift pictures available, ran a 1-column picture of hostage Joseph Subic being escorted to the plane at Tehran and a 3-column photo of Reagan repeating the oath of office. Both the Roeder and Swift photographs provided the human dimension of the hostages' return. Inaugural pictures paled by comparison.

Although many editors were reluctant to subordinate inaugural photo coverage, few were bashful about showing their happiness at the hostages' return. Patriotism burst out in papers such as the *Miami News,* which ran a graphic conception of the flag on the top half of Monday's edition under the headline, "Hostages going free." On Wednesday, the *Houston Post* wrapped itself in a red, white, and blue border. The Allentown *Morning Call* used red color blocks to represent the flag around its "Alive, Well, Free" banner (Fig. 13.69). The *Union Leader* of Manchester, N.H., ran its double

Fig. 13.68.   Fig. 13.69.

banner in red and overprinted an artist's drawing of a citizen waving a red ribbon over the hostages. The ribbon turned yellow later in the week. The *Dallas Morning News* special hostage section was led by the word "FREEDOM" in nearly 2-inch deep red type; dragging broken chains, an American eagle lifted off the *M*.

Some of the headlines were special. The *Philadelphia Inquirer* (Fig. 13.70) relaxed enough to say "They're Coming Home!" The *Topeka Capital-Journal* said, "At last . . . we're all together again." The two favorite headlines were "Free at last," a line with religious overtones, and "Alive, well, and free," a quote from negotiator Warren Christopher.

Fig. 13.70.

Researchers tell us readers do not buy news; they buy editors. Readers expect editors to select the news, rank it in importance, organize it, and explain it. Consequently, editors must be able to focus on the essence of each news day. On January 20, 1981, too many editors confused chaos with excitement and failed to bring order to the unusual combination of news events.

CHAPTER FOURTEEN

Making news-papers colorful

COLOR helps us to communicate the news better. News isn't black and white. Color gives people a more realistic view of the news.

Richard Curtis
ASSISTANT MANAGING EDITOR
USA Today

SCIENTISTS AT THE Institute of Biosocial Research in Tacoma, Wash., found that pink reduces anger, aggression, and physical strength. As a result, holding cells in the U.S. Naval Correctional Center in Seattle were painted pink. Judging from the reaction of some readers to controversial news, perhaps newspapers should print with pink ink.

It has been known for years that color has manipulative power. Red is a favorite color at restaurants, for instance, because it makes you salivate. We also know that color enhances the newspaper's image in the eyes of its readers. Click and Stempel (1976) gave each of 136 people front pages from four newspapers; two had black and white photos, and two had color photos. None of the papers were published near the city where the test was conducted. Respondents were asked to rate the papers on a number of factors by using a semantic differential scale. No reference was made to halftones or color. The pages with color were rated higher on 19 of 20 scales. The differences, the authors concluded, "are large enough that they can't be ignored."

Thanks to improving technology and increasing competition, newspapers are not ignoring color anymore. Five years ago, a color photo in a newspaper was an oddity; today, many newspapers run color weekly if not daily. Ninety-one percent of the 315 respondents to an American Newspaper Publishers Association survey said they printed process color at least once in 1979. The survey also found that 57 percent ran more color in 1979 than in 1978, while

14 percent used less. Editorial color is printed routinely by many newspapers including the *St. Petersburg Times,* the *Detroit Free Press,* the Dover (N.J.) *Daily Advance,* the *Kingsport* (Tenn.) *Times-News,* the *Eugene* (Oreg.) *Register-Guard,* the Orange County (Calif.) *Register,* the *Charleston* (W.Va.) *Gazette,* and the *San Diego Union* and evening *Tribune.* The Edmonton (Alberta) *Journal* published 412 full-color pictures on 191 pages in September of 1980 alone.

To produce that color, newspapers purchase equipment ranging from several hundred to several thousand dollars. A color computer system that makes one separation (a negative for each process color) at a time with an electronic scanner can cost nearly $40,000. On the other hand, newspapers can make separations inexpensively by relying on the process camera, which is standard equipment in offset plants. Newspapers have not embraced color quickly because of the cost, the time needed to prepare it, the press capacity required, and the often disappointing results. The initial investment is usually significant, but it pays off by reducing the time and labor needed for color production. Newspapers that have the proper equipment and trained personnel print good quality color. In the next few years, more newspapers will print color routinely, and journalists must know how it is produced.

Color production

The vocabulary of color production includes the following basic terms:

1. Process color – full- or four-color reproduction achieved by separating each color on individual pieces of film and burning them on separate printing plates.

2. Process colors – yellow, magenta (process red), cyan (process blue), and black.

3. Duotone – one color plus black, achieved by shooting two halftone negatives of the picture and producing two plates for the page. A duotone look can be produced by using a color screen tint behind the black halftone. This merely tints the reproduction.

4. Transparency – a color photograph on slide film. A transparency has excellent detail and is viewed by passing light through it.

5. Color print – a color photograph produced from negative film and commonly referred to as reflection copy because it is viewed by reflected light.

6. Spot color – a single color other than black on paper.

7. Key plate – the printing plate that puts the first image on the paper. To print process color, an image is printed on the page four times, once with each of the process colors. All the printing must be in register (each image must be in exactly the right place), or parts of the picture will overlap.

8. Scanner – a machine that reads visuals and transfers the information

into impulses. Scanners read one color of a photograph at a time and transfer the image to a negative called a separation. Scanners are either electronic or laser.

9. Color filter — a filter that absorbs all but one color. Violet filters permit only yellow to pass through, green filters permit only red, and orange filters permit only blue. To make the black separation, a special filter is used to screen the primary colors.

Technological developments

Before May 1980, the *Detroit Free Press* had never published color in its news section. Since then, the newspaper has published it nearly every day, sometimes several times a day. While the *Free Press* is not typical of the newspaper industry as a whole, it may not be long before more papers embrace color just as enthusiastically. Like the *Free Press,* Long Island's *Newsday* did not run color until 1980. At both papers, the installation of offset presses preceded the use of editorial color. The offset press permits sharper reproduction of all pictures, black and white or color. Smaller newspapers have had offset for years. The 44,000-circulation *Kingsport Times-News* went offset in 1972 and has run color every day since 1979. Publisher Frank Leeming estimates the cost is $70 a color picture, but he believes it is money well spent. Ever since the *Times-News* started running color pictures daily on both Page 1 and the section fronts, the readers have ranked them among the top five favorite features.

Use of color is somewhat of a regional phenomenon. Florida papers, possibly influenced by the example of the *St. Petersburg Times,* run more color as a group than any other state. Papers in the Pacific Northwest and portions of California run color routinely. This is not the case in the industrialized East, however, where few papers use color regularly. Gannett's national newspaper, *USA Today,* uses color more than any other newspaper in the United States.

Offset printing encourages newspapers to print color photographs, and other technological developments have made it possible to make quality separations quickly. The lead time required to print color pictures has been cut drastically just in the last five years. Because additional time was needed to make separations, burn the extra plates, and make sure the press was in register, newsrooms needed the color print early and had to decide exactly where it would be placed on the page. If the news changed dramatically, the only option for a quick redesign was to switch from color to black and white. Now the lead time is more manageable, but it still causes problems. The *Free Press,* in an intensely competitive newspaper city, must get the color print to the scanner operator by 5 P.M. in time for an 8 P.M. press run. There is a 9 P.M. makeover deadline for the midnight metropolitan final. In those three hours, the editors are locked into picture location unless they want to pull the color picture or risk missing color on at least part of the run. It takes about 25 minutes to process the film and another 15 to produce a print. The scanner produces the four separations in about 45 minutes. The introduction of electronic and laser scanners has made it possible for newspapers to produce good quality separations in a reasonably short time, and further improvements are ahead. A laser scanner that can produce a film separation is not far from beaming the same information directly onto a plate. Another development involves digitizing the photographs and storing them in computers that could drive the scanner directly.

Electronic and laser scanners speeded color production and also improved it. Many of them have color enhancement capability. Some can read a print and increase or decrease the amount of color for a separation. However, most of these variations affect the entire print, when only an area correction may be needed. Some advanced systems are even able to offer area enhancement. The computer analyzes the amount of light transmitted through the transparency onto a vacuum easel, controls exposure, and makes filter changes.

Most photographers use transparencies when they shoot color because the quality of the reproduction has always been better, especially in the highlights. However, the *Free Press,* the Edmonton *Journal,* and the Hamilton (Ontario) *Spectator,* believe that the advantages of using color negative film outweigh the disadvantages. Color negative film gives the photographers more room to err on exposure settings. Transparency film is less forgiving, because the picture is lost if the transparency is overexposed or passes the tenuous limits of underexposure. With color negative film, photographers have an opportunity to correct some of the problems in the printing stage, just as they do when working with black and white. No prints are made with transparency film; the image goes directly from the slide to the separation. With color negative film, photographers can dodge or burn portions of the prints. This is helpful because lighting is not constant unless the photograph is taken under controlled laboratory conditions. Although much newspaper color photography is taken in labs (the food-page illustrations, for example), more of it is used in spot news or sports. If a photographer sets the camera for the lighting on a subject's face, another light source in the background can wash out parts of the picture. In spot news or sports situations, the photographer often has insufficient control of the lighting. With transparencies, such problems cannot be corrected; with negative film, they can.

At the *Free Press,* photographers use Kodacolor 400 film. Editors select photos from color contact sheets or, if a deadline is near, view the negatives through a video analyzer on an 8- by 10-inch screen. Color adjustments can be made on the analyzer, and the settings are transferred to an enlarger. After

Plate 14.1

Plate 14.2
YELLOW

Plate 14.3
RED (MAGENTA)

Plate 14.4
BLUE (CYAN)

Plate 14.5
BLACK

A glittering burst of fire superimposed on the colorful precision march of Largo's Band of Gold is a special keepsake of Festival of States' 12th Annual Illuminated Night Parade.

A festival of music and color to welcome spring

◀ The Red and Blue Band of Morgantown High School in West Virginia cuts a colorful figure in the Night Parade. The 'Mohigans' are directed by Michael Roberts.

▲ Clowning around is a big part of festival fun, so these chums put on their happiest faces and strolled through the Night Parade in style.

Plate 14.6

LEWISTON MORNING TRIBUNE

Federal judge overturns Carter's gasoline surcharge

The calm before...

A plume of steam portends another eruption on Mount St. Helens.

Carter, Reagan add to delegate totals

Legislature kills highway funding

By Kevin Roche
of the Tribune staff

See Primary, Page 7A

See Legislature, Page 7A

The inside story

Asparagus season is here. Some simple ideas about how to take asparagus on a picnic and why not to stalk the wild variety. Food and Home, Page 10E.

3A Airline fares may take off for higher altitudes, thanks to the CAB.

1B It'll be Lapwai and Orofino in today's baseball championship game.

1C Potlatch is recalling workers as the timber industry starts to recover.

3C Fire Tuesday morning destroyed a bar and grill in Elk City.

Partly cloudy
(Details, 2A)

Plate 14.7

Plate 14.8

Plate 14.9

editors receive the four prints, one for each process color, a page dummy showing color picture location is prepared and given to the scanner operators. The scanner reads the color copy four times to produce four separations — black, cyan, magenta, and yellow. The separations are burned onto the plates and placed on the press. This is the process that the *Detroit Free Press* used to produce the page with the first in a series of reports from Lebanon (Plate 14.1). The process color adds realism to the photograph and thus to the reportage. To produce the photograph, four separations were made (Plates 14.2–14.5). Process color is produced by laying colors over each other. The rest of the color on the page is spot color, produced by spotting one color in a space.

Although the *Free Press* relies on color negative film, the *St. Petersburg Times* photographers use transparencies with an ASA rating of 64 to achieve high-quality color reproduction. The newspaper combines years of experience with a commitment to excellence to produce pages like that in Plate 14.6.

Using one and two colors

Newspapers commonly use one color, or one color with black type, in both news and advertising. Although spot color can attract attention and even help readers understand illustrations such as maps and charts, it must be handled with care. It is easy to lower the legibility of type by using color over it. Spot color (the use of a single color) often appears in newspaper promotion boxes on Page 1. It can be used effectively with maps, charts, and illustrations, especially with one or more screens. The screens, for instance, can make red appear pink. To the reader, it looks like two colors. Artists can use either colored felt-tip pens or colored overlays (such as that produced by Zipatone) on tissue put over the artwork. Someday, perhaps even the daily weather maps will appear in color in most newspapers. They already are in *USA Today* and the *Chicago Tribune*.

Editors often misuse spot color by placing it on the nameplate or, worse, in a headline. Spot color usually should be used in a mass. When it is used over type, the type should be large (as in feature titles) and preferably sans serif. Some typefaces, such as Bodoni with its thin serifs, are difficult to reproduce in color.

If color is used over text type, the type should be enlarged to about 10 or 12 points. Spot color can also be used in mass as a frame or border around a picture or illustration and as a background against which type can be reversed. When it is used on headlines 72 points or smaller, it has little impact; when it appears randomly on the page, the reader cannot help but wonder why the story is so special that its headline is in color.

Spot color, however, can be effective on the large type that is often used on special news events. When the hostages returned from Iran, the Allentown *Morning Call* used red in a mass around the banner to give the impression of the red stripes of the U.S. flag (see Fig. 13.69). When the *Boston Herald American* ran a banner reporting on the city's financial condition, it used a readin before finishing with large, gothic type (Fig. 14.1):

Even if Boston pays all its school and tax
abatement bills, the city will still be $6–$10 million deep in

RED INK

Fig. 14.1.

The words "red ink" were appropriately in red ink.

Editors should resist the temptation to use color over text type except on short stories or enlarged type. The legibility decreases as the contrast of black letters on a white background drops off. Text type itself should never be printed in color against a white background. Black print on a yellow background and red print on a white background are legible, but neither should be used with text type in any significant amount. Only light pastels should be used over text type. As the background increases in intensity, the print becomes more difficult to read.

The use of two-color pictures can attract attention, but care must be taken that the color and picture are matched correctly. Duotones, produced by using black and one other process color, are most effective on scenic shots. Normally, duotones should be avoided when there are people in the picture. A green face, for instance, is not very appealing. Green is effective on some landscape shots; blue is good in scenes dominated by water or sky. When the Lewiston (Idaho) *Tribune* published a story about the rumbling in Mount St. Helens, it ran a picture of the mountain as a blue duotone (Plate 14.7). The color selection was appropriate because it worked with the title: "The calm before . . ." Blue is a calm color; red is hot. Duotones can be even more effective if no color is printed over the part of the picture that is naturally white. When the U.S. space shuttle Columbia returned from its first flight, the Associated Press distributed a photograph of the white and black plane against a blue sky. Use of blue on everything but the plane would have given the appearance of full color.

Many newspapers merely put a color over a picture and call it a duotone, but that is not a true duotone. Two halftones, called printers, should be made to different specifications. The dark printer is usually used with black ink and contains the lower middle tone and shadow detail. The light printer carries the upper middle tone and highlight detail. Approached this way, the duotone has a longer density range than a single halftone (Adams and Faux 1977).

Avoid the temptation to overuse spot color. When it is available, editors often use it on promotion boxes, pictures, screens over headlines, and index boxes. This undisciplined use only clutters the page and adds nothing to reader understanding of the day's events.

Producing quality color

Producing quality color on newsprint requires the combined talents of everyone from the photographer to the person operating the press. Many newspapers expect the actual printing process to make up for any inadequacies in preparation, but papers with the most experience in producing color put the least amount of responsibility in the pressroom. "Too many newspapers just produce color and then expect the pressmen to print it when it is beyond the equipment's capability," says Bill Howard, color lab supervisor of the *St. Petersburg Times* and *Evening Independent*. "We take an entirely different approach. We don't try to make the press make color. As color separators, we try to give the press good color to print."

Of all the people involved in color production, the press operators are the least able to adjust for poor quality transparencies or separations or to compensate for plates that are not in register. Color can be adjusted on the press, but any adjustment affects the entire picture or page, not just an area of the picture. Press operators should be primarily concerned about getting the press in register once the basic color is adjusted. At the *St. Petersburg Times,* where color is produced almost daily, the responsibility starts with the photographers. Because they use transparencies, photographers must fill in shadow areas, which usually means using flash and flash fill. The scanner operators know that the press gains on blue and loses on red, and they make the separations accordingly. The platemakers must reproduce the separations dot for dot and place the material in exactly the right position on the plate to reduce registration problems. "If this commitment [to quality] is missing from just one department," Howard says, "quality color cannot be achieved." At the *Fort Myers* (Fla.) *News-Press,* production director Don Miller also believes in the team approach: "It takes everybody to do good color — photographers, the separation process, pressmen and good equipment." Miller, who believes in specialization, added, "I hire the experts and the experts do the job. When I know as much as the guy who's working for me, he doesn't last long. There's no way you can keep track personally of all the skills needed of the people in these jobs." Neither can the journalist. But just as editors must understand how to combine type, photographs, and artwork, they must also understand the potential and limitations of using high-speed web presses to produce color on newsprint.

A contrast in color

The dimension that color adds to newspapers was illustrated well in May 1980 by two newspapers 2,500 miles apart. In Cleveland, the *Plain Dealer* promised much ("Adjectives flow as May unfolds so many glories") but delivered little (Plate 14.8). Black and white pictures fitted around a pyramid advertising stack failed to convey the beauty of the colorful flowers that pushed their way through the still-cold soil. Just two days earlier, the *Eugene Register-Guard* had published a page on the same subject (Plate 14.9). The brilliant color, appropriate typeface, and delicate lines combined to communicate the message of spring visually. Because of the typeface selection, the arrangement and sizing of the photos, and the space devoted to the package, the *Register-Guard* page would have been successful even in black and white. The addition of color demonstrated its potential to enhance the message and convey visual excitement. When all the available tools are used — color is just one of them — the potential of the newspaper as a visual medium is realized.

CHAPTER FIFTEEN

The process of redesign

IF they had killed that flag, I'd have taken it all and said "forget it."

Bob Lynn
GRAPHICS EDITOR

WHEN BOB LYNN, former graphics editor of the *Charleston* (W.Va.) *Gazette,* started redesigning the 56,000-circulation paper, he worked behind closed doors of a conference room for five months. He studied other papers, bounced ideas off no less than a dozen *Gazette* employees, and occasionally asked the advertising manager if a proposal would cause any problems. When he emerged, he showed the prototypes to the editor, news editor, and city editor. They liked them. The next day he showed them to the publisher, who liked them so well he wanted to use them in two weeks. Instead, they waited six weeks to work out some details and run a $5,000 promotional campaign to prepare readers for the changes.

The response? A few negative letters were received from readers who said it just was not the *Gazette* anymore, and there were some complaints about the cropping of the columnists' pictures. Some positive comments were also received. Of those subscribers who paid for the *Gazette* by mail, 60 percent said they did not like it and 40 percent said they did. The average age of the respondents was 63, but the average age of the typical readers was 48.

To the majority of readers, the most dramatic change was the nameplate. At that time, the *Gazette* was a 108-year-old newspaper. The redesign was, as the publisher said upon first seeing it, "the *Gazette* of the eighties" (Fig. 15.1). Editor Don Marsh began having second thoughts about the new look and, three weeks after it appeared, asked the editorial board to vote on whether to return to the old flag. The board voted to retain the new one (Lynn interview 1980).

the Charleston Gazette

The State Newspaper—Our 108th Year

Increasing cloudiness,
with rain likely by
evening. High to 19 C
(mid-60s F), lows near 13
C (mid-50s F). Details on
Page 3A.

CLOUDY 20%

Valley edition   20 cents
Charleston, West Virginia

Exiles arrive despite warning

By Mimi Whitefield

KEY WEST, Fla. (UPI) — Cuban exiles battled the Florida Straits in a tattered armada of bought, begged and borrowed boats Thursday to get their friends and relatives out of Cuba despite threats and warnings from Washington.

Commercial skippers were demanding anywhere from $1,000 per refugee to a flat fee of $50,000 to make the 180-mile roundtrip ran across the straits to Cuba. Unable to afford that, many exiles were putting out in small or seaworthy boats that kept Coast Guard rescue officers at full pitch.

Meanwhile the first Cuban exiles to be flown out of Havana since evacuation flights were suspended six days ago arriving in Costa Rica late Thursday, but officials declined to say if it marked the resumption of the emergency airlift.

A Costa Rican LACSA BAC-111 jetliner arrived in San Jose with 97 Cubans aboard. Officials said the plane.

Frank Vella, manager of the Key West city port, estimated late Thursday that 1,500 boats of every description had been put into the water at the city marina since Wednesday morning when the frantic sealift of refugees from the Peruvian embassy in Havana began.

"They've been steady, one right after another," he said.

Late Thursday night, another small boat — the 18th by unofficial count — brought 12 more refugees into Key West. That brought the unofficial count of refugees to 912 since the first boat returned Wednesday.

The State Department in Washington threatened fines and jail sentences for boat captains bringing in undocumented aliens, but the State Department has no power of enforcement and the Immigration and Naturalization Service appeared untroubled by stories about the refugees.

The Coast Guard, busy trying to prevent disasters at sea, was merely warning skippers that bringing in the refugees might lead to trouble.

However, the presence from Washington was having some effect, and many exiles with relatives still trying to get out of Cuba were frantic. Few had the money to pay the enormous prices — as much as $50,000 — commercial skippers were demanding for the trip.

Many of the ill-prepared ships that did leave failed to make it to Cuba. UPI photographer Tom Salyer, flying over the Florida Straits, reported an abandoned

(Please turn to page 3A, col. 1)

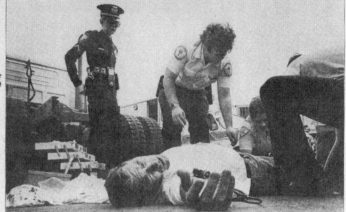

Aid and comfort

First aid is administered to Kenneth Smith, 52, of Charleston after he was struck by a tractor-trailer at the Valley Bell plant in the West Side. Smith, a Valley Bell employee, sustained a fractured left thigh bone and pelvis. He is in stable condition at General Division, CAMC.

Gazette photo by LAWRENCE PIERCE

HUD loans offer housing relief

By Edward Peeks
BUSINESS LABOR EDITOR

New relief appeared Thursday for West Virginia home builders and prospective home buyers who have been turned off by soaring high interest rates which have depressed the housing market.

The relief is in the form of 14 percent loan offers by the Department of Housing and Urban Development for builders to finance the sale of housing inventories. "This will bring relief to builders in the state," said Carl A. Smith, supervisor of HUD's Charleston service office. "It will help families who want to buy a new home," he added, referring to the mortgage program insured by the Federal Housing Administration.

"Upon completion of a home,

builders may obtain FHA financing at the current FHA allowable rate of 14 percent," Smith explained. "The maximum insurable mortgage is limited to 25 percent of the loan available to an owner-occupant on a particular property. The current maximum for the owner-occupant is $67,500."

FHA will insure a mortgage loan up to that amount for the home buyer at 14 percent interest. Smith said. The low down payment is 3 percent of the first $25,000 of the appraised value of a home and 5 percent of the value over $25,000.

For example, the down payment on a $50,000 home comes to $2,000, or $70,000 to $2,000, and on $80,000 it's $3,500.

"By insuring private financial

institutions against loss, the FHA encourages capital investment in the home mortgage market," Smith said.

Lenders charge points on FHA and Veterans Administration loans to make up the difference between interest on government-backed loans and conventional loans. Conventional rates range from 15 percent to 17 percent in West Virginia.

A point is a one-time payment made by the seller or purchaser to the lender. The point spread now is averaging about 3 percent if the amount of the loan. A $50,000 loan, for instance, would require a payment of $1,500 to the lender.

As for the builder, Smith said, the insured mortgages may not be in the name of the construction

company, but in the name of the individual builder or an agent not associated with the construction. This will establish responsibility for repayment of debt if the construction company goes out of business.

Builders may also take advantage of the escrow commitment procedure. Smith said. This permits the builder to obtain a commitment for a maximum mortgage which can be assumed by a home buyer. The builder is required to place a minimum of 15 percent of the mortgage amount in an escrow account held by the lender.

If the builder doesn't sell the property by the due date of the

(Please turn to page 3A, col. 6)

Censuring congressman recommended

WASHINGTON (UPI) — The House ethics committee recommended, 10-2, Thursday that Rep. Charles H. Wilson, D-Calif., be censured by the House on charges of accepting kickbacks and converting campaign funds to his own use.

The panel also recommended that the 63-year-old lawmaker be stripped of the chairmanship of his Post Office and Civil Service subcommittee on postal operations and be denied any other chairmanship during the remainder of the current session.

The censure resolution is expected to reach the House floor for a vote within about two weeks.

If the committee's recommendations are adopted there, Wilson, now serving his sixth term, will have to stand in the well of the House while Speaker Thomas O'Neill Jr. reads the resolution of censure.

The California Democrat was disciplined once before by the House — in 1978 when he was reprimanded for failing to report gifts from Tongsun Park, a South Korean lobbyist.

The ethics committee last week found Wilson guilty of eight counts of misconduct. But it acquitted him of seven other counts, including a charge that he lied to the committee under oath during the investigation.

Ghotbzadeh threatens Persian Gulf blockade

By Sajid Rizvi

TEHRAN, Iran (UPI) — Foreign Minister Sadegh Ghotbzadeh said Thursday Iran will blockade the entire Persian Gulf if the United States tries to block or mine Iran's ports. He said Iran had asked the Soviet Union for military aid.

Ghotbzadeh said Iran was ready to mount a blockade to keep oil tankers of the Persian Gulf out of action, if Iran had been given permission to use Soviet territory as an overland trade route "in the event of an emergency."

the steps that Washington has been reported considering should Iran continue to refuse to free the U.S. Embassy hostages.

In an interview with CBS News, Iranian President Abolhassan Bani-Sadr said the United States had violated a commitment that it would allow Panama to begin extradition proceedings against Shah Mohammed Reza Pahlavi.

When asked by CBS News if he had a message for the American people, Bani-Sadr replied: "That the question of the hostages will not last long and will be solved sooner or later."

In Washington, defense sources

said Iran could blockade the gulf by mining the narrow strait or by stationing warships there.

The sources said it would be easy for the United States to sweep the strait as soon as Iran began to mine them. For that reason, they said Iran might try to blockade the strait with warships.

But the sources also said it was not clear whether the Iranian navy, disorganized and lacking trained manpower, could do that.

Inside glance

A change of direction

The U.S. Chamber of Commerce is planning to launch a program aimed at getting the country back on track. An interview with C. William Verity, president-elect of the Chamber, is on Page 1C.

Verity

Nation/world

VITAMIN B-15, a health food rage, is a "dangerous" consumer deception and may be hazardous," scientists at the American Council on Science and Health said Tuesday.   **Page 9A**

PRESIDENT CARTER, meeting with a group of bitterly divided legislators, Thursday backed his threat to veto legislation that would weaken the Federal Trade Commission.   **Page 4B**

GULF OIL CORP. reported its first-quarter profits rose 56 percent, and Conoco Inc. announced its earnings more than doubled.   **Page 6B**

State

Index

Mobil bows to administration pressure to forgo price hikes

By Lawrence McQuillan

WASHINGTON (UPI) — The Mobil Oil Co., under pressure from President Carter, agreed Thursday to forgo $30 million in price increases to bring it into compliance with administration price standards.

Press secretary Jody Powell announced the compromise at a White House briefing. President Carter had contended — in a March 28 speech designed to bring public pressure on the company — that the oil firm overcharged customers by $48 million.

Carter had used strong words to criticize the oil company last month, and said it had refused to take corrective action.

But the White House statement

released Thursday said Mobil had "endeavored to interpret and apply the price standards in good faith and that honest differences of interpretation caused ... different conclusions" before.

Under the agreement, Mobil will withhold $30 million in price increases that would have been acceptable under administration guidelines on its products through this September.

Eight killed as Iranian rescue effort is grounded

WASHINGTON (UPI) — The White House announced early Thursday an operation underway in Iran to prepare to rescue the American hostages was aborted and eight Americans were killed when two American aircraft collided on the ground at a remote airstrip in Iran.

The White House statement said the mission was "terminated because of equipment failure."

"There were no military hostilities and the president deeply regrets that eight Americans comprise the two aircraft were killed."

Fig. 15.1.

Because of his talents and management support, Lynn was able to successfully redesign the *Gazette* and have it accepted by the management and staff. However, this does not happen often. The success and acceptance of a redesign is more likely when the process involves planning, broad participation, and gradual implementation.

To many editors, redesign means a change of typeface, new logos for the columnists, and perhaps a new nameplate, but design encompasses much more than such variations. It involves a change in the production process to provide for planning, a review of the content, and an evaluation of every element from the nameplate to the spacing between letters in the text. Changing one or two of the elements in the package is tinkering, but reviewing the entire package piece by piece is designing.

A wry joke that travels in management circles describes the six phases of a project as follows: wild enthusiasm, total confusion, disillusionment, search for the guilty, punishment of the innocent, and promotion of the nonparticipants. To avoid getting sidetracked into wild confusion, newsroom managers should plan for the redesign. Whether a staff member or an outside consultant, a designer does not create a new product in isolation. To meet the needs of readers and staff, the redesign should be the product of the combined thinking of both the journalists and readers. The designer's job is to translate that thinking into a usable product. The process of redesign starts with the formation of a committee that represents all segments of the newspaper.

Getting others involved

Just as tapping the creative resources of people in the newsroom results in a better product, so will tapping the resources of a wide variety of the newspaper's employees. The person who has final authority to accept or reject the plans, whether it is the editor or the publisher, should be on the committee. In addition, the committee should include the staff member primarily responsible for graphics; departmental editors and representatives of the copy desk; reporters; and personnel from the production, advertising, and circulation or marketing departments.

Why should nonnews people be on the committee? The news or editorial department may be responsible for content and form, but the marketing or circulation department has to sell it. Unfortunate as it may be, the people in marketing often talk to more customers than editors do. No design is going to be successful unless the production department has the opportunity to point out mechanical possibilities and limitations. At the same time, the production department representative communicates the goals to fellow department employees. No matter how exact a dummy is, the person who actually places the materials on the page is the arbiter of how the page will look. The managers of the Allentown *Morning Call* were aware of this and experimented with having paste-up personnel in the newsroom. Eventually, pagination will bypass the composing room entirely, but production employees should always be key members of a redesign committee.

Advertising representatives are equally important. Column widths cannot be changed in any publication without involving advertising, nor can a move be made toward modular ad display without advertising and management consent. Other policies that may come out of a redesign, such as restrictions on reverse ads and on editorial holes at the top of inside pages, also require involvement of the advertising department. Robert Haiman, who was managing editor of the *St. Petersburg Times* when it underwent a redesign in 1975, knows the value of involving management and advertising representatives. "We knew that unless we could get top management approval of the concept that we were not going to have skinny little spaces across the top," he said, "our work would be academic."

There is yet another important reason to include all these people: It is good management. A broadly based committee offers a variety of perspectives and experiences, and because the members are responsible for the formulation of the plan, they will be more enthusiastic about implementing it. A design cannot be done by committee; that must be the work of one or two people. The committee establishes goals, and the designer translates those goals to paper.

Predesign questions

Design, as we have seen, involves both content and form. Because form follows content, questions about content are very important and must be answered before a redesign is ordered. Susan Clark, editor and publisher of the *Niagara* (Niagara Falls, N.Y.) *Gazette,* emphasized this point in a report on her paper's redesign. "The reader survey has not meant just a redesign of our newspaper. It has meant, most importantly, an examination of what we write and how we write it."

Every publication must answer the following questions before undergoing a redesign:

1. What will the newspaper's policy be concerning jumps from Page 1? The newspaper's jump policy determines the story count on the front page, and the story count determines the marketing approach. A high story count, which is possible only with a policy that permits jumps, offers variety; the readers can shop the front page. A low story count, usually the result of a no-jump or limited-jump policy, permits better display of each story and lowers the irritation level of readers who do not like to follow jumps. The strength of one philosophy is the weakness of the other. However, the front page does not have to follow one or the other strictly. It is possible to have a high item count and a low story count. For instance, a page with three or four complete stories supplemented by digest or promotional boxes has a high item count. Other methods, such as using a synopsis of major enterprise stories (as described in Chapter 12), also help editors avoid the problems posed by jumping stories. The decision regarding jumps is critical to the personality of the newspaper (Bain and Weaver 1979) because it determines the content and looks of the all-important front page. The decision is also influenced by a number of other factors, most of which are considered in succeeding questions.

   2. What are your marketing goals? How many editions do you have and who are the audiences of each? How many newspapers are sold in vending machines? What is the potential for growth? Who subscribes to your paper and why? Who does not and why not?

   3. What are the characteristics of your market? Is it highly competitive? Does the competition come from other newspapers, shoppers, and broadcast or home delivery information systems? What is the white-collar, blue-collar mix? What time do people go to work and get home? What kind of a mass transportation system exists? Are you near lakes, mountains, or forests where people spend hours in recreation? Are you in an urban area where movies, theater, dining out, and sports are important recreational activities? Is there a mix of religions or does one denomination dominate? How would you describe the community—Retirement? Financial? Agribusiness?

   4. How will the paper be divided? Beyond the basic divisions for news (which should be subdivided)—features, sports, and business—what additional sections do you have or should you have for your particular audience? For instance, Dallas is a fashion center, and both newspapers have big fashion sections. The *St. Petersburg Times* has a successful religion section. The *Miami Herald* prints a Spanish-language edition. The *New York Times* has an outstanding books section. Each market has its own peculiarities, and each newspaper ought to reflect them. When answering these questions before a redesign, some newspaper managements, especially if they are consulting with the advertising and marketing departments, may find potential sections that will broaden the newspaper's appeal.

   5. What personality do you want to project? Type used in combination with other devices creates a personality. Ask key management personnel to describe the personality they want the paper to have and compare the responses. If they agree, the management team has a common goal. However, there will probably be severe differences of opinion. Also ask staff members and readers to describe the newspaper's personality. Chances are, there will be differences between the intent of the staff and the perception of the readers. Agreement must be reached on the personality desired before the designer can select the elements to achieve the desired result. Although readers get their first impression from the typography of a newspaper, the content must be consistent with the rest of the message. If the graphics are modern and lively and the copy is dull, the reader soon realizes that something is amiss.

6. What are your personnel limitations? Is the newspaper large enough to have a design editor? How many staff members will be responsible for the daily implementation of the design? Who are they? Is the staff capable of carrying out the design? Will someone watch for slippage and make the necessary adjustments as problems arise? Does the staff have an artist to do the illustrations, maps, and charts?

7. What are the limitations of the management system? If the editorial management does not include a strong graphics voice, the design cannot be executed no matter how well-intentioned the editor may be. The format can change, but lack of visual thinking will not produce good word and picture combinations or a paper that explains with graphs, maps, and charts.

8. What are the limitations of the management system? If color is wanted every day, is there a photo staff capable of producing it, a production staff capable of processing it, and enough press capacity to print it? Are the deadlines so restrictive that screens and double burns are impractical? Is the paper cold type and offset? What limitations does the production process impose on the design?

9. What do your readers think? If sufficient time and money are available, it is useful to question subscribers and nonsubscribers. A semantic differential scale is commonly used to test reader reaction to form. Click and Stempel (1974) used one such scale to test the reader's reaction to front page makeup. Most of the factors in the scale could be used to test the present product and a prototype.

   Evaluative: Pleasant, unpleasant; valuable, worthless; important, unimportant; and interesting, boring.

   Ethical: Fair, unfair; truthful, untruthful; accurate, inaccurate; unbiased, biased; and responsible, irresponsible.

   Stylistic: Exciting, dull; fresh, stale; easy, difficult; neat, messy; and colorful, colorless.

   Potency: Bold, timid; powerful, weak; and loud, soft.

   Activity: Tense, relaxed; active, passive; and modern, old-fashioned.

It is interesting, if not enlightening, to have readers, editors, and staff rank the present paper on a scale of one to ten using the factors just given. The staff often has a perception quite different from management, and the readers may respond differently than either the staff or management. Such a comparison can be used to start discussions on ways to improve the paper. Having readers and nonreaders test both the present paper and prototypes permits the designer to see what impact the changes might have. The semantic differential scale provides guidelines, not answers. Questions about organization and content are not answered with this kind of test.

The Rochester (N.Y.) *Times-Union* tested its prototypes with a representative group of readers in a relaxed group interview called a focus-group session. The participants indicated approval.

The content and organization of the newspaper can largely be determined by the answers to these questions. That is important because design is the proper organization of the content in an artistically pleasing and technically legible package. The only way to reach the point of design is through planning — long-term to establish the newspaper's goals and short-term to produce the stories and illustrations that appear in the newspaper daily.

Implementation

Using the responses to the questions, the designer can begin to organize and label the content and select the elements to achieve the personality desired. If a modern functional look is desired, the popular Helvetica or Univers faces may be appropriate. If the management wants to emphasize the newspaper's long tradition, one of the classic faces such as Caslon or Century may be more appropriate. If the newspaper wants to build a reputation for local coverage, the second section, clearly labeled, could lead off with local news. However, the front-page story selection is also vital to that image. Decisions about the packaging, placement, and playing of columnists must be determined by how hard the editors want to sell them. If the paper has large amounts of record copy (real estate transactions, court news, and police blotter material), decisions are necessary so that the material is gathered efficiently and presented coherently. If sections are involved, special requirements must be outlined.

As the designer tries to solve each of these problems, the redesign committee needs to see and respond to proposed changes. Incorporating some of the committee members suggestions into the redesign will be helpful in getting their support and will save the designer a great deal of time. Problems or disagreements that surface early in the process can be solved much more easily than those that surface at the last minute. A designer who is deeply involved in the project may find it difficult to compromise or separate ego from practicality. If the committee members have seen the various parts of the redesign, they are more likely to approve the whole.

Once the committee has approved the project, it must be sold to both staff and readers. If the staff has been kept informed during the course of the project, the results will not be a surprise. However, the committee and the designer must have enough flexibility to adjust the plan when staff members find weaknesses. Because staff members must work with the plan daily, their support is essential. In addition to the meetings where the philosophy and technical points of the plan are discussed, it is useful to have a manual for staff members, particularly for those who arrive after the design has been implemented. After its redesign, the *Niagra Gazette* held workshops with every department, developed a manual to explain the new sections, posted proofs of the new pages on the walls, prepared layout manuals for editorial and composing room employees, and held an extensive layout workshop with the composing room personnel.

Reader acceptance is also critical. How the redesign is implemented depends on the condition of the newspaper. If the newspaper is operating from a position of strength in the market and has a reasonably high degree of acceptance from readers, the design should be phased in. If a newspaper is failing, management may have to make the changes overnight. That obviously is the last resort. A failing newspaper will not be saved by a redesign. Peter Palazzo redesigned the *New York Herald Tribune* and the *Chicago Daily News* as they lay on their deathbeds. The diagnosis was terminal before the transfusion. The time to redesign is when things are going well. A newspaper that is constantly updating is responding to changing market conditions.

When the *Minneapolis Star* and *Minneapolis Tribune* changed from 8 to 6 columns in 1975, the change was advertised in advance with the help of Laurel and Hardy (Fig. 15.2). When the *Jackson* (Miss.) *Daily News* was redesigned, it was introduced to readers with a quarter-page wide overlay (Fig. 15.3) and a full page explanation (Fig. 15.4).

A close look at the *New York Times* behind its traditional news pages, reveals a surprisingly well-designed variety of sections. The *Times* changed a section at a time, quietly and steadily. Its readers, like those of the *Wall Street Journal,* are consumers of the newspaper's tradition, credibility, and authority. Any dramatic change in format or content could have been disastrous.

At the Rochester (N.Y.) *Times-Union,* work on a redesign began in 1977 but was not fully introduced until 1980. Special sections gave readers a preview of coming graphic changes. This planned change allowed the editors to experiment without shocking what editor Robert Giles described as a conservative market.

Rather than making a shocking change in a competitive market, the *Columbia Missourian* simplified, darkened, and stacked its nameplate when it redesigned in 1982. It also selected Times Roman Bold, a modern face with traditional qualities, to replace Bodoni (Fig. 15.5). The *Missourian* wanted a more modern look without losing touch with its 75-year-old history (Fig. 15.6).

Newspaper reading is a habit. A dramatic change in the content, organization, and appearance of the paper is more acceptable to the staff than the readers. When the Long Beach papers were redesigned, the changes were phased in over a year's time. This is a good policy and not unusual. Depending on the depth and variety of changes, a gradual phase-in, accom-

In The Minneapolis Star and Minneapolis Tribune...

starting May 5, we'll have 6 fat columns instead of 8 skinny ones.

On May 5, 1975, both The Minneapolis Star and Minneapolis Tribune will switch from the old eight-column format to a new six-column page.

This full-size, special section has been prepared to give you a visual description of the new design and to announce its revised mechanical requirements for the preparation of advertising. Editorial content was taken from earlier editions of The Star and the Tribune. Thus, in page make-up and appearance, including advertising, the prototype news pages in this section accurately reflect the new format The Star and the Tribune will adopt in early May.

The six-column format is widely accepted

Many newspaper readers already are accustomed to the six-column format. Among the daily newspapers that are using or will soon convert to the six-column format for news are: Miami Herald, Louis-

ville Courier-Journal/Times, Los Angeles Times, Miami News, Philadelphia Inquirer, Philadelphia Bulletin, all Booth newspapers (Michigan), Kansas City Star and Times, The Minneapolis Star and Minneapolis Tribune, and St. Paul Dispatch and Pioneer Press and most other Knight-Ridder newspapers.

In addition, several other leading newspapers, including the New York Times, are considering the change.

Why a new design?

The new six-column format is consistent with current trends in typography, which indicate that wider columns are easy to read and may, in fact, read faster and reduce eye fatigue.

The basic changes in the new format are in page width, column width and page make-up. Page width will be reduced one-half inch; column width will be increased from 1-11/16 inches to 2-1/8 inches; page columns for both news and advertising will be reduced from eight to six columns.

The Star now uses a modified six-column

format on its front page, but all pages in the new format, except classified advertising, will go to six columns. The Minneapolis Tribune (morning and Sunday) will change from eight columns of news and display advertising pages to six-column pages throughout, except for classified advertising.

Currently, both newspapers publish classified advertising in a 10-column format. This format will remain as it is.

"While readers will find the new format to their liking, it also will conserve newsprint, which is expected to remain in short supply for some time," said Robert W. Smith, publisher of The Minneapolis Star and Minneapolis Tribune.

"We believe too, that in making our newspapers more attractive, our advertisers will benefit as well.

"In short, we want to make the change to a new format a bonus for everyone who reads and advertises in The Minneapolis Star and Minneapolis Tribune. We like it and hope you will, too."

Fig. 15.2.

Why we're changing your

Jackson Daily News

There was a time that men and women got up early and went to the fields or shops, returning in the afternoon to rest, read and talk into the evening.

Today's life, for most, is much more hectic. Men and women are returning from their jobs, trying to get the kids fed, supper on the table, or to go out for the evening. There's a fight for time until the last light in the house is turned off.

Our research strongly indicated that many people these days feel they don't have time for a newspaper in the evening. Many of you told our researchers you found the bulk of information too overwhelming, you had too little time to read, even in an age in which information is increasingly vital.

You were irritated that national, international and local stories were mixed throughout much of the paper.

You were irritated by stories that "jumped" from one page to another.

You found the type too small, too hard to read.

You found it frustrating to search through the paper for the comics or the sports agate.

We listened. We've set out to create the newspaper you're asking for, by:

● Packaging the major national and international news separately. In the package, you get the major stories of the day, with new digests that quickly fill you in on other items, and tell you where you turn if you want more information on particular items.

● There's a new local and state news package in B section, where you can keep up with the community or state. Our editorial pages also move to the section.

● Extensive indexing. A new index on the back of the front section tells you, briefly, about every major story in the newspaper. And where to find it. Each section front tells you what major features are inside that section.

● Bigger type. The body type is 16 per cent bigger, set in a new format that makes reading easier by equalizing spacing between letters in words and between the words themselves.

● "Jumps" of stories from one page to the next are being eliminated, except in extraordinary circumstances. Virtually all stories are completed on the page on which they start.

Fig. 15.3.

Some of the ways we help you read and enjoy the NEW

D<small>AILY</small> J<small>ACKSON</small> N<small>EWS</small>

Mississippi   **B**
• DEATHS pg 2 • METROPOLITAN pg 3 • EDITORIALS pg 6   DAILY NEWS

We've put all our local news in one section, the new Mississippi section of the new Daily News. It's a complete rundown on metro Jackson, regional and state news, and includes our editorial pages. You'll notice all the section "flags" in the new Daily News tell you the major features inside the section.

Sports   **C**
• SCOREBOARD pg 2 • BUSINESS pg 5 • CLASSIFIED pg 7   DAILY NEWS

Sports lovers will find their box scores and other statistical information always on page 2 of the sports section. A sports section that placed third in a national contest last year becomes even better. Friday, there's Sports Weekend to help you get ready for the important games.

Living   **D**
• ABBY pg 2 • ENTERTAINMENT pg 6 • TV pg 7 • COMICS pg 8   DAILY NEWS

You'll find our new Living section a family place, a section filled with items of interest to a wide range of people, stories that deal with everyday problems and offer hints and help. And, there are columnists such as Dear Abby, Heloise, and lots of recipes on Thursday.

The Nation

The headings for The Nation, The World and The Jackson Daily Double represent very special areas of the NEW Jackson Daily News.

Ford Motor Co. has lost a suit with a federal appeals court ruling that the company was negligent in the death of a man who was drunk when his sports car crashed at a speed of more than 105 miles an hour. The court held that improper tires, not drinking or speed, caused the death. Details, Page 4A.

Voyager 1 has started sending "beautiful pictures" of the planet Saturn to Earth. Scientists say better pictures are still to come from the satellite, which is still 64 million miles from Saturn. Details, Page 13A.

The World

The Nation and The World offer the news packaged, with digests like those shown at right that fill you in on the top news, then tell you where to find the full story if you like.

A Soviet tug today began towing a powerless Soviet nuclear submarine from the Western Pacific off Okinawa. The sub was disabled by a fire that reportedly killed at least nine sailors. The Russians have refused aid. Details, Page 8A.

Worker unrest has become a regular part of life in Poland during the last 25 years, and few who know the country expect that to change. An analysis of the situation in Poland indicates that the Communist regime that controls Poland has failed repeatedly to put down unrest. Details, Page 17A.

Jackson Daily Double

The Jackson Daily Double is a special package. One day it could tell you all about an upcoming fair, complete with maps and prices. Another day, it may be an in-depth spread on a major problem in the Jackson area. Whatever it is, it's special. The feature, which gets its name from the plan to center it across a double page, appears Wednesday through Friday.

Our typeface has changed

Our old type

WASHINGTON — Ronald Reagan's economic advisers believe he can knock as much as two percentage points off the rate of inflation by the end of 1981 by using a vigorous attack on federal spending and regulation.

They are ready to challenge the conventional wisdom, expressed by private economists and many officials in the Carter administration, that little, if anything, can be done to bring down the inflation rate next year.

Our NEW type

WASHINGTON — Ronald Reagan's economic advisers believe he can knock as much as two percentage points off the rate of inflation by the end of 1981 by using a vigorous attack on federal spending and regulation.

They are ready to challenge the conventional wisdom, expressed by private economists and many officials in the Carter administration, that little, if anything, can be done to bring down the inflation rate next year.

Today's Daily News

MISSISSIPPI

Parents of a Mississippi murder victim are suing the state of Arizona for $11 million for letting the convicted killer out of jail. PAGE 1A

The final phase of immunization of Mississippi's school children against disease is going into effect this fall. PAGE 1B

The Hunger Coalition is criticizing welfare department appointments. PAGE 1B

Pine beetles' invasion of Mississippi has apparently slowed, but three counties are hard hit. PAGE 1B

Tobacco use is reported down in state, nation. PAGE 1B

THE NATION

Ronald Reagan faced a hostile crowd of blacks in New York today and told them he'd work for jobs for minorities. PAGE 1A

President Carter has approved a nuclear strategy aimed at deterring Soviet attack by focusing on U.S. Retaliation. PAGE 3A

Former priest James Kavanaugh has accused Pope John Paul II of trying to turn back the clock on Catholic reforms. PAGE 3A

Black leaders in New York got a promise from President Carter today that he would propose an economic recovery plan to provide millions of jobs. PAGE 3A

Today's Daily News is a new index on the back page of the newspaper telling you something about every substantial story in the newspaper.

If you're in a real hurry, it'll give you a "headline" gist of the day's news from every section of the newspaper.

If you're in a hurry, but not that big a hurry, it'll let you pick and choose the stories you want to read, or not to read.

It's divided into subject headings of national, international, local, sports and living section news, where in your newspaper you can find a story that strikes your fancy.

Fig. 15.4.

Columbia Missourian

Strychnine found in west coast Tylenol

CHICAGO (UPI) — Tylenol capsules tainted with strychnine poisoned a man in California, officials reported Tuesday, and fears arose that a "copycat" could be imitating a saboteur whose cyanide-laced capsules killed seven people in Chicago last week.

Greg Blagg, 12, a teacher from Creville, Calif., went into convulsions after swallowing capsules of Extra-Strength Tylenol tainted with strychnine last Thursday — the same day publicly broke about the Chicago deaths. He subsequently recovered.

The Food and Drug Administration and McNeil Consumer Products Co., manufacturer of Tylenol, issued an immediate warning against consumption of any type of Tylenol capsule — extra or regular strength.

In New York, trading of stock in Johnson & Johnson Co., McNeil's parent company, plunged more than two points and was halted for more than an hour after news of the California development.

In Chicago, the head of a massive investigation into the cyanide deaths warned against national hysteria.

It would be very counter-productive for people to become hysterical, because that just encourages the arrestsable." Illinois Attorney General Tyrone Fahner said.

Asked if a "copycat" could be at work in the California case, Fahner said, "That's been a constant fear — that other people would do that sort of thing."

Fahner said the FBI would investigate the

strychnine case for links to the Chicago investigation, which has been bogged without substantial leads since the weekend.

The list of suspects in the Chicago investigation "fluctuates but is still about two dozen," Fahner said. At least 20 suspects were reportedly under round-the-clock surveillance.

"There is no single person at even a group of persons that stand at above the rest at a better suspect then the others," he said. "This could go on for quite a while or it could be resolved very quickly."

California health officials began a check of doctors' offices and hospitals in Oroville, a town of about 3,500 people 36 miles north of Sacramento, for possible cases linked to the

man's poisoning.

In San Francisco, regional FDA director William C. Hill said strychnine was discovered in two bottles the man and his wife purchased at the store, plus a third bottle in the store's shelf.

The bottles appear to have been tampered with," Hill said. "You can see pink flecks. It's a tub-ish substance, enough to make you real sick but not enough to kill you."

The FDA dispatched eight investigators to Oroville.

Strychnine is an odorless poison that can kill in large doses and, in smaller doses, can cause nervous systems disorders, including convulsions. Though lethal, it is less potent than the cyanide that killed the Chicago vic-

tims.

In a statement by McNeil said, "We are working with the FBI and the FDA to determine the implications of that discovery. In conjunction with the FDA, we are notifying retailers to discontinue the sale of Tylenol extra strength capsules and regular strength capsules throughout the country until further notice.

"We join the FDA in urging consumers nationwide to discontinue further use of Tylenol extra strength capsules and regular strength capsules also until further notice."

The strychnine-laced capsules were Extra-Strength Tylenol from lot number 1MA764, a designation not previously cited in the Chicago cyanide killings.

Dr. Zuhdi Lababidi, above, demonstrates the procedure he used to help keep Casey Frank, 2, from having to undergo open-heart surgery. At right, Casey sits in his mother's lap.

New technique saves children

By Trisha Ratledge
Missourian staff writer

A University Hospital doctor last month performed a new surgery technique that spared two mid-Missouri children from dangerous open-heart surgery.

Dr. Zuhdi Lababidi, director of pediatric cardiology at the University Hospital and Clinics, operated on Casey Frank, 2, of Jefferson City, on Sept. 23 and six days later on Ashley Creason, 13 months, of El Greenville Court.

The operation, which fully spares narrowed heart valves, has been performed in only three other children in the United States.

The Franks had to think twice and hard before agreeing to the surgery. "We were very frightened but we felt it was a risk we had to take," Deborah Frank said.

The Creasons hesitated as well, even though the technique was the only hope for their child. "I was very receptive at first because the procedure is so new," Linda Creason said.

At birth, Ashley Creason suffered temporary heart failure, Despite Mrs. Creason's fear of the new procedure, she said she agreed to it because it was the only option.

"This was my daughter's life and that was important to me," she said. "She's very special now to our family."

"The procedure, called balloon valvuloplasty, enables physicians to widen narrowed heart valves that feed blood to the lungs, Lababidi said. The operation involves feeding a three-foot wire through a vein in the right leg to the child's heart and then through the reflective valve. A catheter is fed along the wire and a specially designed balloon is positioned in the valve. The balloon is inflated several times for short intervals to open the defective valve.

"Even if the valve is not opened fully, no physicians can buy time before open-heart surgery is required," Lababidi said.

The valve malfunction, which afflicts 7 percent of all children born with heart defects, causes the heart to force blood through the narrow opening. The blood backs up in the heart chamber, enlarging the heart and liver, Lababidi said. The patient eventually dies of heart failure if no corrective action is taken.

Open-heart surgery, the traditional treatment, has a mortality rate of 50 percent with newborns and 3 to 10 percent with children 1 and older.

The new procedure is preferred because it is less complicated and dangerous for the patient, Lababidi said.

Reactions vary to Bond's cuts

By Debbie Coleman and Bill Kates
State capitol bureau

JEFFERSON CITY — House Speaker Bob Griffin, D-Cameron, said Tuesday he was surprised with Gov. Christopher Bond's decision to exempt the state legislature from the $90 million budget cutback.

Bond's exemption includes the legislature, the judiciary level and the governor's office. His decision to exempt the legislature from cuts was made despite the legislature's willingness to accept cuts.

The governor announced the cuts at a televised statewide address Monday night, saying that without the cuts the state could be out of money by the end of the month.

In a recent meeting with Bond, Griffin said he told the governor he thought the legislature's budget should be pared along with those of state agencies.

"Every department should share in the burden . . . including the legislature," Griffin said.

Griffin said he would order the legislature to make cuts in its operating budgets similar to decreases Bond authorized for state agencies.

As Speaker of the House, I plan to institute that budget cuts," he said.

Members of the legislature have been discussing ways to reduce spending in anticipation of a budget shortfall this fiscal year, he said. The added that reductions in supplies, travel and personnel could result.

Most of the legislature's funds are used to pay legislative salaries, however, Griffin said.

"And we can't drop a representative," he said.

Lt. Gov. Kenneth Rothman said he was not surprised that the legislature was exempted.

Although the Missouri Constitution authorizes governors to order cutbacks for the state legislature, most governors exempt legislators from cuts, Rothman said in agreement with that philosophy.

"The legislature is responsible for appropriating state money . . . any cuts ought to be up to the legislature," he said.

Sen. Harry Wiggins, D-Kansas City, concurs. "I personally feel the legislature should do its share," he said. But Wiggins said the legislative

expenditures constitute a small part of the state's budget. Any legislative cuts wouldn't help that much, he said.

Tuesday, Bond set reduction targets for each state agency in a news conference that followed a meeting with his cabinet.

Although several programs described as essential to the public's health and safety were exempted, many agency officials will have to formulate plans to meet the governor's targets.

Most agency officials were not surprised by the governor's request and appeared willing to cooperate. During the meeting, Bond asked how many department directors thought a staff layoff would be necessary to implement the cuts. Seven department directors raised their hands.

Richard King, director of revenue, said Bond was using a scalpel, not a cleaver, to make the cuts.

King's department, however, was spared a massive cutback. The total reduction for the department amounted to $169,000 after essentials were exempted. King said it would not be difficult to find areas to cut to meet the governor's recommendations.

"That can be done by reducing advertising and similar costs and reassigning paperclips," he said.

Other departments did not fare as well. Although they were cut only 5 percent, elementary and higher education cuts involve the largest monetary sum. The governor recommended a $55.6 million cut from the two departments. The figure is more than half of the $90 million in total state reductions.

Social services suffered the next largest reduction with cuts of $32 million. Department Director Barrett Toan said every program would be examined, but none would be eliminated.

"We will be cutting back on the reimbursement levels of some programs," he said.

Bond has left agencies to cut a 5 percent cut in their budgets during the next fiscal year. But higher education is exempted from next year's cut.

Peter DeSimone of the Missouri Association for Social Welfare said he thinks the cuts are insensitive to social welfare agencies.

Crimestoppers finds justice best reward

By Gardner Hatch
Missourian staff writer

Since its creation in March, Crimestoppers of Greater Columbia has helped solve 32 local crimes and has led to the recovery of $8,475 worth of property.

Program coordinator Lt. Tom Hurbon of the Columbia police says anonymous tips from the public have helped solve such crimes as theft, prostitution, assault and burglary.

Crimestoppers so far has paid $1,190 in cash rewards to five anonymous callers. Twenty-seven of the 32 people who have helped police solve crimes, however, did not accept the rewards.

"A lot of people just don't want a reward," Hudson says.

Hudson is optimistic about the program. "It's one of the best things I've seen come along in a long time," he says.

Crimestoppers is a nationwide program that relies on citizen participation and private donations to help police solve crimes. Media publicity is used to alert the public to particular crimes for which police need help in investigation. Persons with information on a crime are guaranteed anonymity in all conversations with the police.

The information is then given to the appropriate division within the Police Department and if the information leads to an arrest, the person

refreives a cash reward.

Reward money appears to be sufficient incentive for some people to supply information to the police. Hudson says that in another city a woman gave information to Crimestoppers leading to the arrest of her boyfriend. She received her $200 reward.

Media cooperation, public involvement, anonymity and cash rewards are essential to the program's success. Hudson says.

"Anonymity is the big thing in the concept of the program," he says. "Joe Public doesn't want to get involved."

Hudson says the organization receives on average of one call per case. The information is usually enough to give investigators "that last effort to solve the case."

Hudson says he thinks the organization is effective by lowering the local crime rate, but that it is impossible to link the program's success to the low August crime index.

Reaching people who don't read newspapers or listen to the radio is a problem the organization will be confronting. Hudson says. Many people might have information about a crime but don't know the police need help.

Egypt lambastes Begin policy; Israelis charge anti-semitism

United Press International

Egypt marked the anniversary of Anwar Sadat's assassination Tuesday with accusations that Israel had violated the peace treaty signed by the slain president. For its part, Israeli officials accused Egypt of anti-semitic media attacks.

The deteriorating relations between Egypt and Israel, following the Jewish state's invasion of Lebanon, were seen as a threat to the Reagan administration's efforts to establish a lasting Middle East peace.

Egyptian Foreign Minister Kamal Hassan Ali, in comments on the eve of the first anniversary of Sadat's Oct. 6 slaying, said Israel was following a "path of violence and destruction."

The Egyptian-Israeli peace treaty contained several references concerning the obligation to establish peace not only between Egypt and Israel, but also between Israel and each of its neighbors, he said in reference to the 1979 pact fostered by the historic Camp David accords of 1978.

"It is with deep regret [that] I state before you here that Israel has violated the letter and spirit of her

undertaking when it committed the splash on the Iraqi nuclear reactor, annexed the Golan and Arab Jerusalem and violated Lebanese territory," Ali said.

"The Israeli aggression against the Lebanese and Palestinian peoples constitutes a grave setback to our peaceful efforts," Ali said. "It threatens the bridges of peace we have tried to build up during the previous five years."

In Israel, officials charged the Egyptian news media with anti-government's appraisal — was waging an "anti-Israeli and anti-semitic" campaign.

The recent articles and editorials appearing in the Egyptian press are absolutely terrible," an official told reporters in Jerusalem. "They are anti-Israel, anti-semitic, anti-everything, no doubt this worries us."

The official said the Israeli ambassador to Cairo made several complaints to Egyptian authorities but was told "the press is not controlled."

As the Camp David process concluded to founder, Reagan administration officials in Israel and Washington attempted to arrange the withdrawal of Syrian and Israeli forces from Lebanon.

In Jerusalem, U.S. envoy Morris Draper, who serves as Philip Habib's chief aide, met Prime Minister Menachem Begin and Defense Minister Ariel Sharon for 90 minutes.

But Begin's aides said he told Draper that Israel insisted all Palestinian guerrillas leave Lebanon before any Israeli and Syrian troops withdraw from the country.

Israeli military sources say there are about 1,000 Palestine Liberation Organization guerrillas in the north of Lebanon, the port city of Tripoli and between 4,000-6,000 PLO rebels with the 30,000 Syrian troops in Lebanon's central Bekaa Valley.

Western intelligence sources say Israel has about 19,000 troops in Lebanon.

In Washington, White House ambassador to Cairo made several complaints of Middle East capitals, would lunch with President Reagan Wednesday to discuss the withdrawal of all foreign forces from Lebanon.

Reagan, worried about a possible escalation of fighting in Lebanon, reportedly asked the State Department to accelerate moves, including setting a timetable for the withdrawal of Israeli and Syrian troops and remaining PLO members.

Fig. 15.5.

Columbia Missourian

75th Year — No. 22   Good Morning! It's Friday, October 8, 1982   3 Sections — 16 Pages — 25 Cents

Classmates of children with cancer exhibit understanding as

Teachers learn from students

By Chris Bartley
Missourian staff writer

A 9-year-old girl, weak with leukemia and bald from chemotherapy treatments, returns to school after being released from the hospital. She is probably scared — of dying, of more sickness, of what her friends will say when they see how she looks.

The release will not be permanent, of course. She probably will be in and out of the hospital for months, even if the leukemia goes into remission.

Another child, not realizing exactly what is wrong with the girl or the fear involved with cancer, walks up to her on the playground. He tells her he's heard she's going to die, and calls her "Baldy."

INSIGHT

According to one member of the Candlelighters, a group of Missouri parents of children with cancer, such scenes are common when a child with cancer returns to school. Leah McNay of Jamestown, Mo., said at a Candlelighters' public seminar Sept. 26 it happened to her daughter, Jennifer, two years ago.

The purpose of the seminar, held at University of Missouri and Climax, was to try to prevent similar scenes by letting teachers know what to do if one of their students has cancer. About 30 people, some of them teachers from local schools, attended.

A panel of six women, all either mothers or teachers of children with cancer, spoke at the seminar. They agreed that the best way to ease tensions caused by a child's cancer at school is to be as honest as possible with the other students.

"Other students are also under stress," McNay said. "They're afraid they might catch it. You need to prepare those children to cope with it too."

Another panel member, Melda Langle, a third-grade teacher in Marshall, Mo., had a boy in her class last year with Burkitt's Lymphoma, a rare cancer of the lymph system. When she first heard he had cancer, she worried about how the rest of the class would react.

But she read some books about cancer, and when the felt she could answer most of the students' questions, she told them why the boy, Dustin Burton, had been absent for so long, and now gathered they knew for him if they wanted to.

When Dustin returned to school after 2½ days in the hospital, he was wearing a hat to hide his chemotherapy baldness. Langle wanted to see how the students would react.

"It amazed me how sensitive they were, and how protective," she said.

When Dustin got in a fight one day with some boys from another class who had called him a "bald eagle," she said, the whole class was very upset, and talked about it for several hours.

Sometimes teachers go too far, though, and overemphasize the child's illness. This can lead to the child feeling excluded from his peer group. The panel said the best way to treat a child with cancer is the same way you would treat any child normally.

According to McNay, the only special treatment the teacher needs to give is quiet caring, understanding of what the child and family are going through, and concern.

"A parent doesn't want a teacher to be distressed with grades or give them anything they don't deserve," McNay said. "When they get something they know they don't deserve, immediately they begin to think, 'Am I not doing as well as the nurse or my parents expected?'"

Above, Dustin Burton, 9, of Marshall, Mo., takes a break during lunch hour. He recently completed chemotherapy treatment. At left, Dustin and Burton sit with Dusty Campbell, 10, also of Marshall. Like Dustin others have difficulty when returning to school after treatment for cancer. Many of their class mates don't know how to react to them.

Even when the student is too ill to attend school, the education should continue, the panel said, so that when he returns to school he won't be far behind. Missouri laws guarantee the right to an education with homebound tutors to any student who can't attend school.

Béyan Cline, a panel member and a Catholic, Mo., kindergarten teacher whose class includes a leukemic girl, said the child usually doesn't want special treatment. Besides, she said, the other children in school don't give special treatment to the child, so adults shouldn't either.

For example, the first time Jennifer McNay wore a wig to school, her teacher worried that the other students might tease her about it, even

though they all knew of Jennifer's illness by then. During class, she entered that Jennifer's new black hair was attracting a lot of stares and laughs.

Before Jennifer became she and the whole class to the school restroom, as usual. The boys finished in the usual time, but even after 18 minutes, not one of the girls had returned.

The teacher thought she heard a commotion, and perhaps someone crying, in the girls' restroom. Immediately she thought the girls were making fun of Jennifer's wig, so she hurried into the restroom. What she saw stopped her in her tracks with surprise.

The girls were giggling and parading in front of the mirrors as they took turns trying on Jennifer's wig. And Jennifer was laughing hardest of all.

Like a phoenix, Charter reborn

By Dennis Stone
Missourian staff writer

Charter Medical Corp., whose application to build a psychiatric hospital was rejected only a month ago, got a new lease on life Thursday that could lead to two psychiatric hospitals being built in Columbia.

The state Health Facilities Review Committee resurrected the hopes of Charter Medical Corp. by voting to consider the company's application for a certificate of need. Charter needs that certificate to build a psychiatric hospital here.

More than likely, the committee will approve the application at its Nov. 9 meeting.

The committee members have discussed it, and have decided they would not mind approving this application," said Susie Bradshaw, the committee's vice chairman.

On Sept. 8, Encompass Midwest Inc. of Indiana and Charter of Macon, Ga., made appeals before the committee to build psychiatric hospitals in Columbia. Encompass was granted a certificate of need. Charter's request was denied.

Charter's reconsideration hinged on one of the committee members who was absent for that original vote. "I have come to an erroneous decision," said Sen. Richard Webster, R-Carthage, as he brought the motion to the floor to reconsider Charter's application.

Webster cited a letter from Dr. Hugh Stephenson, chief of staff at the University School of Medicine,

endorsing Charter. He also said that support for Charter by four of five local psychiatrists prompted him to request Thursday's vote.

Despite claims that Columbia could not support two hospitals, both Charter executives and officials of their hospital would not agree with those at the Encompass hospital. Charter's psychiatric hospital would have adolescent, young, adult, adult and geriatric units while Encompass will have adolescent, adult, alcohol and drug abuse units, said Tom Gustauen, Charter executive. "No doubt we could support two now, in addition, our service area is larger than Encompass's."

Encompass's only representative at the meeting disagreed. "At the September meeting, the services be not presented as both institutions were considered by the some staff and communities, and it was decided there was need for only one psychiatric hospital," said Dan Flora, Encompass attorney.

Boone Hospital Center has an agreement with Charter to trade services and Columbia Regional Hospital has an agreement with Encompass to close its psychiatric ward if Encompass builds here.

Committee Vice Chairman Bradshaw said, if Charter can prove it can survive, it's likely it will be approved.

M.U. officials seek funding cut answers

By Daryl Kannaberg
Missourian staff writer

University system officials now are saying there is still a possibility no new cuts will be passed down to individual companies.

Indeed, the two most talked-about plans continue to be use of available contingency funds and a special one-time only student fee surcharge tacked on to next semester's tuition. Such actions would mean that campuses would not have to lay off employees or reduce programs, said Duane Stucky, Columbia campus director of institutional research and planning.

But no definite solutions had emerged as University officials met Thursday continuing to seek ways to battle cutbacks in state funds.

University President James Olson's staff and the four campus chancellors kicked around ideas to lessen the impact of the University's latest financial crunch.

The meeting was closed to the media and public.

In the meantime, plans are at a standstill in the Columbia campus as to what types of moves will have to be made, if any at all, Stucky said.

"It is break during the meeting, Olson said he would need the Board of

Curators and campus officials a framework of planned ideas early next week, he said that the $1.4 million in systemwide cuts two Christopher Bond ordered Monday. Olson would not say in what three terms he would recommend making the cuts.

If the cuts were passed across the board to all four campuses, the Columbia campus would have to find $1.4 million to trim.

The curators still meet next Thursday and Friday in Columbia.

University of Missouri-St. Louis Chancellor Arnold Grobman has not mentioned ideas were thrown out for discussion among the proposed which looked more than four hours cities and the mailing was an opportunity to meet with his staff and get some ideas on how to react. "I have not analyzed a specific amount to the campuses," he said.

Stucky said campus administration is geared to take on the cuts if any are passed in down by the system.

Budget woes during the last three years have impressed campus budget planning, Stucky said.

"We're in better control of our destiny," Stucky said. "We know the options we have for the funds are, where we have threshold.

September unemployment rate to be highest since '40

WASHINGTON (UPI) — Industry and labor economists predicted Thursday the September unemployment rate will set a post-Depression record of at least 10 percent, and Democrats appear ready to use that information like a mortar gun at the Alamo in the November elections.

Even before the Labor Department's Bureau of Labor Statistics releases the data today, President Reagan's foes have made the case an integral part of many campaigns in the congressional elections only 24 days away.

In Michigan, the state with the highest unemployment rate — 15.2 percent — Democratic candidates are harping on joblessness and Indiana, anticipated layoffs at International

Harvester are a major focus of the campaign where four-term Democrat Rep. Floyd Fithian is trying to unseat Republican Sen. Richard Lugar.

Unemployment of near 20 percent in Duluth and near 40 percent among miners and steelworkers in Minnesota's Iron Range has made it the major issue between Sen. Dave Durenberger, R-Minn., and Mark Dayton, the Democratic-Farmer-Labor challenger.

Joe Smolnja, president of a United Steelworkers union local in Virginia, Minn., thinks the wrong election is being held in November.

"The problem is we can't vote on the right guy (ecause Reagan isn't running," he said.

The predictions of many of the economists that the jobless rate could reach as high as 10.5

percent relied on a report of joblessness among those covered by unemployment insurance.

The Labor Department Thursday reported nearly 4.4 million claimants for unemployment insurance benefits during the week ended Sept. 18, the week the Census Bureau surveyed households to determine the overall September unemployment rate.

That kept the seasonally adjusted insured unemployment rate at 3 percent. A percentage points above what it was at the time of the survey for the August rate of 9.8 percent a peak World War II high.

"Based on that, I would guess the unemployment rate would be about 10.1 percent," said

Martin Lefkowitz, director of economic trends for the U.S. Chamber of Commerce. He also noted an upsurge in layoffs, and initial claims for jobless benefits.

Mary Eccles, economist for the congressional Joint Economic Committee, said there is a "strong possibility" of a 10 percent rate, and a labor economist forecast 10.2 percent because of a record 290,888 new claims for unemployment benefits and "general worsening of the situation."

Although Reagan acknowledged the rate may climb into double figures for the first time since 1940 when it was 14.6, he told a group of GOP candidates Wednesday the rate was 1.4 percent when he took office so if it hit 10 percent, he would "take blame for 2.4 percent

---

Panel approves land-use plan

By Aimee Cunningham
Missourian staff writer

Ridgeway neighborhood residents want another option: the City Council's.

After almost three years of research and revisions, the city's updated 10-sector land-use plan Thursday night won the unanimous approval of the Columbia Planning and Zoning Commission.

The plan designates part of the Ridgeway area on Providence Road for office buildings instead of homes, and that has elicited persistent opposition from resi-

dents. Thursday's meeting was no exception.

The Ridgeway neighborhood residents want another option: the City Council's.

After almost three years of research and revisions, the city's updated 10-sector land-use plan (which was the only portion of the citywide land-use plan to spark heated testimony during recent public hearings. The plan tracts are located in Providence Road between Rosann and Hickman avenues on the east side and between Austin and Hickman on the west.

The residents claim that office buildings would be an encroachment on their inner-city, namely on the west.

But residents Thursday night said office buildings would be an encroachment on their inner-city, namely on the west.

See RESIDENTS, Page 8A

City mails out help with utility bills

By Robert Dutch
Missourian staff writer

Columbians are receiving something extra in their water and light bills this month. Tucked into the envelope is a form allowing customers to make a tax-deductible donation to help the elderly and handicapped pay their winter utilities.

The group launching the authorization is Citizens Assisting Senior Citizens and the Handicapped, administered by the city's Health Department.

So far, response to the program has been good, according to Steve Gray, an assistant Energy administrator in the city Finance Department, which keeps Poverty on the program.

By Wednesday, Mr. Gray said, CASH had 1,005 pledged per ceipts from 500 people. The bus also had four one-day donations totaling $596 for the program.

"We have several donations of $10 and up with 75 of the 500 donations we received yesterday," 15 were $5 donations."

The idea for CASH was suggested at a spring city staff meeting by Dirk Malon, director of the Water and Light Department.

Customers can earmark a dollar or some per-month for the CASH programs by returning the form with their utility payments. The paid will be distributed to the Health Department, Hargrove said, helping for the needed such as referrals from various social agencies in the city.

An energy audit will be made of CASH recipients' homes to catalog ways to cut utility costs. Hargrove said that this year the council has already backed $79,000 for insulation and $25,000 for weatherization of eligible homes.

Hargrove said low-income houses often have high utility bills because they are poorly insulated. Some bills, he said, run as high as $200 per month during the winter.

Hargrove emphasized the need for proper heating for the elderly and handicapped because "they are homebound and are at their homes in more extensive cold."

Authorization forms are available at the Water and Light Department billing area or the County-City Building.

Inside

Business 7A
Classified 5-6A
Opinion 4A
Record 2A
Sports 1-4C

8:30 a.m. to 4:30 p.m. Old master drawings in Display Fine Arts Gallery, Stephens College.

2:30 p.m. High school home cooking parade starting at Business and College Avenue.

7:30 p.m. Performance Maena, South Campus Auditorium, Stephens College.

7:30 p.m. Homecoming to In-finity, Daniels Theater, Gentry Hall basement program.

8 p.m. High school football pep rally at Jefferson City, Hickman Field.

8 p.m. High school football Rock Bridge vs. Mexico, Rock Bridge Field.

8 p.m. Ken Haas, lecture and concert on Brahms and his own compositions, Jesse Auditorium. University tickets $4.

Fig. 15.6.

panied by promotional advertising and columns explaining the changes, will reassure present readers and attract the attention of new ones. A phase-in is likely to result in some unpleasant typographic effects as both the old and the new appear on the same page, but that will be more bothersome to journalists than readers in the short run. The readers will be affected, however, if the clash of materials continues for an extended period.

When is the design work done? For some, like J. Ford Huffman of the Rochester *Times-Union,* the answer is, "never and that's the best part about our new format. Each time we try to package the news of the day, we discover different ways to use the typographic elements we have." A dynamic publication is one that is constantly finding better ways to report and explain the world to its readers. Progress should not come in five-year intervals.

GLOSSARY

Agate — Traditionally, 5½-pt. type, though now commonly used for type up to 7 points; agate line is an advertising space measurement ¹/₁₄ of an inch deep.

Ascender — That part of the letter that extends above the body of the type.

Balance — Placement of elements to produce a harmoniously integrated page.

Banner — A large headline that extends across the top of the front page above the most important story of the day.

Bar — In type, a horizontal or slanted line connected at both ends.

Baseline — Line on which the center body of type rests.

Bastard type — Type set a different width than the standard column setting.

Black letter — *See* Text letter.

Bleed — An illustration filling one or more margins and running to the edge of the page.

Blurb — A quote or a small part of a story displayed in type larger than the text, usually 14 to 18 points.

Body type — *See* Text type.

Boldface — Type that has thicker, darker lines than the medium or lighter weights of the same face.

Border — An ornamental rule.

Bowl — In type, the line enclosing a space.

Burn — To transfer type and images to a sensitized plate.

Byline — Line crediting the writer, photographer, or designer. Most commonly, it refers to the writer's credit at the top of the story.

Cathode ray tube (CRT) — An electronic tube used to transmit words and pictures onto paper or film.

Characters per pica (CPP) — Measurement of the width of a typeface, computed by counting the average number of letters that will fit in a given horizontal space and dividing by the number of picas.

Cold type — Type produced by a photographic process rather than by pressing inked metal forms against paper.

Color filter — Filter that absorbs all but one color.

Concord — Blending of typographical elements to form a uniform impression.

Contrast — Effect achieved by varying shapes, sizes, and weights of the elements on the page.

Contrast and balance — Layout technique in which a page is balanced by using contrasting shapes and weights.

Counter—White space within the letter.

Cursive—Race of type that is a stylized reproduction of formal handwriting. Also known as script.

Cutline—Information under a picture or artwork; also called a caption.

Cutoff rule—A line used to separate elements on a page.

Deck—One or more lines of display type that are smaller than the main headline.

Descender—That part of the letter that extends below the body of the type.

Design—A system of planning in which the person who arranges the elements on the page has some control over the collection and selection of those elements.

Display type—Type larger than that used for text. In newspapers, display type ranges upward from 14 points.

Double truck—Facing pages in which the space between the pages is also used.

Dummy—The page, usually half the size of the page being produced, on which the editor shows where all the elements are to be arranged. The blueprint of the page.

Duotone—One color plus black, achieved by shooting two halftone negatives of the picture and producing two plates for the page.

Dutch wrap—Extending copy beyond the headline; also called a raw wrap.

Ear—The distinctive stroke at the top right of the letters *g* and *r*.

Em—a unit of space equal to the space taken by the capital *M* of the type size being used.

En—Half an em, or half the size of the capital *M* of the type size being used.

Family—In type classification, typefaces that are closely related in design and share a common name. They differ in width, weight, and form.

Flag—*See* Nameplate.

Flush—Term combined with either right or left to indicate that the element starts at the left or lines up with the right edge of the column.

Flush left—Type that begins at the left-hand edge or border of the column.

Flush right—Type that ends at the right-hand edge or border of the column.

Focus—Starting point on the page, achieved by selecting a dominant element or elements.

Font—A complete set of type of one style and size.

Gutter—The vertical white space between columns of type.

Hairline—The thin stroke of a letter.

Halftone—Reproduction in which tones have been photographed through a screen to break up the areas into dots, whose size determines the dark and light areas.

Hammer—One- or two-word headline in large type, usually over a deck.

Inset—Photograph or copy contained within the borders of a photograph.

Italic—Serif type sloped to the right.

Jim dash—Cutoff rule that does not cross the entire column.

Justified type—Type set so that the lines are all of equal length by hyphenating words and placing more or less space between words.

Kenaf—A fibrous plant that is being tested as a substitute for wood pulp as a raw material in making newsprint.

Kerning — Touching the letters of type.

Key plate — Printing plate that puts the first image on the paper.

Kicker — Three or four words that are set about half the size of the main headline and usually appear flush left above the main headline.

Layout — Arrangement of elements on the page, usually done without any voice in the preparation or selection of those elements.

Leading — Sometimes written "ledding," this is the space between lines of type.

Legibility — Measurement of the speed and accuracy with which type can be read and understood.

Letterpress — Method of printing in which raised letters are inked and pressed against paper.

Logo — An insignia of type, art, or both that ties together stories in a series or identifies a regular feature such as a columnist.

Loop — The curved part of letters such as *o*, *c*, and *e*, which is often drawn distinctively.

Masthead — A listing of the publication's editors, name of the paper, date, volume, and sometimes the publication's creed.

Modern — Sometimes used to differentiate among types in the roman race. The type is geometric and symmetrical.

Module — A rectangular or square shape; to run a story in modules means that éach column of type is the same depth.

Mortise — Overlapping of two or more photographs or of a headline and a photograph.

Nameplate — The newspaper's name as it appears at the top of Page 1. Also known as the flag.

Novelty — *See* Ornamental.

Oblique — Sans serif type slanted to the right.

Offset — A printing method in which the inked image transfers from plate to rubber blanket to paper. It is based on the principle that grease and water do not mix.

Old style — Sometimes used to differentiate among types in the roman race. The type is asymmetrical and less formal looking than other roman faces.

Optimum format — The layout in which columns are set at the most legible line length. For broadsheet newspapers, this has been six columns, but with pages becoming narrower, five columns is becoming more legible.

Ornamental — Race of type specially designed to create such a specific mood or emotion that it is not useful for other uses. Also known as novelty.

Pagination — System of producing pages from a photocomposition machine, thus eliminating the need for a composing room.

Photocomposition — Method of producing type by exposing negatives of the characters on film or paper or reproducing them digitally.

Pica — A unit of measurement; 6 picas equal 1 inch.

Plate — The metal on which the photographic image of a page is developed by exposing it to a negative. The plate is then placed on the press.

Point — A unit of measurement; 12 points equal 1 pica. Headlines are measured vertically in points.

Process color — Full- or four-color reproduction achieved by separating each color on individual pieces of film and burning them on separate printing plates. The process colors are yellow, magenta, cyan, and black.

Proportion — Proper relation among the elements on the page.

Pyramid format — Arrangement of advertisements in a stack up the right or left side of the page.

Quad — An empty printing unit for spacing; an em quad is the square of the type size.

Race — The broadest category of type classification. Type is divided into six categories; roman, square serif, sans serif, text letter, cursive, and ornamental.

Ragged right type — Type set with a fixed left starting point but with an irregular ending point at the right of the line.

Readability — Measurement of the difficulty of the content.

Readin — Type subordinate in size to the main head and placed above it. The main head completes the thought started in the readin.

Readout — A deck that reads directly out of the main head. Unlike the deck, it is written in a conversational tone.

Roman — A race of type characterized by serifs and thick and thin strokes; also used to mean straight-up-and-down type as opposed to italic or oblique.

Rule — A plain line that ranges upward in width from ½ point. *See* Border.

Sans serif — Race of type without serifs and with uniform strokes. Also referred to as gothic.

Scanner — Electronic or laser machine that reads one color of a photograph at a time and transfers the image to a separation.

Screen — Glass or film used in cameras to break copy into halftone dots. The number of lines per linear inch of the screen determines the fineness of the reproduction; the higher the number, the better the reproduction.

Script — *See* Cursive.

Separation — A negative containing elements to be printed in one of the process colors. A full-color picture normally requires four separations.

Series — The range of sizes in a typeface. With photocomposition and digital typesetting, the range of sizes includes fractions of points.

Serif — The cross-stroke at the end of the main stroke of a letter.

Sidebar — A secondary story intended to be run with a major story on the same subject.

Side-saddle — Placement of type to the left side of the story rather than over it; also called side head.

Slug — One-word designation for a story as it moves through the production system.

Spot color — Any color printing other than process.

Square serif — Race of type with monotone strokes and squared-off or blocked serifs.

Stereotype — A flat or curved metal plate cast from a papier-mâché mold; the process.

Stroke — The primary line of the letter.

Stress — The thickness of a curved stroke; the shading of the letter.

Tabloid — A publication whose pages are approximately half the size of a broadsheet or full-size newspaper and usually printed on newsprint.

Teaser — A graphic written and designed to draw readers' attention to something in the publication, usually on an inside page.

Terminal — The distinctive finish to the stroke on sans serif type.

Text letter — Face of type that has a medieval appearance of early European hand-lettering. Also known as black letter.

Text type — Also referred to as body type; is used in the stories and editorials. In newspapers and magazines, it usually ranges from 8½ to 12 points.

Tombstoning — Bumping of two or more headlines.

Transitional — Sometimes used to differentiate among types in the roman race. The type has characteristics of both old style and modern faces.

Transparency — A color photograph on slide film.

Typography — The arrangement and effect of type.

Unity — Harmony among the elements on a page and among the parts of the publication.

Video display terminal (VDT) — Electronic typewriter with a televisionlike screen.

Well format — Arrangement of advertisements in the shape of a U on a page.

W-format — A layout in which one column is run about 50 percent wider than the others.

Wrap — A column or leg of type. Type set over six columns would have six wraps.

X-height — Height of the lowercase x, the standard for measuring type.

REFERENCES CITED

Adams, J. Michael, and Faux, David D. 1977. *Printing Technology: A Medium of Visual Communications.* North Scituate, Mass.: Duxbury Press, pp. 143–44.

Alexander, Charles T. Graphics explosion III: Modern outscores traditional. 1974. *The Bulletin, ASNE* July/August: 10–12.

Bain, Chic. 1980. Newspaper design and newspaper readership: A series of four experiments. Center for New Communications Res. Rep. 10, School of Journalism, Indiana University, Bloomington.

Bain, Chic, and Weaver, David H. 1979. Newspaper design and newspaper readership. Paper presented to the Graphics Division, Association for Education in Journalism, Houston.

Back, Paul. 1980. Packaging and design. *Design* (Society of Newspaper Designers) March:28.

Becker, D., Heinrich, J., Von Sichowky, R., and Wendt, D. 1970. Reader preferences for typeface and leading. *J. Typogr. Res.* 1(Winter):61–66.

Benton, Camille. 1979. The connotative dimensions of selected display typefaces. Paper presented to the Association for Education in Journalism, Houston.

Clark, Ruth. 1979. Changing needs of changing readers. American Society of Newspaper Editors Newspaper Readership Project, May, p. 30.

Click, J. W., and Stempel, Guido H. III. 1974. Reader response to modern and traditional front page make-up. American Newspaper Publishers Association News Research Bull. 4, June.

_____. 1976. Reader response to front pages with four-color halftones. *Journalism Q.* 53:736–38.

Curley, John. 1979. PILOT research tailored to unique needs of each newspaper. *Gannetteer* March:8.

Curley, Thomas. 1979. Readers want latest news, consistent and complete newspapers. *Gannetteer* March: 6–8.

_____. 1980. What the readers want – And how newspapers can give it to them. Editorially Speaking. *Gannetteer* May:2–4.

Dowding, G. 1957. *Factors in the Choice of Typefaces.* London: Wace.

The Editor's Exchange. 1980. *ASNE* May:1.

Emery, Edwin, and Emery, Michael. 1978. *The Press and America,* 4th ed. New Jersey: Prentice-Hall, p. 236.

Fabrizio, R., Kaplan, L., and Teal, G. 1967. Readability as a function of the straightness of right-hand margins. *J. Typogr. Res.* January:90–95.

Hartley, James, and Barnhill, Peter. 1971. Experiments with unjustified text. *Visible Language* 5(3):265–78.

Haskins, Jack. 1958. Testing suitability of typefaces for editorial subject matter. *Journalism Q.* 35:186–94.

Haskins, Jack P., and Flynne, Lois P. 1974. Effect of headline typeface variation on reading interest. *Journalism Q.* 51:677-82.

Hays, Harold T. P. 1977. The push pin conspiracy. *New York Times Magazine.* March 6, pp. 19-22.

Holmes, Grace. The relative legibility of black print and white print. 1931. *J. Appl. Psychol.* 15(June):248-51.

Hurlburt, Allen. 1976. *Publication Design.* New York: Van Nostrand Reinhold, p. 7.

Hurley, Gerald D., and McDougall, Angus. 1971. *Visual Impact in Print.* Chicago: American Publishers Press, p. 45.

Hvistendahl, J. K., and Kahl, Mary R. 1975. Roman v. sans serif body type: Readability and reader preference. ANPA News Res. Bull. 2, January.

Itten, Johannes. 1964. *Design and Form.* New York: Reinhold, p. 98.

Kobre, Kenneth. 1980. *Photojournalism, the Professionals' Approach.* Somerville, Mass.: Curtin and London, p. 9.

Lerude, Warren. 1979. Reno newspapers stress graphics, production quality after PILOT. *Gannetteer* March:13-15.

Lynn, Robert. Interview with the author, August 20, 1980.

Mott, Frank Luther. 1945. *American Journalism.* New York: Macmillan. (Most of the dates contained in this discussion of evolution of design are taken from Mott's book.)

Pitnof, Barbara Bell. 1980. The front page. *Nieman Reports* Summer:46-49.

Poindexter, Paula M. 1978. Non-readers: Why they don't read. ANPA News Res. Rep. 9, January.

Poulton, E. C. 1955. Letter differentiation and rate of comprehension of reading. *J. Appl. Psychol.* 49:358-62.

Puncekar, Sandra. 1980. Presses: Technology is catching up. *Presstime* June:4-6.

Robinson, David O., Abbamonte, Michael, and Evans, Selby. 1971. Why serifs are important: The perception of small print. *Visible Language* 5(Autumn):353-59.

Roethlein, B. E. 1912. The relative legibility of different faces of printing type. *Am. J. Psychol.* 23(January):1-36.

Siskind, Theresa G. 1979. The effect of newspaper design on reader preferences. *Journalism Q.* 56:54-61.

Sissors, Jack Z. 1974. Do youthful, college-educated readers prefer contemporary newspaper designs? *Journalism Q.* 51:307-13.

Tannenbaum, Percy, Jacobson, Harvey K., and Norris, Eleanor L. 1964. An experimental investigation of typeface connotations. *Journalism Q.* 41:65-73.

Terry, Art. 1980. Photography for editors. Unpublished master's thesis, University of Missouri, Columbia.

Tinker, Miles A. 1963. *Legibility of Print.* Ames: Iowa State University Press, pp. 88-107.

Tinker, Miles A., and Paterson, D. G. 1929. Studies of typographical factors influencing speed of reading: III. Length of line. *J. Appl. Psychol.* June:205-19.

Tipton, Leonard, 1978. ANPA newspaper readership studies. ANPA News Res. Rep. 13, July, p. 4.

ADDITIONAL READING

Allen, Wallace. 1981. *A Design for News*. Minneapolis: Minneapolis Star and Tribune Company.

Arnold, Edmond C. 1969. *Modern Newspaper Design*. New York: Harper and Row.

Bain, Eric K. 1970. *The Theory and Practice of Typographic Design*. New York: Hastings House.

Berry, W. Turner, and Johnson, A. F. 1953. *Encyclopaedia of Type Faces*. London: Blandford Press.

Burt, Sir Cyril. 1959. *A Psychological Study of Typography*. London: Cambridge University Press.

Dair, Carl. 1967. *Design with Type*. Toronto: University of Toronto Press.

Ernst, Sandra B. 1977. *The ABC's of Typography*. New York: Art Direction Book Co.

Evans, Harold. 1973. *Newspaper Design, Book Five*. New York: Rinehart and Winston.

Gregory, D. L. 1970. *The Intelligent Eye*. New York: McGraw-Hill.

Hopkins, Richard L. 1913. *Type*. Morgantown: West Virginia University Bookstore.

Hurlburt, Allen. 1978. *The Grid*. New York: Van Nostrand Reinhold.

Johnson, A. F. 1966. *Type Designs*. Norwich, England: Jarrold and Sons.

Lieberman, J. Ben. 1978. *Type and Typefaces*, 2d ed. New Rochelle, N.Y.: Myriade Press.

Merrinian, Frank. 1965. *A.T.A. Type Comparison Book*. Advertising Association of America.

Nelson, Roy Paul. 1978. *Publication Design,* 2d ed. Dubuque, Iowa: William C. Brown.

Polk, Ralph W., and Gage, Harry L. 1953. *A Composition Manual*. Washington, D.C.: Printing Industry of America.

Rehe, Rolf. 1979. *Typography: How to Make It Most Legible*. Chapel Hill, N.C.: Source Publications.

Rosen, Ben. 1967. *Type and Typography,* 2d ed. New York: Van Nostrand Reinhold.

Seybold, John. 1979. *Fundamentals of Modern Photocomposition*. Media, Pa.: Seybold Publications.

Smith, Charles. 1965. *Color—Study and Teaching*. New York: Van Nostrand Reinhold.

Turnbull, Arthur, and Baird, Russell. 1980. *The Graphics of Communication,* 4th ed. New York: Holt, Rinehart and Winston.

White, Jan V. 1974. *Editing by Design: Word and Picture Communication for Editors and Designers*. New York: R. R. Bowker.

Zachrisson, Bror. 1965. *Studies in the Legibility of Printed Text*. Stockholm, Sweden: Almquist and Wiskel.

INDEX